The Music *of* Tchaikovsky

The first page of Tchaikovsky's manuscript for the Piano Concerto
No. 1 in B-flat minor, Op. 23

Note the crossed-out dedication at the top of the page. Tchaikovsky originally
intended to dedicate the concerto to Nikolai Rubinstein. But Rubinstein's response
at the first hearing of the piece was so unfeeling that the composer, overcome with
rage, decided to dedicate the piece to Hans von Bülow instead.

The Music
of
Tchaikovsky

Edited by GERALD ABRAHAM

W · W · NORTON & COMPANY · INC · New York

Contents

CONTENTS

Preface

THIS IS A MUSICAL BOOK planned on novel lines; it consists of chapters on various aspects of Tchaikovsky's music contributed by well-known critics. It is hoped that by careful planning and co-ordination the most common weaknesses of collaborative works, looseness and diffuseness, have been avoided. Thus a real book is produced; and not merely a collection of separate essays bound together. The volume has been planned to cover the whole of the composer's output, or at any rate all of it that matters, and the omission of a long biographical section has made possible a much more thorough and detailed discussion of the music than would otherwise be possible in a book of this size.

The need for a serious, large-scale study of Tchaikovsky's music has been apparent for a good many years. As I have remarked elsewhere: "It is customary not to criticize Tchaikovsky's music but to sniff at it, or to admire the tunes. One either likes it or one doesn't. Yet an extraordinarily large proportion of his music—probably nearly two-thirds of it—is largely unknown even to intelligent musicians, while anything worth calling criticism of Tchaikovsky is practically nonexistent except in the U.S.S.R." I think it can be claimed that this book removes that reproach.

The fact that so much of Tchaikovsky is so little known is reflected in the space devoted to certain aspects of his work. It is, for instance, the only excuse for what at first sight may appear to be a disproportionate number of pages allotted to his dramatic music. The same remark applies to the chapter on the songs, written by a distinguished Soviet critic whose magnum opus on Tchaikovsky is awaited with keen interest. Professor Alshvang's essay has the additional value of representing a typical contemporary Russian view of Tchaikovsky, markedly different in some respects from that generally taken in western Europe. The other contributors, even though allowed complete freedom of critical judgment, show a surprising unanimity on many general points.

G. A.

1

Tchaïkovsky the Man.

By

Edward Lockspeiser

A T FIRST SIGHT he seems a benign old gentleman, with snow-white hair, full features, not especially striking in appearance, not recognisably Slavonic, but decidedly old for his years. In his forties he has already approached old age. In the year of his death, at the age of fifty-three, he looks like a man of seventy. A photograph taken in his youth shows a triangular face with a pointed chin, an aquiline nose and a massive forehead. So at any rate he looked when a law student. A few years later he was wearing long hair in the romantic manner of the 1860's, and his large eyes, which we are told were of a ' wonderful blue,' were beginning to show signs of suffering. None of these photographs, however, different from each other as they are, seems to correspond to the character of the man as we are able to judge it from either his letters or his music. A more convincing portrait is the one taken at the age of thirty-nine, two years after his marriage. It does not appear in any of the Tchaikovsky biographies, and was published in Russia only in 1935. Here undoubtedly is some suggestion of that terror of the mind against which he fought for the greater part of his life. There is nothing idealised in this picture. The knit brows, the agonised stare, the heavy, despondent expression give for the first time a glimpse of the man in mental torture.

Peter Ilyich Tchaikovsky was the second of six children, of whom the eldest was Nicholas. Following Peter were Alexandra, his only sister, Hippolyte and finally the twins, Anatol and Modest. From his early years he showed a sensitiveness which, if it gave him a keener perception, also made him more vulnerable. He was fortunate enough to have a governess who refrained from punishing him, but who was powerless to deal with his abnormal nervous excitement. As a boy he impressed everyone with an unusual charm of manner, a charm of which he was well aware and which he was quick to use to his own ends. He was often moody, capricious and irritable. He showed great energy and persistence, but he was at the same time, so

9

Modest tells us, ' as malleable as wax.' He was less than eight years old when he could reproduce at the piano arias from *Don Giovanni* which he had heard played on an ' orchestrion.' ' He found such delight in playing,' says Modest, ' that it was frequently necessary to drag him by force from the instrument. Afterwards, as the next best substitute, he would take to drumming tunes upon the window-panes. One day, while thus engaged, he was so entirely carried away by this dumb-show that he broke the glass and cut his hand severely.' Whereupon the question of his musical education was seriously considered.

Inseparable from this early passion for music was his devotion, no less passionate, to his large family. Indeed, his early family attachments were so strong that they not only conditioned but stifled his relationships with men and women throughout his life. In later years he ate his heart out in a wretched state of loneliness, and often it seems that his existence was made possible only by his memories of a childhood which was probably not without some premature experience of love. Shortly after the birth of his twin brothers he told his governess that whenever he saw them he thought they were ' angels come down to earth.' To Modest he was specially drawn, and in later years he was always hankering after a maternal love from his sister. At the age of thirty-one he tells her : ' I have already told you what an important part you play in my life, although you do not live near me. " If things go very badly with me, I shall go to Sasha," I say to myself; or " I think I will do this, I am sure Sasha would advise it "; or " Shall I write to her? What would she think of this? " ' Tchaïkovsky had little reticence in describing his feelings. Even in the letters of his middle age he would sometimes gush like a schoolgirl.

Tchaïkovsky's father, Ilya Petrovich, a government Inspector of Mines, seems to have been a simple, good-natured man though he does not seem to have distinguished himself either by a brilliant intelligence—it took him twenty years to rise to a rank corresponding to lieutenant-colonel—or by shrewdness of judgment. He showed a very poor understanding of his son's musical abilities. When, after the performance of Tchaïkovsky's early opera *The Oprichnik*, Modest asked the father whether such an artistic success was not worth more than the Order of St. Anne which Tchaïkovsky might have gained had he pursued the career of a government official, Ilya, then in his eightieth year, obstinately replied : ' The decoration would certainly have been better.' Even worse was the ignorance Ilya showed of the young Peter's emotional difficulties; and as we shall see later, at the time of Tchaïkovsky's marriage he blundered atrociously. In his outward manner Tchaïkovsky, in later years, was far too conventional ever to express any hostility towards his father or even to allow himself to think of such a feeling. Nor is there ever any suggestion of antagonism in his correspondence; the letters he wrote to his father, though few and far between, are consistently affectionate. But one cannot avoid the suspicion that he was merely paying lip-service to a sentiment which was probably less profound than he would care to believe. On receiving the news of his father's death he wept, but he seems to have been far more concerned by the fact that he had received no word of praise after the performance of a recent work. Before marrying Tchaïkovsky's mother, Ilya had been married to a German (by whom he had a daughter who was for a short time responsible for Peter's care), and he married a third time after her death.

Alexandra Andreevna, the composer's mother, was the daughter of a French emigrant named Assière who, according to Modest, was an epileptic. Exactly what was meant by the term 'epilepsy' in those days (approximately the end of the eighteenth century) it is difficult to ascertain. It may have been the disease known by this name to-day, but it is possible, too, that it was another form of mental disorder. Modest states unequivocally that Tchaïkovsky's 'one certain inheritance seems to have been an abnormally neurotic tendency' and that this 'probably came to him through his grandfather Assière who suffered from epilepsy.' Without raising the thorny problems of heredity, one can at least suppose that he acquired his mental constitution from his mother. And it was to his mother that he showed the most passionate attachment of his life. Modest, whose understanding of his brother was anything but superficial, draws attention to this attachment in a description of her departure after a visit to Peter at boarding-school :

> When the actual moment of parting came, he completely lost his self-control and, clinging wildly to his mother, refused to let her go. Neither kisses, nor words of comfort, nor the promise to return soon, were of any avail. He saw nothing, heard nothing, but hung upon her as though he were part and parcel of the beloved presence. It became necessary to carry off the poor child by force, and hold him fast until his mother had been driven away. Even then he broke loose, and with a cry of despair, ran after the carriage, and clung to one of the wheels, as though he would bring the vehicle to a standstill.

Such a scene may not be altogether unusual in the life of an affectionate and nervous child. In Tchaïkovsky's case, however, it appears to be the first symptom of that fierce identification with his mother from which he was never able to free himself. Modest speaks of this episode as the ' first great trouble of his life ' and adds significantly that he ' could never recall it without a shiver of horror.' When Peter was fourteen his mother died. We have no record of its immediate effect on him at the time, but twenty-three years later, in the course of a letter in which he is discoursing at length on the meaningless of immortality he suddenly contradicts his whole argument by saying : ' I shall never reconcile myself to the thought that my dear mother, whom I loved so much, actually *is not*, or that I shall never be able to tell her how, after twenty-three years of separation, she is as dear to me as ever.' In another letter he admits that ' her death had a great influence on the fate of myself and our entire family.'

Tchaïkovsky's first attempt at composition dates from the month of his mother's death. ' Undoubtedly,' he confessed many years later, ' I should have gone mad but for music.' Those words are to be taken literally; and they provide, too, one of the clearest cases of an emotional conflict exteriorised in art. There is never anything concealed in the workings of Tchaïkovsky's mind. The love for his mother remained, in its adolescent state, so powerful that her death would have threatened the stability of his mind had he not found an expression for his pent-up passion in music. The evidence for this statement is not in the music, now lost, which he composed at the age of fourteen. It is in the Fourth Symphony and his opera *Eugene Onegin* which he wrote at the time of a similar crisis in his life twenty-three years later. At that time when the same root conflict had reached an intolerable state of intensity he did lose the balance of his mind and came very near to losing his life as well. Tchaïkovsky's mind, seen for a moment from a scientific viewpoint, constitutes a text-book illustration of the borderland between genius and insanity. If by genius we mean that abnormally acute vision of human values brought into reality by a highly organised mind, then insanity, too, reveals the same abnormal vision, no less true in its fundamental elements, but incapable of any creative expression and condemned to chaos and destruction.

It is only by constant effort and suffering that an artist of Tchaïkovsky's mental constitution can manage to orientate his mind towards sanity and productiveness. The explanation of his prolific output must surely be that he felt compelled to produce ceaselessly so as to create some sort of equation between his work and his unsatis-

fied and insatiable passions. Often in his youth he had to proceed by
trial and error. At the age of twenty, when working at his First
Symphony, he suffered from hallucinations and collapsed. Yet he
seems to have known himself sufficiently well to have seen the
danger coming. Three months before this breakdown—the first of
a periodical succession—he wrote to his brother Anatol:

> My nerves are altogether shaken. The causes are: (1) the symphony,
> which does not sound satisfactory; (2) Rubinstein and Tarnovsky have
> discovered that I am easily startled, and amuse themselves by giving
> me all manner of shocks all day long; (3) I cannot shake off the convic-
> tion that I shall not live long, and shall leave my symphony unfinished.
> I long for the summer and for Kamenka [his sister's house] as for the
> Promised Land, and hope to find rest and peace, and to forget all my
> troubles there. . . . I hate mankind in the mass, and I should be
> delighted to retire into some wilderness with very few inhabitants.

These perpetual fears which made social life impossible for him,
his despondency and his self-pity are all signs of his failure to divert
his energies into music completely. He struggled incessantly, but
however real his efforts a part of his mind remained imprisoned and
unable to conquer the worst of his fears. The pattern of his feelings,
so vividly coloured by his early allegiances to his mother and to
Sasha, developed soon into a warped or inverted conflict from which
he was never able to escape. His life would have been difficult enough
had he to bear the burden alone of an exceptional artistic temperament
with the constant threat of insanity in the background. That is, after
all, a price paid for creative power. But far worse than this and what
is really the tragedy of Tchaïkovsky was the denial, forced upon him,
of normal love. His neurotic character, of which he was perfectly
aware, not only forbade an intimacy with women but drove him into
homosexuality with all its attendant complications of furtiveness,
deception and guilt.

It is not always necessary, in the study of an artist's character, to
delve into the malformation of his mind. In some cases it may have
no more effect on his creative powers than a physical ailment that
incapacitates without in any way obscuring the artist's vision. It is
admittedly difficut to indicate where the inroads of a neurosis com-
mence and still more difficult to isolate it and say: 'Here is the
idealism and here is the cancer that corrodes and distorts it.' When
Oscar Wilde said that he put only his talent into his work, keeping
his genius for his life, I think he must have been speaking symboli-
cally. For talent we may read fantasy and for genius the chaotic conflicts which he was manifestly able to exclude from his art. The

poetry of Verlaine similarly reveals very little of the unbelievable sordidness of his neurotic character. But these were artists whose work displays moderation and reticence. Moreover, homosexuality in its various manifestations and degrees of intensity is not always—in fact, is probably seldom—revealed as a psychological disturbance. In Tchaïkovsky's character, however, the neurotic elements are inseparable from his development as a composer. The man and his music are one—unsatisfied and inflamed. An interesting sidelight on the unusual dual nature of his inspiration is provided by the origin of his *Romeo and Juliet* overture, a work which might well be held to refute this argument. Begun shortly after the abortive love affair with Désirée Artôt, *Romeo and Juliet* was not a subject of his own choosing. It was suggested to him by Balakirev, to whom it is dedicated, and who was allowed to supervise its lay-out and instrumentation.

Romeo and Juliet was performed in 1870. Seven years later the terrifying experiences that form a background to the composition of the Fourth Symphony and *Eugene Onegin* disclose the root conflicts of his disturbed mind. The gruesome story has been told before, and if it is repeated in detail here it is because of its importance as showing how it was that such music could have been written by such a man.

Towards the end of 1876 Tchaïkovsky received a commission to arrange some of his small pieces for violin and piano. The commission came from Nadezhda Filaretovna von Meck, a woman to whom he very soon became bound in a relationship as intimate as it was unreal. For fourteen years they carried on a correspondence of the most personal nature made possible only by their mutual agreement never to meet each other. Madame von Meck provided Tchaïkovsky with a handsome allowance, thus freeing him from his irksome duties as teacher of composition at the Moscow Conservatory and, what is still more significant, thus re-establishing another manifestation of maternal dependence. There can be no other explanation of this freakish relationship which has surely had no parallel in history since the guileless poets of the Middle Ages dedicated their verse to women who were of necessity to remain unknown and unseen. Tchaïkovsky, however, was less guileless than they. The long correspondence, collated with the letters to Modest, contains many examples of shuffling and insincerity. ' He is conscious,' writes Olga Bennigsen on this correspondence,

> that Madame von Meck's generosity has forged chains which bind him —however easy and golden, they are still fetters. ' I confess with regret,' he writes to his brother, ' that our relations are not normal and

at times I am keenly aware of this abnormality.' In his frequent
' moods ' he occasionally complains to his brothers of Madame von
Meck's undue solicitude for his comfort which he resents as indiscreet
interference; he indulges in not-too-kind sneers at her tender outpour-
ings; and he voices his misgivings concerning her suspected desire to
trespass upon his solitude. Having to write her wordy epistles often
bores him, and he complains of this tedious duty. These asides are in
glaring contrast with all he says in his letters to his benefactress, which
abound in protestations of love, devotion and gratitude. The reader
can hardly be blamed if he questions Tchaïkovsky's sincerity. But in
justice to him one should say that he was conscious of his faults and
shortcomings, and made no secret of them. He frankly admits ' the
duality of my nature . . . I think in one way and act in another.'

In justice to him, too, one should not overlook the gushing tone
of some of Madame von Meck's letters, which could be as insufferable
as some of Tchaïkovsky's worst manifestations of self-pity. She was
herself a recluse, sick in imagination and morbidly introspective,
though she had previously been a woman of exceptional energy and
devotion. Nine years Tchaïkovsky's senior, she had married at an
early age and during twenty years of married life had had eighteen
children. Of the eleven who survived when her husband died, only
a few months before the correspondence with Tchaïkovsky opens,
seven were still living with her. Her husband also left her an immense
fortune acquired largely through her own intelligent foresight.
Almost immediately after his death she was able to sublimate herself
in a passion for Tchaïkovsky's music and in what she imagined to be
his personality.

There is something wildly ecstatic in Madame von Meck's new
cult. A few months after the correspondence had begun, on March
18/30, 1877, she wrote apropos of a short piece she had asked him to
arrange from his opera *The Oprichnik* :

> Your march is so wonderful, Peter Ilyich, that it throws me—as I
> hoped—into a state of blissful madness, a condition in which one loses
> consciousness of all that is bitter and offensive in life. . . . Listening to
> such music, I seem to soar above all earthly thoughts, my temples throb,
> my heart beats wildly, a mist swims before my eyes and my ears drink
> in the enchantment of the music. I feel that all is well with me, and I
> do not want to be reawakened. Ah, God, how great is the man who has
> power to give others such moments of bliss![1]

Earlier, Madame von Meck had taken the initiative in this

[1] This seemingly extraordinary march was an arrangement of Natalya's arioso in
G flat in Act I : chromaticism and a sweeping melody produce a familiar Tchaikovskian
effect.

esoteric liaison. On February 15/27, 1877, she made the following confession set out almost in the form of a challenge :

> I should like to tell you a great deal about my fantastic feelings towards you, but I am afraid of taking up your leisure of which you have so little to spare. I will only say that this feeling—abstract as it may be—is one of the best and loftiest emotions ever yet experienced by any human being. Therefore you may call me eccentric, or mad, if you please; but you must not laugh at me. All this would be ridiculous, if it were not so sincere and serious.

Or, she might have added, so pathetic. Three weeks later she admits having taken ' every opportunity ' of hearing what was said of him. ' I stored up every remark, every fragment of criticism,' and she adds laconically, ' I must confess that just those things for which others blamed you were charms in my eyes—everyone to his taste! ' She makes it clear that any sort of personal acquaintance, at one time desirable, is now out of the question. ' I feel the more you fascinate me the more I shrink from knowing you.' At last Tchaïkovsky responds in terms displaying a corresponding infatuation. His letter of March 16/28, 1877, is a clear proof of what this new affection meant for him and is worth quoting at length.

> You are quite right, Nadezhda Filaretovna, in thinking that I am able fully to understand the peculiarities of your spiritual organism. I venture to think you're not mistaken in considering me a kindred spirit. Just as you've taken the trouble to study public opinion about me, I on my part have lost no chance of learning something about you and your way of life. I've always been interested in you as a human being in whose moral character are many traits common to my own nature. The very fact that we both suffer from one and the same malady draws us together. This malady is—misanthropy, but misanthropy of a peculiar kind, at the base of which there is certainly no hatred and contempt for people. People who suffer from this complaint fear not the harm that may be caused by intrigues but the disillusionment, the craving for the ideal, which are the consequence of every intimacy. There was a time when I was so possessed by this fear of people that I nearly went out of my mind. The circumstances of my life were such that I couldn't escape and hide myself. I had to fight it out with myself, and God alone knows what this struggle cost me.
>
> Now I've emerged from this struggle so far victorious that life has long ceased to be intolerable. Work saves me—work which is at the same time a pleasure. Thanks to a few successes which have fallen to my lot, I have taken courage, and depression, which used to amount to hallucinations and insanity, rarely visits me.
>
> From what I have said above, you will easily understand that I'm not at all surprised that, loving my music, you do not strive to make the acquaintance of its composer. You are afraid of not finding in me those

qualities with which I have been endowed by your imagination with its tendency to idealisation. And you are absolutely right. I feel that on closer acquaintance with me you would not find that congruence, that full harmony between the musician and the man, of which you dream.

Now allow me to thank you for those expressions of love for my music, of which your letter is so full. If you only knew how pleasing and consoling it is to a musician when he knows there is one soul which feels so strongly and so deeply all that he himself felt when he was planning and writing his work. Thank you for your kind and warm remarks. I won't say, for the sake of becoming modesty, that I'm unworthy of them. Whether I write well or ill, one thing is certain— that I write from an inward and irresistible impulse. I speak the language of music because I always have something to say. I write *sincerely,* and it is extraordinarily consoling to me to meet in you someone who values this sincerity.

He found consolation, but also material support. He had already received from Madame von Meck several highly paid commissions, and by May he was asking her for a loan of 3,000 rubles. In the same letter he announces his intention of dedicating his Fourth Symphony to her. The opening theme of this work, ' our symphony,' as he calls it, represents ' a force which, like the sword of Damocles, hangs perpetually over our heads and is always embittering the soul.' It is not irrelevant to point out that in his letters to Modest he refers to this same ' sword of Damocles which always hangs over my head " to convey the fear lest his perversion be exposed. This perversion is never named outright; he speaks of it enigmatically as *That.* The wretched man was riddled with guilt. At the end of May 1877 he made the desperate decision to marry in order, as he had put it some months earlier, ' to shut the mouths of all despicable gossips.'

At the very time Tchaïkovsky met Antonina Milyukova, 'a rather pretty girl of spotless reputation,' though ' no longer very young '— she was actually twenty-eight—he was working on the letter scene of *Eugene Onegin.* In the opera Tatyana's love for Onegin is cruelly rebuffed. Tchaïkovsky confessed that he was ' in love with the image of Tatyana and furious with Onegin for his heartlessness.' On this evidence the view has been put forward that Tchaïkovsky found in his future wife, who was certainly as forward as Pushkin's heroine, a Tatyana in real life. But this is an over-simplification of the problem. Antonina, like Nadezhda von Meck, developed a purely idealised love for Tchaïkovsky. The difference was that Antonina was not content to live in a world of fantasy; if her dreams were not to be realised, she threatened suicide. Tchaïkovsky entered into marriage, therefore, at the pistol-point. He had no love for the girl; he

B

had no intention of forming anything more than a Platonic union; the main merit of his marriage, as he makes quite clear, was that it would serve to obscure his perversion from the world. He also seems to have imagined, naïvely enough, that by such a marriage he could conquer his nature.

A month before the marriage took place he gave a detailed account of the whole affair to Madame von Meck (in a letter of July 3/15, 1877):

> In the latter part of May, in the most unexpected manner, I *became engaged to be married*. This is how it happened. Some time before this I received a letter from a girl whom I knew and had met previously. From this letter I learned that she had long honoured me with her love. The letter was written so sincerely, so warmly, that I decided to answer it, which in such cases previously I had carefully avoided doing. Although my answer did not give my correspondent any hope that the feeling could be mutual, an exchange of letters began. I won't tell you the details of this correspondence, but the result was that I agreed to go to see her. Why did I? It seems to me as if the power of fate had drawn me to that girl. When I met her I again explained to her that I felt no more than sympathy and gratitude for her love. But when I left her I began to think over all the thoughtlessness of what I had done. If I don't love her, if I don't want to encourage her feelings, then why have I been to see her, and how will it all end?
>
> From her next letter I came to the conclusion that if I suddenly turned my back on this girl after having gone so far, I should cause her real unhappiness and drive her to a tragic end. So I had a difficult alternative: either to save my freedom at the price of the girl's ruin (*ruin* is not an empty word here: she really loves me to distraction) or *to marry*. I could not do otherwise than choose the latter. One thing that helped me to this decision was the fact that my eighty-two-year-old father and all those near to me think of nothing but my getting married. So one fine evening I went to my future wife, told her frankly that I didn't love her but that I would be a devoted and grateful friend. I described in detail my character, my irritability, variable temperament, my unsociability, and finally my circumstances. Then I asked her if she wished to be my wife. The answer, of course, was in the affirmative. I have no words to tell you the awful feelings I experienced during the first few days after that evening. It's understandable. Having lived thirty-seven years with an antipathy to marriage, it's very hard to be goaded by the force of circumstances into the position of a fiancé—moreover one not in the least attracted by his bride. One must alter one's whole way of life, one must think of the welfare and peace of mind of the other person to whom one's destiny is bound—all this is not very easy for a bachelor hardened in egoism.
>
> In order to think it over and adjust my mind to such a future, I decided not to change my original plan but to go to the country for a month. I did so. The quiet country life, surrounded by people very dear

to me, as well as the beauties of nature, had a most beneficial effect on me. I decided that I could not avoid my destiny and that there was something predestined about my meeting with this girl. Also I know from experience that very often in life, what frightens and appals sometimes results in good, and on the other hand, something we have striven for in the hope of happiness and success, disappoints us. Let what is to be, be.

The letter continues with a description of Antonina and ends with the dubious protestation that its writer's 'conscience is clear.' The marriage took place on July 6/18, the news giving his eighty-three-year-old father such happiness that he 'crossed himself and jumped for joy.' A few days later he was telling Anatol of his ' ghastly spiritual torture ' and that Antonina had become ' physically absolutely repulsive ' to him. With his marriage, he told Madame von Meck, 'music, for the best part of me, had perished for ever.' It is just possible that he really believed it. But in August when Antonina went alone to Moscow to prepare their home, and Tchaïkovsky to his sister at Kamenka, he is fed and inflamed by his thwarted passions and resumes work on both the Fourth Symphony and *Eugene Onegin*. The collapse, however, is inescapable. The day following his arrival in Moscow he is panic-stricken. ' My only desire is for the chance to run away somewhere. But how and where? It is impossible, impossible, impossible! ' A fortnight later the climax to the dreadful episode comes in a fit of combined insanity and cowardice. Gerald Abraham[1] has here given the authentic account :

> One bitterly cold night he waded in to the river ' almost up to his waist,' hoping to catch pneumonia, and told Antonina, on his return, that he had been fishing and had fallen in accidentally. But his robust physique defeated him. Finally, having induced Anatol to send a faked telegram in Nápravnik's name, he fled to Petersburg on September 24/October 6 ' in a state bordering on insanity.' Anatol took him straight to a hotel where, after a terrible nerve-storm, he lay unconscious for nearly forty-eight hours. The verdict of the doctor, a mental specialist, was that nothing but complete change would save his reason; there must be no renewal of conjugal relations, and it would be advisable for Tchaïkovsky never even to see his wife again.

Tchaïkovsky parted from his wife, but only to plunge still more deeply into the illusory alliance with Madame von Meck, who now maintains him with a handsome allowance until, three years before his death, she suddenly severs all connections, ostensibly for financial reasons but actually, it seems, because of an erratic nature that was

[1] *Tchaïkovsky : A Short Biography* (Duckworth, 1944).

beginning to preclude any constancy of sentiment. They were certainly birds of a feather, these tortured souls. Beginning with the Fourth Symphony and *Eugene Onegin*, Tchaïkovsky's music now reflects all the indulgent yearning and the garish exteriorisation of a composer who can never refrain from wearing his heart on his sleeve —if, indeed, it is not music which suggests a less modest image than that.

Yet the elements of his music are unchanged. His friend Taneev was the first critic to perceive the origin of his very personal style in ballet music, its pretty tunes and dainty effects distorted by an ecstatic, self-lacerating personality. ' In my opinion,' Taneev says (in a letter of March 18/30, 1878),

> the [Fourth] Symphony has one defect to which I shall never be reconciled: in every movement there are phrases which sound like ballet music—the middle section of the andante, the trio of the scherzo and a kind of march in the finale. Hearing the symphony, my inner eye sees involuntarily our *prima ballerina* which puts me out of humour and spoils my pleasure in the many beauties of the work.

Tchaïkovsky admitted the criticism, but attempts to defend himself by saying that he ' can never understand why " ballet music " should be used as a contemptuous epithet. The music of a ballet is not invariably bad, there are good works of this class—Delibes's *Sylvia* for instance.'

Those words go a long way towards defining the difference between Tchaïkovsky and the Russian nationalist composers. He had more facility than Mussorgsky, more skill than Borodin, more passion than Rimsky-Korsakov, more sustained inspiration than Balakirev. But he had neither their drama, nor their fantasy, nor their originality. The derivation of his later, characteristic style is still the conventional idiom of his contemporaries in France. It is doubtful whether he was aware of this derivation, though a letter to Madame von Meck of February 5/17, 1883, suggests that he was. ' In the modern French composers,' he says, ' you do not find that ugliness in which some of our composers indulge in the mistaken idea that originality consists in treading underfoot all previous traditions of beauty.' He persisted in placing the lesser French composers of the nineteenth century on a much higher level than their German contemporaries. ' Bizet stands head and shoulders above the rest,' he continues, ' but there are also Massenet, Delibes, Guiraud, Lalo, Godard and Saint-Saëns. All these are men of talent who cannot be compared with the dry, *routinier* style of the contemporary Germans.'

A preference for 'ballet music' is obvious enough in this judgment—
a preference which, incidentally, brings us a little nearer to understanding how it was that Mozart could have been the idol of such
an un-Mozartian composer as Tchaïkovsky. It must surely have been
a Mozart of Dresden china that he worshipped.

This strange use of the ballet idiom overlaid, as it is, with an
almost hysterical emotionalism[1] is only another aspect of that conflict
that never lies far beneath the surface of Tchaïkovsky's music. We
have already seen that *Eugene Onegin* and the Fourth Symphony
were the outward manifestations of his divided allegiances during the
year 1877. And in one form or another this conflict persists to the
end of his life, his forked sexuality condemning him to subterfuge
and duplicity, though at the same time he presents a picture of the
perfect bourgeois gentleman, working regularly, travelling abroad,
a benevolent uncle, playing patience at night and concerned with his
physical ailments. The voluminous correspondence with Nadezhda
von Meck is full of pages of dull, minute details—pages which Olga
Bennigsen describes as 'more suited to his medical adviser than to a
lady-friend.' 'The reader has difficulty in realising,' she observes,
'that the letters are written by a young man and not an old dotard
whose interests are centred in his digestion and minor ailments of a
senile organism.' Sometimes, too, he makes no effort to conceal a
schoolgirlish sentimentality. 'Do you love flowers?' he asks his
benefactress in all naïvety. 'I am passionately fond of them, especially
the wild flowers of the field and forest. To my mind the queen of
flowers is the lily-of-the-valley. Modest, who is equally fond of
flowers, is all for the violet, so that we often fall out on the subject'—
and so on for the rest of the page. Towards the end of his life, at his
house at Maidanovo, the would-be country gentleman followed a
routine existence from which he seldom deviated 'by more than a
minute or so':

> He rose between seven and eight, drank tea and read the Bible, then
> studied English or read serious books and took a short walk. He
> worked from half-past nine to one o'clock, which was his dinner hour.
> After dinner, no matter what the weather, he took a solitary two-hour
> walk, unaccompanied even by a dog, and it was during these afternoon
> walks that he did most of his creative work, jotting down memoranda
> in innumerable little note-books. These notes were afterwards worked
> out at the piano into the 'sketch' or reduced score, and his full orches-
> tral scores seldom differed materially from the 'sketch.' When he was

[1] It is impossible, in view of Tchaïkovsky's admiration for Delibes, not to suspect
the origin of the scherzo of the Fourth Symphony in such a seemingly remote work
as the 'Pizzicato' from *Sylvia*.

not composing on his walks, he would recite aloud—usually in French. At four o'clock he had tea, worked from five to seven; then took another walk, this time with company if any were available, before supper at eight o'clock. After supper he would read or play cards—patience, if alone—talk or play the piano till eleven, when he retired.

He told Madame von Meck that ' under normal conditions there is no hour of the day in which I cannot compose.' His boast that ' when there is question of an order I am ready to set a corn-plaster advertisement to music ' reminds one of the application of certain French composers, of Rameau who was prepared to set the *Journal d'Hollande* to music, and of Darius Milhaud who actually did set a catalogue of agricultural implements.

But there his affinities with the French ideals stop short. No composer ever showed a greater lack of *pudeur*, that word for which there is no equivalent in English, expressing an almost pious respect for sensuousness, or an honest sense of shame without any suggestion of priggishness or hypocrisy. Behind the exterior of a successful composer, decorated by the Tsar, journeying to Cambridge to receive an honorary doctorate or to America for a concert tour, there is the whining tone of so many of Tchaïkovsky's declarations, and that parading of his inmost thoughts with the persistence of an exhibitionist. ' I often think that the whole of my discontent,' he says, ' is due to the fact that I am very egotistic, that I am unable to sacrifice myself for others, even those near and dear to me.' He accused himself not only of egotism but of insincerity and sham. ' To whomever I write and whatever I write about, he once confided to his diary, ' I always worry about the impression the letter will make, not only on my correspondent but on any chance reader. Consequently, I pose. Sometimes I strive to make the tone of the letter simple and sincere, i.e., to make it appear so. But, except letters written in moments of aberration, I am never my true self in my correspondence.' This admission is bad enough, and as if to show that he deserves not to be condemned but to be pitied for such duplicity he adds, ' These letters are constant sources of remorse and regret, sometimes even very painful ones.'

As the years go by references in his diaries to drunkenness become more and more frequent, and there are many cryptic entries regarding a certain ' sensation Z.' His servant Alexey Sofronov, who had entered Tchaïkovsky's service at the age of fourteen and remained with him till his death in 1893, is mentioned in the most amorous terms, and later a similar passion is displayed for his nephew (nicknamed 'Bob') Davïdov. The most revealing documents on Tchaïkovsky's intimate life appear to have been destroyed at the composer's request, yet they could hardly have added much to the existing evidence of his character, detailed and complete enough as it is, a formidable contradiction of genuine passion and hypocritical sham. Less than a year before his death, Tchaïkovsky began his last symphony, which he dedicated to his nephew, informing him that its 'programme shall remain an enigma for everyone—let them puzzle their heads over it.' It was Modest who suggested the title *Pathétique* —certainly an appropriate title, as it turned out, for two weeks after its first performance Tchaïkovsky died of cholera and Vladimir Davïdov eventually committed suicide in his uncle's house at Klin.

And yet pathos, despite the fervour of his suffering, is not a quality that Tchaïkovsky could express with any sense of nobility. The man and his music combine to show that his grief and sorrow remain imprisoned within himself, so that it is never pity that he expresses, but self-pity and with it self-love and self-hatred. The dignity of suffering was unknown to him, but not its pleasures. He is the musician of indulgence. Power is evident in his character, but one suspects at the same time a strain of impotence which, far from reducing his creative force, excites and enhances it with an unnaturally vivid imagination. It may be unorthodox in modern musical criticism to point, in a symphony, to a sense of guilt or of sin; but they are there, in his letters as in his music, expressed with the same horrifying terror as in the poetry of Baudelaire. If there is no humour in his character there is also no irony, no embittered sarcasm. Nor is there cleverness in Tchaïkovsky. His is not the 'art of concealing art'; it is music to gorge on, shameless in its sensuousness and splendour. And it was no accident that such music was conceived by a warped neurotic, shy and tortured.

2

The Symphonies

By

Martin Cooper

IT IS DIFFICULT to speak of Tchaïkovsky's development as a symphonic writer because, in the words of his brother Modest, he moved in 'spiral convolutions.' His nature was so emotional and so quick to respond to external impulses, his emotions themselves were so violent and mercurial, than any logical evolution of style could only have been unnatural, the forced product of theorising. Tchaïkovsky only theorised when he was hard put to it; and though his criticisms of his own works are often astonishingly shrewd and sensible his compositions are so much the fruit of the emotional *élan* of the moment, so spontaneous and immediate in their inspiration as in their effect, that each work has to be accepted on its own merits, without too many preconceived ideas in the listener's head. This is one of the reasons why Tchaïkovsky has always been a popular composer, often encountering scorn or cold disapproval among critics; and just as no works of his are more popular than his last three symphonies, so no works have met with more criticism from the severely minded critics.

Although he himself professed to despise the 'programme symphony' we shall see that his conception of the symphony was, in fact, purely romantic and differed more in name than anything else from programme music: that the sonata form demanded by the first and last movements of the classical symphony was frankly a bed of Procrustes on which he was sometimes forced to torture his happiest inspirations, and that he was at his happiest in the two middle movements of the symphonic scheme, which allow great latitude both in content and in form. The real test of the symphonist, properly so called, is his handling of sonata form, and it would have been strange if Tchaïkovsky had found this test an easy one.

The Romantics were never natural symphonists, because music was to them primarily evocative and biographical—generally autobiographical—and the dramatic phrase, the highly coloured melody and the ' atmospheric ' harmony which they loved are in direct opposition to the nature of the symphony, which is primarily an architectural form. The movement away from the architectural towards the dramatic, from line to colour, was implicit in the later works of Beethoven. It is clearer in Schubert; and with the full growth of the Romantic movement it led quickly and .inevitably to the cultivation of new forms, more vague, more intimate and more easily moulded to the ebb and flow of the composer's emotion —to the fantasia, the ballad, the impromptu. The most typical of the Romantics were never symphonists at all: Chopin and Schumann were pianists, Weber and Wagner operatic composers, Liszt a rhapsodist in every genre. Even the return to symphonic form in Schumann, Mendelssohn and Brahms was not really a return to linear, architectural music: it was at best an attempt to fuse the two elements, most successful in Brahms because in him the violence and directness of emotional expression was somehow veiled and muted and therefore least apt to disturb the balance and proportion of the form.

The true successor of the symphony is the symphonic poem, in which Liszt and Berlioz first tried to combine large-scale orchestral writing with the ragged violence and brilliant colour of Romanticism, with a literary programme which was to be evoked and suggested by every device of harmony, melody, rhythm and colour. Every symphonic poem is really an extended fantasia, for a fantasia is the basic romantic form. Some of these works may conform, to a certain extent, to the old form of the symphony, but the underlying process is quite different: it is rather a rhapsodising of the composer within a certain emotional mood, a free play of the emotions over the surface of some story (in case of works with an avowed programme) or some *idée fixe* in the ostensibly more abstract compositions. The rough outlines of the old symphony were useful, as pegs on which to hang this loose, brilliant, often diaphanous material; or Liszt again evolved the technique of the cyclic form, the perpetual recurrence under various different aspects of a single motive which would give at least superficial unity to the work. Tchaïkovsky was more or less aware of this process.

You ask [he wrote to Nadezhda von Meck about the Fourth Symphony] if I stick to established forms. Yes and no. In certain compositions, such as a symphony, the form is taken for granted and I keep to it—but only as to the large outline and proper sequence of

25

movements. The details can be manipulated as freely as one chooses, according to the natural development of the musical idea. For instance, the first movement of our symphony is handled very freely. The second theme, which tradition places in a related major key, is here minor and unrelated. In the recapitulation of the same movement the second theme appears only in part, etc. The Finale also deviates from conventional form.

In fact, the symphony is to him simply a form, a convenience, no longer the natural, instinctive channel for his musical imagination. Form was always a difficulty to the Romantics, and inevitably, since the emotions which they were trying to express were of their essence vague and refused to assume regular, symmetrical shapes. Hence comes the Romantic insistence on colour, the enormous widening of the harmonic field and the development in orchestral technique: for these—harmony and timbre—can give new and quite different significance to the melodic phrase. But they cannot solve the problem of form, and so, in despair, the old forms were taken over, although more often than not the new wine burst the old skins.

All my life I have been much troubled by my inability to grasp and manipulate form in music. I fought hard against this defect and can say with pride that I achieved some progress, but I shall end my days without ever having written anything that is perfect in form. What I write has always a mountain of padding: an experienced eye can detect the thread in my seams and I can do nothing about it.

Tchaïkovsky is often unusually frank and shrewd in his criticism of his own work. He understood and admired the genuine symphonic ideal: Mozart was a god to him, and he must have been blind if he could not see the difference between his symphonies and Mozart's, not simply as music but as symphonies. This distinction is worth making because many writers about music have often spoken as though a lack of the specifically symphonic gift, a temperamental distaste for sonata form, were in itself a sign of a composer's inferiority. Now this is to erect a certain form which was admirably suited to the music of a given period into a categorical imperative for all time, simply because the music of that period has never in actual fact been surpassed—although we have had only two hundred years in which to surpass it. It is on a par with the once-popular argument that, because no more beautiful and satisfactory churches than the Gothic cathedrals of the Middle Ages have been built since, therefore all churches should be built in the Gothic style. If, however, we accept sonata form as one proved successful in a number of great compositions, and Gothic as an architectural style proved successful by the same test, we find a parallel development in each art. From the union of the Gothic with the new ideals of the Renaissance and the Counter-Reformation there developed a new style—the Baroque—which is not simply a decadent form of the Gothic but a genuinely new architectural style, an organic development from the Gothic but as different in individuality as a child from its father. In much the same way the symphonic poem grew from the symphony, by cross-fertilisation with the Romantic ideals of colour, emotional expressiveness and dramatic intensity; and to judge a symphonic poem by the same standards as are applied to a symphony is to judge, say, the Peterskirche in Vienna by the same standards as those applying to Notre-Dame. The two styles, though related, are quite distinct, each with its proper excellence.

Something the same is true of the romantic symphonic poem, in which a new range of emotions meets the old classical symphony, whose whole nature is thereby changed and widened. It is useless to discuss the respective merits of the two forms, which will always appear different to different temperaments. What must be borne in mind is that the same principles do not apply absolutely to the two genres and that a symphonic poem is not simply a bad symphony.

Tchaïkovsky himself admitted that his Fourth Symphony was ' programme ' music, and, by implication, he seems to admit it of his other symphonies. Replying to Taneev's charge that the symphony ' gives the effect of a symphonic poem to which the composer has slapped on three more movements and called it a symphony,' he wrote:

> As to your remark about my symphony being programmatic, I quite agree, but don't see why you consider this a defect. On the contrary, I should be sorry if *symphonies that mean nothing* should flow from my pen, consisting solely of a progression of harmonies, rhythms and modulations. Most assuredly my symphony has a programme, but one that cannot be expressed in words : the very attempt would be ludicrous. But is this not proper to a symphony, *the most purely lyrical of musical forms?* Should not a symphony reveal those wordless urges that hide in the heart, asking earnestly for expression? . . . As a matter of fact the work is patterned after Beethoven's Fifth Symphony—not as to musical content but as to the basic idea. Don't you see a programme in the Fifth? [The italics are mine.—M.C.]

In fact, to Tchaïkovsky the only difference between a symphony and a symphonic poem lay in the vagueness of the programme underlying the one and the explicitly literary programme of the other.

A symphony without a programme was a 'symphony that meant nothing.' Perhaps even more revealing is his description of symphony as 'the most purely lyrical of musical forms'—'lyrical meaning, it would seem, that emotion or mood which can be expressed in no other art but music, the spontaneous expression in sound of those fears, longings and desires which are both too vague and too violently definite to be expressed in words. Now, that lyrical emotion should find its natural expression in sonata form is perhaps not unthinkable, but only if that form is so natural to a composer, both by instinct and habit, that it has come to be really an acquired instinct, a 'second nature,' as we say; and this was certainly never true of Tchaïkovsky, who confessed his difficulties in one of his letters to Nadezhda von Meck:

> I write my sketches on the first piece of paper that comes to hand, sometimes a scrap of writing-paper, and I write in very abbreviated form. The melody never appears in my head without its attendant harmony. In general, these two musical elements, together with the rhythm, cannot be conceived separately: every melodic idea carries its own inevitable harmony and rhythm. If the harmonies are very complicated, one must indicate the part-writing in the sketch. . . . Concerning instrumentation, if one is composing for orchestra, the musical idea carries with it the proper instrumentation for its expression.

And in a second letter, written next day:

> Talking with you yesterday about the process of composing, I did not express myself clearly concerning the work that follows the first sketch. This phase is especially important: what has been written with passion must now be looked upon critically, corrected, extended and, most important of all, condensed to fit the requirements of the form. One must sometimes go against the grain in this, be merciless, and destroy things that were written with love and inspiration. Although I cannot complain of poor inventive powers or imagination, I have always suffered from lack of skill in the management of form. Only persistent labour has at last permitted me to achieve a form that in some degree corresponds to the content. In the past I was careless, I did not realise the extreme importance of this critical examination of the preliminary sketch. For this reason the succeeding episodes were loosely held together and seams were always visible. That was a serious defect, and it was years before I began to correct it, yet my compositions will never be good examples of form because I can only *correct* what is wrong with my musical nature—I cannot change it intrinsically.

This was written shortly after the Fourth Symphony, and it shows a very clear understanding of his own defects. Invention and imagination were never any difficulty: ideas were plentiful.

But to force those ideas to 'develop' and to grow organically, to curb the natural tendency of every Romantic to improvise, to force a free fantasia into sonata form, was pain and grief to Tchaïkovsky; and, as he says, the seams are often enough visible.

It is not difficult to see, by examining the actual thematic material of the great classical symphonies, that the original themes from which a symphonic movement is built up do not need to be in themselves striking or of great intrinsic beauty. The first subject of the first movement of the *Eroica* is in itself a banal enough arrangement of the notes of the major triad: and the second subject of the first movement of Schubert's Unfinished Symphony is such a melody as a child might pick out for itself on the piano. But this is, of course, only true of the primitive germ-cell, so to speak, from which these themes start: their growth and future development depend entirely on the genius of the composer. Not that a composer of genius can construct a great symphony on any theme, or combination of themes, whatever. That architectural principle which we call ' sonata form ' demands certain qualities which may be present in an apparently banal theme and lacking in one of striking beauty; in fact, it would be almost true to say that a theme of striking intrinsic beauty is probably unsuited to a movement in sonata form, and for an excellent reason. The principle of sonata form is the principle of contrast, but it is also the principle of unity in diversity. First and second subject must be contrasted—whether we preserve the old categories of masculine and feminine or not—but they must also be united, capable of organic growth and development during which they can come into direct contact with each other, coalescing and separating, contrasted and yet fundamentally at unity. A melody of great individuality is impatient of this process, it tends to dominate the whole movement in which it is placed, to refuse equal rights to any other melody and thus to ruin the balance and proportion which are the proper beauties of sonata form. With the symphonic poem, the symphonic fantasy which preserves the shell of the old structure only for convenience, the case is different. Tchaïkovsky confessed his difficulty in ' correcting, extending and, most important of all, condensing to fit the requirements of the form.' That is to say, his development sections—since he insisted on preserving a show at least of sonata form—will be naturally weak, and this we find to be true.

Musical development is a kind of creative evolution or unfolding of the latent possibilities—rhythmic, melodic and harmonic—of a given theme, or of a single limb or phrase of that theme. This is a purely musical activity and has little or nothing to do with the free fantasia, the rhapsodising in a given atmosphere or upon a given poetic idea, which was the forte of the Romantics. Some melodies lend themselves very much more than others to this process; and Russian folk-song, on account of its repetitive character and its tendency to be itself a microscopic set of variations, is peculiarly unsuitable. So, too, is the evocative, atmospheric melody loved by the Romantics, which appears already in full bloom, as it were, charged with all the emotion and all the musical interest which it can bear. With both these types of melody there is but one course open to the symphonist, and that is to substitute a form of repetition for true development, to say again in a rather different way what has already been said once and to trust to the beauty and significance of what are fundamentally variations to supply the place of the 'development section' demanded by sonata form. This was, in fact, the course adopted by Tchaïkovsky. If his symphonies are to be judged—as he would certainly, I think, have wished them to be —by the strict academic tests, by his manipulation of sonata form in the appropriate movements, then they may be fine music but they are poor symphonies. If, on the other hand, they are judged as a hybrid species, a cross between the primarily architectural form of the symphony and the primarily 'literary' or 'poetic' form of the symphonic poem, they are completely successful. Individual temperament will probably always decide—as with the rest of Tchaïkovsky's music—whether the listener tends to take the indulgent or the censorious point of view.

It is not that Tchaïkovsky's development sections lack interest —at least in his later, mature symphonies. It is, in fact, rather in the immature first three, where Tchaïkovsky is less sure of himself and therefore adheres more closely to the classical pattern, that the interest is least. This is perhaps particularly true of the Third Symphony, which is in every way the least individual, the most academic of the six. Here he borrows the manner, but nothing of the fundamental spirit, of the classical symphony. In the First Symphony his handling of sonata form in the first movement is rather weak and thin, but not positively irregular. He had not yet the skill or the individuality to break away from the academic forms and to create anything really original in its place. In the Second he was perhaps conscious of his poverty of developing-power, and therefore introduced the theme of the introduction into his development section. By the time of the Fourth Symphony he had found his own genius, and inspiration was stronger than scruple. The development section of the first movement is little more than a free fantasia on the persistent rhythmic figure of the first subject and within that same restless, hectic emotional atmosphere. Musical growth seems to demand a certain tranquillity, or at least serenity, of atmosphere—a relaxation of tension and stress—and this was virtually unknown to Tchaïkovsky. His attempted fugato passages are always held up suddenly by some scarlet danger signal (cf. Sixth Symphony, pp. 35–6 in the miniature score[1]) or they peter out for lack of vitality (cf. Fifth Symphony, pp. 28–9 in the miniature score). One of Tchaïkovsky's methods of avoiding this dilemma was the use of a pedal point, in the broadest sense of the term—either the persistent repetition of a rhythmic figure, as in the Fifth and Sixth Symphonies *passim,* or a succession of short phrases repeated at mounting intervals, as in the Fourth.

Mention has already been made of the cyclic form evolved by Liszt and Berlioz in order to give at least a superficial unity to the symphonic poem. A single motive recurs throughout the work in different forms or under different aspects, varying in fact but remaining recognisably the same. This technique was, of course, only another instance of the substitution of repetition for development. Tchaïkovsky makes a certain limited use of it by opening all his symphonies, except the first, with a solemn, intensely ' atmospheric ' passage of unmistakable character, which returns in some cases throughout the first movement, in others right through the whole work. In the Second Symphony it is introduced, as we have seen, to enliven the flagging development section, and then does not appear again. But in the Fourth the fanfare of ' destiny ' with which the symphony opens is, in Tchaïkovsky's own words, ' the germ of the entire symphony '; and its reappearance, dictated by pro-grammatic rather than purely musical considerations, gives at least a poetic unity to the first movement, although it does not appear again later. In the Fifth Symphony the theme of the introduction reappears, typically ' transformed ' (cf. the Mephistopheles move-ment in Liszt's *Faust Symphony*), into a valse rhythm which enhances its sinister character (p. 126 in the miniature score) and again, in another form, as an introduction at the beginning of the fourth movement (p. 128). In the Sixth Symphony Tchaïkovsky

[1] Miniature score references to Philharmonia (Hawkes) for Nos. 4 and 5, to Eulenburg for No. 6.—M.C.

31

proceeds rather differently, for here the introduction is the genuine musical germ from which the first subject of the first movement grows; and the only other reference to it is at the end of the last movement, and this is rather a return to the same orchestral pitch and colour than a restatement of the identical phrases of the introduction.

This unification of a work by subtly varied forms of repetition was brought to a fine point by Tchaïkovsky, who neglected no possible opportunity. His extreme sensitiveness to orchestral colour, to the timbre of each instrument and each combination of instruments, was far more than a mere natural gift for orchestration; it amounted to a real source of inspiration in itself, and sometimes acted as a unifying principle.

> You ask how I work in regard to orchestration. I never compose in the abstract—never does the musical idea come to me except with suitable exterior form. So I find the musical thought simultaneously with the orchestration. When I wrote the scherzo of the [Fourth] Symphony, I imagined it just as you heard it. It is impossible if not performed pizzicato. If played with the bow it would lose everything. It would be a soul without a body and all its charm would disappear.

In a letter written four months after this (July 1878) Tchaïkovsky admitted that ' one often changes the instrumentation later '; but internal evidence—the unfailing correspondence between a theme and its instrumentation, between the musical idea and its expression in sound—points to Tchaïkovsky's first thoughts being almost invariably right, his instinctive knowledge of the genius of each instrument almost infallible. Instances of this felicity in orchestration, this intimate relationship between a theme and its exponent instrument, are spread throughout Tchaïkovsky's symphonies from the very beginning. In the second movement of the First Symphony the long melody (see Ex. 2 at end of book) is entrusted first to the oboe, although the title of the movement (' A land of gloom, a land of mists.') would suggest some darker-coloured timbre, some thicker orchestral texture, to most beginners who took their ideas of orchestration from text-books rather than personal inspiration. But the oboe does, in fact, sound reedy and harsh, as well as conventionally suave; and here it calls up the voice of a marsh-bird, suggesting with the greatest economy of means the desolation, the sinister emptiness of a deserted winter landscape as the fog descends. The horn solo (an Ukrainian variant of the folk-tune ' Down by Mother Volga ') with which the Second Symphony opens (Ex. 3)

is an early example of the great importance Tchaïkovsky attached
to the exact grading of tone-details which he was always most careful to show, particularly in the many passages for solo instruments
which occur throughout the symphonies (cf. introduction of the
Sixth). His predilection for the lower register of the wood-wind,
especially noticeable in the later symphonies, is already suggested
in the second movement of the Second Symphony (the original
nuptial march from the opera *Undine*) which opens with a hollow,
nocturnal-sounding version of the march entrusted to the clarinets
in their lowest register and the bassoons. The middle section contains a solo passage for clarinets in the same register also.[1] This is
the predominant timbre throughout the introduction and the first
statement of the first subject in the Fifth Symphony; it returns
again in the third movement (pp. 121 *et seq*. and 126 in the miniature score) and again in the opening of the finale. In the Sixth
Symphony the combinations are more sophisticated, and the dark
registers of the strings (the low register in all but the viola, whose
higher register has a thin, unearthly effect far more melancholy
than the lower) take the place of the chalumeau register of the
clarinet.

Roughly speaking, one may say that the musical atmosphere of
each of the symphonies is given at the opening, either in the introduction or in the opening passages of the first movement. The flutes
and bassoons, at two octaves' interval and set against a tremolando
in the strings, prepare the gentle and elegant, rather Mendelssohnian
atmosphere of the First Symphony (Ex. 1) : just as the horn fanfare at
the beginning of the Fourth Symphony sets a kind of ' brazen ' note
which persists throughout the first movement (cf. the Meyerbeerian
passage on pp. 31 *et seq*. of the miniature score), returns in the trio
of the scherzo (p. 113) and dominates the whole last movement
again. Tchaïkovsky's use of the brass has often been criticised as
vulgar (perhaps it is one of the devices fastidiously hinted at in
Grove as used ' *ad captandum* '); but such criticisms are based—as I
hope to show later—on false premisses and are too vague to com-
mand very much attention. Brilliant and effective it certainly is;
and yet the ear is very seldom tired, as it is so often in Wagner, by the
constant presence of brass timbre. Tchaïkovsky's temperament was
too naturally volatile to continue very long in any one vein; and if he
does offend in this manner it is more in the piling of climax upon

[1] Cf. also Third Symphony, third movement (solo bassoon passage), and Fourth
Symphony, second movement (beginning of più mosso).

climax in the top register of the strings, as in the first movement of the Fourth, and the first and second movements of the Fifth Symphonies, where such passages as occur on pp. 94–5 of the Fifth Symphony do more than tear the heart (as indeed they are meant to do) but also affect the nerves like an exhibition of hysteria (with which they are very possibly related). This tendency reaches its climax in the last movement of the Sixth Symphony, where the perpetually repeated descending phrase with which the strings open the movement is raised to a hysterical pitch of emotion on pp. 197 *et seq.*, following very shortly after the climax already reached on pp. 192 *et seq.* There is something quite unbalanced and, in the last resort, ugly, in this dropping of all restraint. This man is ill, we feel: must we be shown all his sores without exception? Will he insist on our not merely witnessing, but sharing, one of his nervous attacks? These moments are almost physically painful, and what agony they must have sprung from in the composer himself hardly bears thinking of. This, perhaps, was the secret of his passion for Mozart, the passion of a man dying of thirst in a desert, for a green field with a stream running at the bottom of it.

Apart from these 'crises,' however, Tchaïkovsky's use of the strings was often extremely sensitive and delicate. The scherzo of the Fourth Symphony is an obvious example, although there the effect was probably suggested more by memories of a balalayka orchestra[1] than by pure string tone. But in the middle section of the valse movement of the Fifth and the whole of the third movement of the Sixth Tchaïkovsky's purely ornamental string-writing is unsurpassable. The accompaniment of the second subject in the first movement of the Fourth Symphony is an excellent example of Tchaïkovsky's blending of wood-wind and string tone, and the more effective for its following close on the hectic, insistent rhythms of the first subject. He uses the violoncellos again towards the end of the slow movement (pp. 102–3) although his usual preference was for a combination of two solo instruments, as in the slow movement of the First (oboe and bassoon), the scherzo of the Third (violin and clarinet), the slow movement of the Fifth (horn and clarinet, and later clarinet and bassoon) and the first movement of the Sixth Symphony (wood-wind combinations in the

---

[1] Cf. Mr. Lockspeiser's suggestion on p. 21. Another possible ancestor of this movement is a chorus in *A Life for the Tsar*, where Glinka actually uses pizzicato to suggest balalaykas.—ED.

moderato mosso on pp. 17 *et seq*). On the whole Tchaïkovsky carefully avoids using the wood-wind *en bloc* in the manner beloved
of Brahms, and the occasional instance of this thick, organ-like tone
(as in the slow movement of the Fourth Symphony, pp. 85 *et seq.*
in the score) stand out unpleasantly from the usual clarity and
purity of Tchaïkovsky's orchestration.

Thematic material, melodic, rhythmic and harmonic invention,
never presented any difficulty to Tchaïkovsky. He seems to have had
an inexhaustible reservoir, a quick and spontaneous flow of musical
ideas drawn from widely differing sources but completely assimilated to form his own personal, unmistakable individual idiom.
The provenance of these various streams of inspiration, however
various, is not difficult to determine. In the first place, there was
the folk-song pure and simple. He wrote of himself to Nadezhda
von Meck:

> As regards the Russian element in general in my music (*i.e.*, the
> instances of melody and harmony originating in folk-song), I grew
> up in the backwoods, saturating myself from earliest childhood with
> the inexplicable beauty of the characteristic traits of Russian folk-song,
> so that I passionately love every manifestation of the Russian spirit. In
> short, I am *Russian* in the fullest sense of the word.

This purely Russian music formed the background for all his
other musical experience, a subconscious musical atmosphere in
which all other musical experiences were saturated, so that even
the most cosmopolitan form, such as the valse, takes on an indefinable but unmistakable Russian air. Of actual folk-songs Tchaïkovsky did not make so much use as the Mighty Handful in St.
Petersburg: this was indeed part of their complaint against him. But
folk-song was so deeply sunk in his whole musical being that it is
often difficult to determine whether some of his melodies are his
own creation or a memory of a song heard, perhaps, as a child and
not consciously remembered. The very opening phrase of the First
Symphony (Ex. 1) might easily be a memory.[1] The structure of
the melody, circling between the intervals of the third and the fourth,
the growth of each succeeding phrase from the last notes of the preceding, and the almost soporific reiterations are typical of Russian
folk-song and of so many of Tchaïkovsky's melodies, particularly
in his early days. The same is true of the adagio of the First
Symphony, where Tchaïkovsky builds his whole movement round

[1] The theme of the slow introduction to the finale, used later as second subject
of the allegro maestoso, is an actual folk-song.

35

another melody of the same kind (Ex. 2), merely adding an ornamental counterpoint or varying the colour and emphasis of the single theme. The Second Symphony is, of course, consciously constructed on Ukrainian folk-songs, and it is interesting to see how little they differ from Tchaïkovsky's own melodies at this time. The long horn solo (Ex. 3) which opens the first movement has just the same characteristics as Tchaïkovsky's own melody with which he started the first movement of the First Symphony (Ex. 1), only here the tendency of the second half of the melody to become little more than a variation of the first is even more marked, in fact, the folk-song introduced in the middle of the scherzo is little more than a series of repetitions of the interval of the third. This characteristic of Russian folk-music makes it as unsuitable as possible for the conventional treatment demanded by sonata form. Melodies which themselves consist of a series of variations round a single germ-interval are, in a sense, fully extended, their potentialities are already exhausted and they obstinately refuse to expand or 'develop' further. Tchaïkovsky obviates this difficulty in the Second Symphony by making his folk-song no more than an introduction and taking a far more conventional theme (Ex. 4) as the first subject, where the first two phrases only are genuinely connected with the introduction and the second and third are lame additions from the conservatoire.[1] This is a glaring instance of the incompatibility of Russian folk-music and the predominantly German symphonic models which are given to all students of composition. Tchaïkovsky may have been aware of this incompatibility when he wrote his Third Symphony and made no direct reference at all to folk-song. But even here the second subject of the first movement,

---

[1] We must remember that the Second Symphony as we know it, after the drastic revision of 1879–80, differs materially from the original, unpublished version of 1872. And despite the composer's own opinion that the final version is much the better, his close friend S. I. Taneev expressed a very different view. Writing to Modest Tchaïkovsky (December 15/27, 1898). Taneev says he has just compared the two scores: ' My God, what a difference! How good the old allegro is, despite some imperfections—rambling modulations, which could be dispensed with, a beautiful first theme, a melodious, graceful second. How weak by comparison with this is the new allegro! A poor first theme consisting of a three-note motive many times repeated, a still less interesting second theme worked in as counter-melody to a snatch of the original first theme, a little bit of the original allegro artificially stuck into the new one as a pretext for keeping fragments of the original development section: all this is manufactured, in no definite mood, laboured. It seems to me that in some future concert you ought to let people hear the real Second Symphony, in its original form. . . . The only things lacking are the parts for bass drum and cymbals in the finale. But it would be very easy to put them in from the printed score—the finale, except for one big cut, remains in its original form. When I see you I will play both versions and you will probably agree with me about the superiority of the first.'—ED.

which starts with an impeccably ' Western ' phrase, immediately reverts to type and starts varying and repeating itself as soon as it is stated (Ex. 5). An instance of the really satisfactory treatment of a folk-song is provided by the last movement of the Second Symphony, which is little more than a series of variations on a single theme (Ex. 6). Here Tchaïkovsky allowed his natural instinct full play: there is no attempt to ' develop ' the theme, which is re-stated (eighteen times in direct succession at the beginning of the movement) in varying orchestral combinations, so that the ear merely receives the impression of kaleidoscopic variation, a fantasia of orchestral colour rather than a musical construction. Much later Tchaïkovsky was to return to the same kind of treatment, carried out with infinitely greater skill and sophistication, in the third movement of the Sixth Symphony.

The more he travelled the more aware Tchaïkovsky became of the profundity of his own national feeling. He never ceased to be violently homesick for Russia; the mentality of the cosmopolitan ' expatriate ' was absolutely foreign to him. But he had always been aware of other, non-Russian music. A creature of emotion and impulse, it was impossible for him to refuse any musical experience that made an immediate appeal to him or to reject, on theoretical grounds, any form of beauty which aroused his natural admiration. It was this absence of nationalistic scruple which antagonised the St. Petersburg composers, who prided themselves on their nationalistic exclusiveness, their cultural protectionism. Tchaïkovsky was twenty-three, and his musical taste was set at least in its main orientations, before he came into contact with the music of Bach and Beethoven. German music was temperamentally alien to him, and his genuine admiration of its masterpieces was of the head rather than the heart. He was horrified when Tolstoy started a conversation with him by stating that Beethoven was bereft of talent; he paid honour to all genius which he could distinguish as genius, but he was too sincere and spontaneous, too good a judge of the nature of his own gifts, to force his admiration to take the form of imitation. He felt a certain kindred spirit in Mendelssohn, whose urbanity and charm naturally attracted him; and in the tenderness, the rather wistful poetry of Schumann. But it was with Mozart alone of Germanic composers that Tchaïkovsky felt completely in tune. Nadezhda von Meck had one day written slightingly of ' that epicurean Mozart ' and compared his music unfavourably with that of Tchaïkovsky himself :

You say that my worship of Mozart is quite contrary to my musical nature [he wrote in answer]. But perhaps it is just because, being a child of my day, I feel broken and spiritually out of joint, that I find consolation and rest in Mozart's music, wherein he gives expression to that joy of life which was part of his sane and wholesome temperament, not yet undermined by reflection.

And he goes on to quote Berlioz's passion for Gluck as a parallel example of a musician admiring another who is his complete antithesis. Tchaïkovsky had, of course, the conception of Mozart which was almost universal throughout the nineteenth century:

> Mozart was an inspired being, childishly innocent, mild as a dove and modest as a maid: he did not belong to this world. One can find no conceit in him, no self-applause: he never seemed to suspect the grandeur of his genius.

He used to speak of him as 'the Christ of music.' But if he rather misconceived the character of Mozart the man, his appreciation of his music was real and profound. Here he saw the flawless form which he knew he could never achieve himself, the exact correspondence between an idea and its expression, the perfect balance and the effortless vitality, the emotional reserve and serenity which were in such complete contrast to his own tortured and twisted feelings. Mozart, then, was an ideal which Tchaïkovsky knew very well that he could never achieve, although he could and did achieve some of the exterior, superficial grace and elegance which is all that the musical Philistines—then and now—see in Mozart. These too he valued, perhaps as all shy and sensitive people value good manners, the suavity and urbanity which makes everyday life pleasant and easy and can even for long periods conceal the bitterness and frustration which Tchaïkovsky felt to be the very root of existence.

It was this 'civilised' quality which he felt and admired in Latin civilisation and in Latin music. Before he had heard a note of the German classics Tchaïkovsky was a passionate opera-goer, and the operas which he heard during the 1860's in St. Petersburg were almost all of the Italian school. Rossini, Verdi and Meyerbeer were the operatic gods of the day, and in their worship Tchaïkovsky was an enthusiastic devotee. Tastes acquired at such a formative period in a man's life are never wholly lost, and although the influence of this music was naturally strongest in Tchaïkovsky's own operas, where it was at first quite overwhelming, it is not difficult to find traces of this early enthusiasm throughout Tchaïkovsky's whole life, re-appearing strongly in the Sixth Symphony in particular. Meyerbeer was a supreme master of the theatrical manner. Not content with a dramatic situation, he must always underline and demonstrate its drama to his audience, exaggerating the bliss or the despair of his characters, surrounding them with every possible splendour and acting as showman, rather than interpreter, of their emotions. His music is vulgar and effective, contrived and planned to the last detail, often moving in a frankly stagey way but fundamentally hollow. Paris had taken this music to her heart, and Meyerbeer and Offenbach were the gods of the Second Empire. Success at the Paris Opéra could only be achieved by music which had the same qualities, and when Verdi was asked to write his *Vespri Siciliani* for the Opéra (1855) he modified his own style to meet the Parisian public's demand for splendour, grandeur and noise. But even in this second, 'Parisian' manner Verdi still has all his vigour, his directness and magnificent emotional vitality. The influence of Meyerbeer was purely superficial, and he remained his intensely Italian self, the proud and conscious heir to the great musical tradition which had never wholly died in Italy. It was the vigour and sanity, the emotional vitality and spontaneity of expression of the southerner which won Tchaïkovsky's heart in the music of Verdi. He was too much a child of his age not to be impressed, not to have his breath taken away by the blaring brilliance of Meyerbeer. The peasant who lives not far beneath the surface in every Russian was inevitably fascinated by anything so highly coloured and glittering, so large and so magnificent; and his weak nervous system, stimulated as though with a drug by the violence and brilliance of the music, found an escape from reality in these most 'operatic' of operas. Here was another strand in Tchaïkovsky's musical make-up which militated against his being a skilful manipulator of conventional symphonic form. The actual appearance of distinctively operatic phrases or melodies in the symphonies is rare, of course, though in the Second Symphony Tchaïkovsky did use a march from his opera *Undine* as a second movement: and very effective it is, with its purely Verdian moments.

But generally speaking, the operatic influence is more vague and diffused. The opening of the Fourth Symphony, for example, is almost in the vein of a more sophisticated Meyerbeer or the Verdi of *Don Carlos*. The barking, hammering brass rhythms in the first movement of the Fifth, the emotional abandonment of the second subject, the voluptuous gloom of the slow movement with its repeated climaxes mounting almost to hysteria, the sudden brutal interruption, the pause and the return of the melody over the pizzicato chords in the strings—all these are devices of the theatre, or at any rate first learned in the theatre rather than the concert-hall. Even in the first two symphonies, where operatic influence is oddly less evident, Tchaïkovsky shows a predilection for the sudden dramatic pause, the silence which is one of the most effective methods of focussing the attention of the audience on what is to follow. In the scherzo of the First Symphony (a transposed version of that originally written for the C sharp minor Piano Sonata), the middle section is introduced by Ex. 7. Or he would use a brass fanfare to heighten the emotional tension, as in the first movement of the First Symphony, where the recapitulation is announced by Ex. 8 in the horns and basses, followed by a three-bar pause, staccato chords in the brass anticipating the pizzicato in the slow movement of the Fifth Symphony (miniature score, p. 86), and then a repetition of the fanfare.

These horn-calls became almost a mannerism with Tchaïkovsky. The Fourth Symphony is dominated by the familiar 'destiny ' motto-phrase; they interrupt the slow movement of the Fifth (p. 84) and recur throughout the finale of the Fifth and the first and third movements of the Sixth. They are always, from the time of the Fourth Symphony onwards, sinister—a reminder of the ' Damocles ' sword, hanging over the head in constant, unremitting, spiritual torment. Again and again, in Tchaïkovsky's words, they say ' But no, this was only a dream and Destiny awakes us,' until in the Sixth Symphony there is hardly a moment of complete escape. Here the horror is expressed in a language which is almost entirely operatic in its origin. It is even possible that the introduction and some of the dominant phraseology of the first movement were directly suggested by the last act of Verdi's *Otello,* which had appeared in 1887. If we compare the opening with the appearance of Otello in Desdemona's room, the long solo passage for the double basses punctuated by staccato semiquavers in the violas and the persistent recurrence of the staccato figure in the basses, followed at first by a single ' note of doom ' in the brass (Ex. 9), we are irresistibly reminded of the poco più animato (pp. 12–16 in the miniature score) of the Sixth Symphony. Here the Italian operatic idiom seems to have been assimilated and transmuted much as it is in the florid, dramatic manner of Liszt. The whole movement is broken into short, nervous bursts of energy and violently opposed moods in much the same way as in Liszt's B minor Piano Sonata. The allegro vivo which ushers in the fugato of Tchaïkovsky's development section (p 28 in the miniature score) suggests the più mosso in the recapitulation section of the sonata (pp. 27–8 of the Peters edition of the sonata) where Tchaïkovsky's descending trumpet scale against the violin semiquavers is almost exactly paralleled. These similarities arise, of course, not from any conscious imitation but from an emotional kinship, a natural violence and lack of reserve in both men and a persistent operatic tendency which they shared. Tchaïkovsky did not in actual fact admire Liszt's music. 'Liszt's compositions leave me cold,' he wrote to Nadezhda von Meck. 'They show more poetic colouring than true creative power, more paint than drawing. In short, what he writes, though dazzling, is devoid of inward structure.' But Liszt's faults were akin to his own, and this is seldom an endearing trait in a fellow artist.

There was another aspect of Latin civilisation which, as Mr. Lockspeiser has already pointed out, played a considerable part in determining Tchaïkovsky's style. Italian music attracted him by its vigour, its clarity, its sensuousness, its directness and its emotional violence. French music, equally Latin but entirely different in quality, appealed to Tchaïkovsky's love of charm, elegance, grace, urbanity—the social virtues in which the French excel. It was not until after the Franco-Prussian War that music enjoyed a renaissance in France. Gounod and Saint-Saëns had done years of pioneer work in the 'fifties and 'sixties with next to no recognition, but after the tragedy of the defeat and the Commune music seemed to be inspired with the new hopes and desires of national regeneration. A number of young musicians banded themselves together in the Société Nationale and, taking 'Ars Gallica' as their motto, set out to create a genuinely national art, free from the slavish following of Rossini and Meyerbeer, and determined to show the world what the music of France could really be. One of the most gifted of these young musicians was Bizet, and it happened that Tchaïkovsky was in Paris at the beginning of 1876, when *Carmen* had just been put on at the Opéra-Comique. He at once conceived a passion for this music, an 'almost unhealthy passion which Bizet's death three months later seemed to exaggerate,' as Modest Tchaïkovsky said:

> To me [he wrote], this is in every sense a *chef d'œuvre*, one of the few pieces which will some day mirror most vividly the musical endeavour of a whole generation. It seems to me that the era in which

we live differs from the preceding in one way: our composers are *searching*—and first of all they are searching for pretty and piquant effects—a thing which Mozart and Beethoven and Schubert and Schumann never did. What is the so-called New Russian school, if not the cult of various spicy harmonisations, eccentric orchestral combinations and all kinds of purely exterior effects? The musical idea has become merely the excuse for new sound effects. Where they once composed and created, they now, with a few exceptions, dovetail and invent. This is a purely rational process: modern music, therefore, though very ingenious and piquant, remains cold, unwarmed by feeling.

And suddenly appears a Frenchman in whose music these piquant and spicy passages are not the result of ingenuity but flow freely. They please the ear, but at the same time they touch and trouble. It is as though Bizet said to us: ' You are not seeking for something lofty and grandiose: you want something pretty. Well, here is a pretty opera.' And, indeed, I know of no music which has a better title to the quality of what I should call prettiness—*le joli*. From beginning to end it is charming and delightful. In it one finds a number of striking harmonies and entirely new combinations of sound, but these do not exist merely for themselves. Bizet is an artist who pays tribute to modernity, but he is warmed by true inspiration.

And what a wonderful subject for an opera! I can't play the last scene without tears. Here is the mob at the bull-fight with its coarse merriment and excitement—and to balance this, a terrible tragedy and the death of the two principals, who through fate—*fatum*—reach at length a climax and their own miserable end.

Tchaïkovsky found, of course, in *Carmen* traces of Meyerbeer, of the rather blatant brilliance with which he was already familiar; but he found also things which Meyerbeer could never have conceived. Here was a savage and tragic story treated with grace and charm, yet perfectly sincere: music which is both pretty and cruel, urbane and tragic, entertaining yet profoundly moving. It was this combination which attracted Tchaïkovsky; and when he was writing his Fourth Symphony, the year after he heard *Carmen*, it was perhaps a combination of this kind at which he was aiming when he made the first subject of the first movement a kind of strangled, despairing valse. There may even be an unconscious echo of Carmen's song over the cards in the third act (' En vain pour éviter les réponses amères, en vain tu mèleras ') which has just the same air of tragic inevitability and fatalism; and, musically, there are the same lay-out of the strings, the same key and the same chromatic alterations in the melody to bear out the hypothesis. In the same way the last bars of the overture and bars 12 to 15 of Tchaïkovsky's introduction are at least moments from the same musical world, if they are no more.

Carmen was not the only work of the new French school which impressed Tchaïkovsky, nor Bizet the only composer. Massenet's *Marie Madeleine* moved him to tears, he confessed—the facile tears of an over-emotional man, no doubt, but Massenet could stir them by his elegant, tremulous phrases and rather saccharine emotion. But the composer whose music he really admired most highly after Bizet was Delibes, whose ballet music *Sylvia* appeared in the same year as *Carmen*; its probable influence on the third movement of the Fourth Symphony has already been mentioned.

Tchaïkovsky's passion for the valse lasted all his life, and he was the originator of the tragic or nostalgic valse, that form of which Sibelius's *Valse Triste* has become the norm. It was not the brio and gaiety of the Viennese valse, so much as the prettiness and elegance, the ballroom glamour, of the French, which attracted him; and he did not hesitate, as we have seen, to make use of valse rhythm in the most tragic movements of his symphonies. Apart from the third movement of the Fifth Symphony and the first of the fourth —which are both marked as valses—the second movement of the Sixth Symphony, although in 5/4 time, is really a kind of distorted valse, the limping valse of some macabre vision. In the Third Symphony Tchaïkovsky had made use of the Austrian country cousin of the valse—the *Ländler*; but it was the polite, social character of the drawing-room valse which he understood so well how to use for his own ends. It is hardly ever allowed to remain simply a dance: almost always there is a suggestion, as in the Sixth Symphony, that there is some impending doom, that one of the partners might be a skeleton, that the dance is the dance of death. Even the third movement of the Fifth Symphony, in which Tchaïkovsky uses part of a Florentine street-song[1] as the foundation for his valse, is not a pure escape from the gloom of the first, and the luxuriant self-pity of the second, movements. A clinging melancholy, a scented nostalgia pervades the whole movement, emphasised by the feminine phrase-endings which recur in the droop of the theme. The middle section of this movement is a typical instance of one of Tchaïkovsky's favourite devices. The valse theme returns in the oboe (miniature score, p. 119) with staccato semiquavers in the strings, running in and out of the melody and giving the effect of an embroidery. The same device is used in the slow move-

[1] The whole melody is used as the song ' Pimpinella,' Op. 38, No. 6; cf. footnote on p. 118 and the composer's letter to Nadezhda von Meck of February 20/March 4. 1878).—ED.

ment of the Fourth Symphony (p. 89 of the miniature score), in the last movement of the same symphony (p. 145), in the first movement of the Fifth (pp. 41–2 of the score) as well as in the Third; in the second movement of the Sixth (pp. 76–7 of the score); and a similar technique all through the third movement. In itself it is not very remarkable, but Tchaïkovsky uses it so skilfully that it does on each occasion give an air of lightness and brilliance quite out of proportion to its intrinsic interest.

The same is true of another device of Tchaïkovsky's: the achievement of climax, the darkening and thickening of the musical texture, and so of the emotional atmosphere, by means of a descending or ascending chromatic scale, generally in the brass. There is an early and unsophisticated example of this in the first movement of the First Symphony (see Ex. 8); but it is most frequent in the last two symphonies. In the Fifth it is to be seen on p. 37 of the miniature score: particularly noticeable in the slow movement (e.g. p. 75 and parallel passages) and in the third movement on pp. 104 *et seq.* It appears as internal harmony in the return of the second subject in the first movement of the Sixth Symphony and again, as a straightforward pizzicato scale in the coda of the same movement (pp. 63–70 in the miniature score); again and again in the descending triplets of the march (third movement); and in ascending instead of descending form in the last movement (pp. 199 *et seq.*).

Tchaïkovsky has been criticised for what has been called the intrinsic unimportance of these figurations and for their obvious and immediate appeal, just as he has been criticised for the 'vulgarity' of his orchestrations. These criticisms are, of course, based on the myth that beauty and artistic worth are in some profound way connected with what is hidden and difficult, and that therefore all which is immediately pleasing and accessible must, of its very essence, be inferior. Like so many of such almost unconscious beliefs, this is rooted, of course, in the old Manichæan or ' Puritan ' heresy, the belief that matter is of itself evil and that anything which immediately pleases the senses must in the last resort be of the devil. It is the same mentality which accords higher honour to an artist in whose work the pains of creation are visibly present, the conflicts and storms of some struggle instinctively felt to be moral, than to the apparently effortless creator, the natural ' singer ' in whose work everything—even personal misery, doubt and distress—is transmuted to a divine serenity, a pure flow of inspiration in which human imperfection is felt as something which has been transcended, something negative which has been drowned in a flood of affirmation. Thus Mozart and Schubert are somehow felt to be intrinsically 'lesser' than Beethoven and Brahms; and German music, in which the element of struggle, brooding, pain and effort generally predominates, is automatically considered to be in a higher category than the spontaneous affirmation, the immediate unpondered emotion or the delight in sonorous beauty for its own sake, which characterise the best of non-German music. 'What is difficult is " better " than what is easy '—and in the moral life this is very often so; but to apply this canon to artistic creations is to introduce a wholly alien principle which has no validity whatever outside its own world. This is not to deny that the moral failings of an artist may very easily—very often do—have a bad effect on the works which he creates; Tchaïkovsky's own temperamental weaknesses are perfectly reflected in his music, because that music was frankly autobiographical, admittedly written as an emotional release, a kind of solution of a private problem. Even so, and granting that Tchaïkovsky's music is a perfect reflection of his personality, there is no reason to expect vulgarity or triviality in the music of a man who, with all his faults, was neither vulgar nor trivial. In the æsthetic world there can be no awards for hard work, moral effort and the like unless the work they produce is satisfactory on· purely æsthetic grounds; and contrarily, there can be no penalties for facility of invention or immediacy of appeal, unless these morally suspect qualities do·actually give rise to what is æsthetically unsatisfying —to the flaccid melody or rhythm which soon palls or the gaudy colour and stagey gesture which soon disgusts. But there is no question of this in the mind of Tchaïkovsky's critics. They merely feel that what is essentially simple and immediate in its appeal *must* be blameworthy, however successful it is in actual practice. And no one can question the effectiveness of Tchaïkovsky's style. His saving grace is, of course, his absolute emotional sincerity. You may dislike his emotional world—the panting, palpitating phrases, the strident colours, the sobs and the short bursts of hysterical defiance, but you can never for one moment doubt that this was Tchaïkovsky's inmost self; that self which he found it almost impossible to reveal to any but his very dearest friends or relations here stands revealed for all the world to see.

Tchaïkovsky's six symphonies cover his whole life as a composer, from his gifted amateur's beginnings to his complete flowering as an artist of genius and one of the most polished craftsmen of the nineteenth century. They are in almost every way representative of him, both as a man and as an artist; and the last three of them are more, for they are the authentic voice of the cultivated Russian world of Tchaïkovsky's day and generation.

3

Works for Solo Instrument and Orchestra

By

Eric Blom

I T WOULD BE INTERESTING to know exactly what happened at the famous quarrel between Tchaïkovsky and Nicholas Rubinstein, when the latter savagely criticised the most popular of all concertos: the B flat minor. But we have only the composer's incomplete and necessarily one-sided account, according to which Rubinstein behaved abominably. He may have done so, like a temperamental artist in a disagreeable mood or like a pedagogue peevishly aware that the time has come for him to let a genius off the leading-strings; but there is little profit in pretending to disclose the secrets of an imaginary psychiatrist's case-book.

What Tchaïkovsky does report Rubinstein to have said on that stormy Christmas Eve of 1874 is, more or less, that (a) he thought the composition bad as a whole, (b) the music was worthless and repellently trivial, and (c) the pianoforte passages were manufactured, clumsy and unplayable. It took some courage to disclose such destructive criticism even in a private letter to Nadezhda von Meck, and if we do wish to indulge in a little amateur psychology we may say that Tchaïkovsky could obviously bring himself to mention the matter only by working himself into a fit of indignation about it. For that would automatically give Rubinstein's strictures an air of wild exaggeration and conceal from Tchaïkovsky's correspondent—as indeed from himself—the realisation of any possible truth they might have contained. Did they contain any truth? If we examine each point separately we shall certainly find some, of a kind.

(a) Is the composition bad as a whole? Yes, in one important respect it is, though it must have required extraordinary astuteness on Rubinstein's part to notice that at a mere preliminary run-through. The Concerto is a very oddly lop-sided structure. So, of course, are Chartres, Ely and Strasbourg cathedrals, which we nevertheless admire for their beauty and grandeur. Well, comparing the less

47

great with the great, so we admire Tchaïkovsky's work for other qualities it possesses; but the point here is that we cannot in music, as we do in architecture, make so many allowances for lack of balance in design, or indeed even find such lack of balance alluring for reasons connected with history, practical 'expediency, widespread division of labour in planning and execution, and enormously protracted periods elapsing between conception and completion, periods that involve all manner of changes. A concerto, written within six months or so and left in the hands of a single creator-craftsman, has no excuse for being faulty in design, though other qualities may make us indulgent towards that defect.

A diagram outlining the ground-plan of Tchaïkovsky's first Piano Concerto (in its main features only) will show at a glance that there is something radically wrong with it as a piece of musical construction. Here it is:

1st Movement		*2nd Movement*			*3rd Movement*
Introduction.	Allegro in sonata form.	Andantino semplice.	Prestissimo.	Tempo I.	Allegro in modified sonata form.
? MOTTO-THEME	EXPOSITION	NOCTURNE	INTERMEZZO	NOCTURNE	EXPOSITION
D flat maj.	1st subject	D flat maj.	F maj.	D flat maj.	1st subject
	B flat min.		D maj.		B flat min.
	2nd subject		B flat maj.		2nd subject
	A flat maj.		F maj.		D flat maj.
	WORKING-OUT				WORKING-OUT
	RECAPITULATION				(with 2nd subject
	1st subject				in E flat maj.)
	B flat min.				RECAPITULATION
	2nd subject (I)				1st subject
	B flat maj.				B flat min.
	Cadenza (= WORKING-				WORKING-OUT
	OUT, cont'd)				(cont'd)
	G flat–B flat maj.				RECAPITULATION
	2nd subject (II)				(cont'd)
	B flat maj.				2nd subject
	CODA				B flat maj.
	B flat maj.				CODA
					B flat maj.

Principal Key B flat minor.

It will be seen that there is a beautifully balanced scheme here, but for one disturbing feature. The allegros of the first and last movements are almost perfect counterparts, certainly quite as satisfying in that respect as two such movements need be, since even in classical concertos the formal difference between them is often much greater, the first being always in sonata form but the finale often a rondo. The slight oddity in Tchaïkovsky's finale—his beginning a quite regular recapitulation in the principal key before he has nearly done with the working-out section—need not worry us, for it could quite easily be accounted for (if that were really nece; ary) by saying that if this telescoping is unusual in a sonata-form movement, it quite justifiably introduces a rondo element into this finale by letting one of the subjects appear three times in its full extent, apart from incidental developments. Nor is it particularly disturbing that while its first appearance as a second subject is made conventionally in the relative major and its third in the equally conventional tonic major, its interpolated re-statement is in the sub-dominant major (E flat), a key which, it will be observed, is nowhere else insisted on as a structural feature. For that second statement occurs in the working-out section, where anything not wildly irrelevant may happen, even in a classically correct work.

These two large symmetrical movements are not the whole design, however. Another glance at the diagram will show that between them stands a smaller group, representing the usual slow movement, which itself makes a perfectly balanced pair enclosing a centre-piece of different character: a gossamer-light intermezzo that may be regarded as a miniature scherzo sandwiched between two sections of the slow movement instead of being given an independent place before or after it. That slow movement I have ventured to describe as a nocturne, for it resembles Chopin's pieces of that name in shape and character rather than any middle movement in a classical concerto.

So far as we have considered the diagram, then, all is well. Even the main key-scheme, which keeps on the side of the flat tonalities so far as the principal features are concerned (there are, of course, many incidental modulations in other directions), is consistent, and the one deviation to a sharp key (D major) occurs in the very centre, approached and again led away from through the nearest key the composer can get to on the flat side—F major—with which the intermezzo opens and closes. The nocturne is in the relative major of the principal key of the whole work, and the first and last movements continually hover round keys of from two to six flats, four and six (A flat and G flat major) being made extended use of in two episodes of the first movement, five and three (D flat and E flat major) in the same way in the finale. The rest is all tonic minor and major. We are faced with a symmetrical building of an appearance something like this:

as indeed the diagram on p. 48 shows if we disregard what stands at the extreme left. But we cannot overlook this; neither can we reconcile it with the scheme as a whole. For some reason, probably for no better one than that he happened to have some most admirable material left over, Tchaïkowsky decided to run up an annexe on one side of his building, which now looks like this:

Not that the mere appearance of a wry-looking diagram necessarily suggests the condemnation of a musical structure it is intended to illustrate. Music and architecture work in vastly different media, and what may be hopelessly asymmetrical in the latter may sound perfectly satisfactory in the former. Slow introductions not thematically connected with the music that follows can be not only unexceptionable, but actually very valuable in composition, as for instance in Handel's overtures and Haydn's symphonies. But neither Handel nor Haydn—nor indeed any other musical master-builder—would ever have dreamt of writing an introduction in the wrong key, and D flat major, although the relative of B flat minor and bearing the same key-signature, is quite decidedly the wrong key in which to begin a work cast in the latter, even if, as here, the opening bar is nominally in the right one. Throughout this broad introduction Tchaïkovsky insists on D flat major: it is, in fact, a complete piece in that key, so that however much we may deplore its having been so used as the musical theme of a film and even played at concerts of sorts, we cannot fairly complain about such vandalism. Indeed, we could hardly resent it if Tchaïkovsky's annexe were pulled down once and for all. The only reason why we might hesitate to consent to this is that it is so fine a thing in itself. It is a grand tune, too grand to be dropped by us or—what is more to the point—pushed aside by Tchaïkovsky. No wonder that a delightful professed amateur and professional enthusiast not only expressed his admiration of it a good many years ago, but quite recently showed that his belief still holds good.[1] He wrote with enviable penetration that he ' found that mighty, mouth-filling song a thing to shout, while the great sea itself put in the crashing chords of the pianoforte part.' But from the structural point of view the very quality and bigness of this tune is a glaring defect. It overshadows everything that comes after, especially the first subject of the first-movement allegro, which comes tripping in like a mouse delivered by a mountain. The great tune's strutting upon the stage at the rise of the curtain, like an actor-manager in a leading part, and then vanishing suddenly and completely, leaves the hearer disconcerted and dissatisfied. He feels as though he were witnessing a performance of *Hamlet* in which the Prince of Denmark is killed by Polonius at the end of the first scene. It is this even more than its appearing in the wrong dress of D flat major which makes Tchaïkovsky's introduction, for all its magnificence, or at least magniloquence, one of the most baffling solecisms in the music of any great composer.

How came it that Tchaïkovsky did not himself want to shout this theme out again at the end of the first movement or, better still, at the end of the whole work? One feels that it is exactly this exulting vociferation which would have chimed in with his mood there, and it would have been so obviously the right thing for just the sort of climax the music finally drives at, even purely formally considered. True, the second subject of the finale itself does well enough, but the fact remains that the theme of the introduction has been wantonly thrown away after having been merely stated and never adequately developed.

A re-statement of what in the diagram I took upon myself to indicate as a possible motto-theme intended to permeate the whole concerto would have been difficult at the end of the first movement, because at the change to the allegro con spirito the composer forsakes its 3/4 time for 4/4. But the finale is in 3/4 again, and the key of D flat major, though not the principal one of the work, has by that time cast a strong influence over the music. We have seen that it is the key of the slow movement and that the second subject of the

[1] J. D. M. Rorke, *A Musical Pilgrim's Progress* (revised edition, Oxford University Press, 1933); *A Latch-key to Music* (Oxford University Press, 1942).

finale makes its first appearance in it. It is as though Tchaïkovsky had, consciously or otherwise, come nearer and nearer his original tune again. One can positively hear him groping towards it. It seems almost impossible that he should have missed noticing that it was waiting just round the corner, anxious to pounce and take possession of the music once more. Not only has the turn into his second subject prepared the right key for it, but the pace of that subject is very much, if not quite, the same as that of the introduction.

Is it too fantastic to suggest that Tchaïkovsky had some sort of return of his initial theme up his sleeve and really did intend it to assume the functions of a ' motto,' but that somehow in the heat of composition he failed to let this part of his plan take shape? One cannot do more than formulate some such theory, but it is quite possible to make it appear credible if one takes the trouble to think it out.[1] Perhaps he took such a fancy to the second subject he had invented for the finale—another good, broad lungful of a tune— that he felt it could well take the place of the ' motto,' which one does not merely regard as called for at some important juncture of the finale, but positively aches to hear again, as though quite un- wittingly Tchaïkovsky had reserved the fit and proper place for it towards the end of the concerto. But lo and behold! he could have brought it in without ever discarding the new subject at all, for it could have been contrapuntally combined with that subject—not, it is true, without some changes in the harmony to make a slight com- promise at one or two points where the two themes would not have fitted with the original harmonisation, but certainly not with any awkwardness that it would have been beyond the ingenuity of a composer like Tchaïkovsky to overcome. He would have done it vastly better than I, but Ex. 10 is a sketchy attempt at showing the kind of thing he might have produced.

I am not suggesting that the introductory theme ought necessarily to have crowded out the second finale-subject at its first appearance, where it is stated in the same key, much less that the two should have so far anticipated the climax of their combination, which ought no doubt to have been reserved for the coda. Even at its second appearance—in E flat major—the finale's own theme does very well as it is. But it returns a third time in the coda, as we have

---

[1] This was first attempted by me in *The Monthly Musical Record* for March–April, 1943, in an article some passages from which are quoted here by kind permission of the Editor of that periodical.

seen, in the tonic major, and it is here, in this B flat major peroration, that Tchaïkovsky might—or dare one say 'ought to?'—have
let his first song ring out once more, entwined with its companion.
If only this had happened, we should never have felt that something has gone askew in the composition of this concerto. It did
not happen; but if we like to imagine that the second subject of
the finale is nothing else than the introductory tune in fancy dress
and that the composer had in mind some such solution as I suggest, if only subconsciously, we shall be able to feel that even as
it stands the B flat minor Concerto is at least potentially satisfactory
in form.

The other points of Rubinstein's criticism, so far as we know it,
must now be dealt with:

(b) Is the music worthless and repellently trivial? There is no
harm in agreeing frankly that there is some truth in this, though
only priggish cultivators of exclusive tastes would accept the adverb.
The concerto certainly lacks any sort of nobility of thought. There
is not a theme in it, whether invented or borrowed by Tchaïkovsky
(and at least three are said to be borrowed), which can be certain
to escape the charge of vulgarity. But having said this one must
make sure that the word 'vulgarity' is not understood in the sense
of 'indecency' which it has unfortunately acquired in the larger
public's understanding. The work is simply written in a musical
equivalent of the 'vulgar tongue,' which includes not only the
language of the guttersnipe, but at the other end of its wide field
the magnificent one of the English Bible and of the great writers
it influenced, with Milton at their head. There is nothing Miltonic
about the B flat minor Concerto, but neither does it descend into the
gutter, though it may be pushed into it by commercial enterprise.
It is just honest theatrical ranting on the level, let us say, of Nicholas
Rowe or Mrs. Inchbald.

In the matter of thematic invention the concerto touches rock-
bottom early in the first movement: the first subject of the allegro,
as I have already suggested, is paltry in the extreme, though perhaps
only because of the jerky triplet rhythm into which it is broken up
(Ex. 11). It is said to be one of the borrowed themes, a Malo-
Russian (Ukrainian) folk-song, which, however, does not appear to
have been issued in any folk-song collection in Russia or anywhere
else. In the form in which Tchaïkovsky uses it there is no sort of
singable tune about it at all, which may seem suspicious. However,
he was quite at liberty to turn a folk-song into what he may have

regarded as a characteristically pianistic form, since he was writing an instrumental work; and it is by no means beyond conjecture that the original may have been something like Ex. 12. I transpose it into A minor because the leading-note in the second bar may well have been flat, if the tune was a genuinely old one; that is to say, the song was quite possibly in the Aeolian mode.

The second subject is one of Tchaïkovsky's best lyrical inventions. Its two strains—which are later separated by the cadenza to pull the recapitulation and the coda together and make them one solid whole in which even the cadenza is a structural feature prescribed by the composer, not an improvised excrescence—are both very individual. The first (Ex. 13) could not possibly be imagined to belong to any other composer; the second (Ex. 14), first heard on muted strings, recalls the dreamy theme following the great, sweetly drawn-out tune in the love episode of his *Romeo and Juliet*. It will be noticed that the accent of the phrases is at first made to fall on the wrong beat, for no good reason that one can see, while at the second appearance it is put right.

Good as the ideas of the second subject are, it might easily have failed to take a satisfactory place in the whole first-movement scheme, as lyrical second subjects often do fail in the work of composers whose inventiveness outruns their symphonic gifts. But Tchaïkovsky had such gifts, for all that he sometimes expressed over-anxious doubts about them and feared that his music did not hang together. He was, in fact, very good at making a large-scale movement sound all of a piece; as good as a dramatic craftsman who knows how to make each act of a play a thing of logical continuity, with the entry of each character carefully prepared and a series of graded climaxes effectively arranged. (It is curiously significant to find how often one is tempted to discuss Tchaïkovsky's art in theatrical terms.) The entry of this second subject is very cleverly foreshadowed before the first has fully run its expository course, as though the hero were made to mention the heroine before her entry (Ex. 15). This occurs so naturally that one could not possibly say whether Tchaïkovsky had first invented the second subject independently and then devised this premonition of it or whether the snatch quoted in the second bar of Ex. 15 first came to him as an indefinite glimmer and gradually developed into a theme; and it is precisely this impossibility of detecting his procedure which proves that we have here an example of spontaneous ingenuity, not of mere mechanical contrivance.

The working-out beginning with a large orchestral exposition of Exs. 11 and 14, followed by a fantasy on Ex. 13, is also very well stage-managed, and the transition to the recapitulation is made almost imperceptibly, yet without any hesitation in design. We have already seen how cunningly the rest of this highly dramatic first act has been planned to keep up the pressure of events to the fall of the curtain.

The second movement, one would think, even Nicholas Rubinstein in one of his most irascible moods could not have called worthless, repellent or trivial. It is the most refined portion of the work; some people would say the only refined one. Apart from the personal distinctiveness that characterises the whole concerto, it has a special delicacy. The one thing that may be said to come near vulgarity—and even that does not do so in the opprobrious popular sense of the word—is the second borrowed tune, occurring in the prestissimo middle section I have ventured to call an intermezzo intruding into a nocturne. There is some mystery about this, as about Exs. 11–12. It is said to be a little French *chansonnette* sung by Désirée Artôt and introduced by Tchaïkovsky as a sentimental recollection of his broken engagement to her. The words are supposed to have been ' Il faut s'amuser, danser et rire;' but they fit the tune very badly, as will be seen from Ex. 16, even if one allows for the fact that French, like other Latin languages, can be set to music with very little regard for accentuation. The story of this quotation is thus hardly convincing. However, there it is, told by Tchaïkovsky's brother Modest, and we must accept it for what it may be worth.

A curious point arises at once at the beginning of the slow movement. The flute begins the tune with the phrase shown in Ex. 17 as figure *a*, but when the soloist repeats this melody, the opening bar is turned up as shown in figure *b*. As it invariably recurs in the second form later, a mistake on the composer's or printer's part has been suspected, and indeed some conductors have taken it upon themselves to correct it and let the phrase appear at once in its later form. This certainly makes for consistency; but one must after all accept and present a work of art as it was left by its creator, unless there is very definite evidence of a slip of the pen or a misprint. It is quite possible that Tchaïkovsky, having first hit on the less striking form of the phrase and then introduced the more telling one in the piano part, decided to let the discrepancy stand in order to give the solo an added importance by making it heighten the significance of his theme.

Perhaps one more detail in the slow movement might be pointed out: the capricious little spray of figures shown as Ex. 19, which knits together the nocturne and the intermezzo by occurring in both in almost exactly the same form, but of course at a very different rate of pace. Tchaïkovsky cleverly preserves the unities by letting, as it were, the same character, if only a minor one, appear in two different scenes which would otherwise have remained utterly unconnected.

The first subject of the finale is a sort of Cossack dance, as Russian as anything could be; it is, in fact, an Ukrainian song, ' Come, come, Ivanka.' Many upholders of the school led by Balakirev look upon Tchaïkovsky, who certainly was a good cosmopolitan, with more than suspicion as an upholder of the nationalist cause; but it remains a fact that many a theme invented or borrowed by him is as Russian as anything they ever used. What probably annoys the anti-Tchaïkovskians is that he often developed such material in symphonic ways they regarded as German and academic instead of merely exhibiting it in picturesque settings that left it unsophisticated.

Tchaïkovsky's theme does engender developments, and the cross-rhythm of two 3's against three 2's that is added to it at the second statement by the strings is very effective. After an unpleasantly rough and noisy orchestral tutti a passage beginning with Ex. 20 forms a bridge to the second subject, already shown in combination with the introductory theme in Ex. 10. It creeps in unobtrusively in the violins. Its further uses have already been made clear in the diagram on p. 48 and it only remains to say that dotted semiquaver figures serve to link the two main subjects together in the working-out.

We now come to Rubinstein's third objection:

(*c*) Are the piano passages manufactured, clumsy and unplayable? The last adjective is disposed of very quickly and conclusively by the mere observation that these passages[1] have now been played by hundreds of pianists, many of them probably less technically gifted than Rubinstein was himself. ' Manufactured ' they may be —perhaps, though, the better word is surely ' contrived,' and the criticism falls to the ground' as soon as one considers that in concerto-writing any composer has to set his mind to the devising of matter that shall not only get his music across to the hearer in the most telling way, but must at the same time confront the player with

[1] The ' completely revised version of 1889 ' mentioned in the ' Tchaïkovsky ' article in *Grove* seems to be a pure myth.—ED.

interesting and difficult technical problems. Even a cursory glance through the score of the B flat minor Concerto shows that what. Tchaïkovsky did manufacture here, if one likes to use that term, was a long series of keyboard devices which are extremely difficult almost without exception and most decidedly possess the interest not only of their difficulty, but also of a quite astonishing variety. One has only to compare this concerto of his with Rakhmaninov's in C minor, which consists very largely of tunes accompanied by various forms of arpeggios, in order to see Tchaïkovsky's technical superiority, which is the more remarkable because he was not, like Rakhmaninov, himself a virtuoso pianist. His fertility in pianistic invention could be adequately shown only with the aid of dozens of musical examples. Three (one from each movement) must suffice to give a bare idea of his resourcefulness (see Exs. 18, 19 and 20).

As for clumsiness, no doubt there is something in that stricture. There are some fearful handfuls in this score for the pianist to tackle, some terrifying runs in four octaves and many breakneck jumps with notes widely stretched apart at one moment and closely bunched together the very next; and much of the figuration is so unusual as to demand a great deal of special study for which no other composer either of concertos or of technical exercises will prepare the player. But that is only another way of saying how original Tchaïkovsky's keyboard writing is. What is more, it almost everywhere repays the effort made to master it. There are a few, a very few passages where the orchestra covers up the soloist while he vainly endeavours to impress the hearers with a particularly heartbreaking effort—where, in other words, the composer does not hold the balance fairly between means and ends. But on the whole his piano part is astonishingly rewarding; and difficult, sometimes even awkward, as it is, it has the great merit of being so enticing that it makes the performer play better than he would think himself capable of doing on looking at the forbidding pages of his part.

So far as we know, Nicholas Rubinstein did not call the B flat minor Concerto conventional. Perhaps it was part of his grievance that it is not so in any way, except possibly in the codas of the first and last movements, where it ceases to talk its own particular language and perorates with a sort of false, empty excitement in a musical Esperanto that other composers have used in almost exactly the same way at similar junctures of their piano concertos. It is enough to compare the Tchaïkovsky with the Schumann and Grieg concertos to see what is meant by this assertion. Leaving the minor for the major key is part of this standard procedure, and the working up of a strepitoso is as much a professional trick in concertos written for the player's sake as in opera devised to show off singers together in a finale. There are, of course, concertos written for music's sake (including Schumann's and perhaps Grieg's). Tchaïkovsky's, even at their best, do not belong to this class; but among virtuoso works the B flat minor and the Violin Concerto at least take top rank.

The Second Piano Concerto (in G major, Op. 44) reflects no disturbing personal experiences, only a kind of detached pleasure in good workmanship. Tchaïkovsky has taught his audiences to expect excitement from his best or at any rate his most characteristic works on a large scale, and it must be said that the Second Piano Concerto is unexciting. So are other things of his which we accept with pleasure for their neatness and their special flavour—the ballet music or the String Serenade, for instance, but what we look for in cases like these is not only superior craft, such as we may also find in this concerto, but distinctive invention of a peculiarly Tchaïkovskian kind that is not sufficiently conspicuous in this work. Hence its neglect, which, though rightly deplored by those who like to see changes in concert-room routine, is on the whole understandable.

Compared with the B flat minor, the Second Concerto is not only lacking in the sensational dramatic appeal with which the former takes hold of the hearer whether he likes it or not; it is also deficient in memorable melodic material. The B flat minor, as we have seen, is so rich in this as to become wasteful: it recklessly drops a first-rate introductory tune. The G major contains little we are tempted to hum on leaving the concert-room, much less while occupying the bathroom.

The principal subject of the first movement, allegro brillante e molto vivace, is a case in point. It is a good theme for symphonic development, which the introductory tune in the First Concerto so obviously was not that Tchaïkovsky got rid of it before he began to work out his material at all; it is, on the other hand, melodically quite undistinguished (Ex. 21). This sort of thematic raw material can only be laboured, and Tchaïkovsky does labour it in the course of a movement that is inordinately long even in the edition revised and cut by Alexander Ziloti with the composer's consent. A second subject, in E flat major, more lyrical but not very much more engaging melodically,[1] with one strain for the orchestra and another introduced by the piano, is also subject to a good deal of treatment which elaborates but does not noticeably advance or enhance it.

All the same, though the development is mechanical, Tchaï-kovsky's manufacture is superbly efficient. If there is not much in this movement to appeal to the emotions or to the mind, it does yield a kind of physical pleasure by the mere technical skill with which it is put together as a symphonic movement. A third theme, brilliantly handled by the soloist, seems at first to be added purely for the sake of pianistic display and rhetorical climax heightened by modulation; but it turns out to have a greater importance, for it serves as a kind of pivot on which the music swings back to the first subject.

Developments are ingeniously delayed—so much so that there would be every excuse for protraction if only the material in itself deserved all the attention the composer demands for it. The first subject is not allowed to do more than raise its head for the moment, for the orchestral strain of the second now claims more extensive treatment in a new key (C major) while the piano is silent. But the solo instrument re-enters with the second strain of that subject, which it now develops extensively in Tchaïkovsky's best inflated keyboard manner, which seems intent on showing that a pianoforte can shout down an orchestra. The latter has to deploy all its tutti force and to present a more magniloquent version of the first subject to assert itself against the pianist's rattling octave passages, marked *fff brillante*. However, the orchestra wins for the moment and embarks on a short development of the first subject that comes as near as anything in this movement to generate that tension Tchaï-kovsky could produce in his hearers with such masterly assurance, but for which this concerto is not on the whole distinguished.

An enormous solo incident—almost an interlude—follows. It is not a cadenza, but takes the place of one and may be described as being what cadenzas improvised or written by other people than the composer so often are: an additional development of material already sufficiently developed elsewhere. But there is the difference here that this extra working-out is the composer's own and consistent with the rest of the movement. It cannot, therefore, be called super-fluous, although it comes near being undesirable by heaping up

[1] It is closely related to the chief melody of the slow movement of the First Symphony (cf. bars 5–6 and 9–10 of Ex. 2).—ED.

difficulties in thick profusion and tightening thematic matter into climax after climax.

The recapitulation, however, begins with some compensating abbreviations and leads to a coda in which a brief stretta, containing some beautiful sweeping modulations reminiscent of late Verdi, makes a brilliant conclusion that is not too superficial for a rather shallow movement.

The slow movement, in D major, is linked to the first by a short modulating passage. It is marked Andante non troppo, a direction that will convey nothing to anyone who fails to understand what is meant by ' at a walking pace, but not too much so.' It may easily suggest slower or quicker than plain andante. The music of this piece, however, leaves no doubt about its pace. Nobody will wish to play or hear it dragged, for that would make it sound maudlin. Taken at the right speed it is at least gracious and mellifluous, if not especially arresting or characteristic of the composer. One might guess it to be Gounod as soon as Tchaïkovsky. In the middle section it becomes a trio for violin, 'cello and piano, with the last merely filling in an accompaniment. This incident exploits one of Tchaïkovsky's favourite tricks: that of repeating a melody with a new and equally important one set against it. The final pages seem to swoon away in a sort of amorous ecstasy, like an operatic love-duet.

The finale does not often overstrain virtuosity at the expense of its playful and humorous character. The keyboard writing is difficult enough to suit a concerto, but it is not bloated, as it often becomes in the corresponding movement of the B flat minor Concerto. In comparison with the first movement this is so short that when the recapitulation arrives one is at first under the impression that it is the return of a rondo subject after a first episode. But there was a real second subject (in E minor) which returns in the recapitulation (in D minor), and the feeling of episodic treatment was due mainly to the fact that what is actually a brief working-out section had developed the second subject only and left the first alone. At any rate it kept going the characteristic rhythm of that subject, which is Schumann's favourite four quavers with the first dotted. The slightly more animated coda introduces some new but perfectly relevant music of great harmonic charm.

Except that the public likes to see the antithesis between pianoforte and orchestra exploited dramatically rather than decoratively, there is no reason for the neglect of that very agreeable work, the Concert Fantasia, Op. 56, beyond the fact that it is not a full-scale concerto. And that is not a good reason, for it is difficult to say why shorter concert works of quality for solo instruments with orchestra have fallen into all but complete disuse. If ever their desired revival comes about, Tchaïkovsky's Concert Fantasia will again take its place in the repertory with such things as Mendelssohn's *Rondo brillant* and Schumann's *Introduction and Allegro appassionato*.

The first of the two movements of which the Fantasia consists, entitled ' Quasi Rondo,' is purely decorative in form and only moderately eloquent and emotional in content; the second, ' Contrasts,' makes dramatic promises in its title, but does little to carry them out. There are two entirely different themes in it, but they do not exploit the possibilities of sonata form in opposing two subjects to each other (and sometimes, in the working-out, making them clash) in such a way as to advance the musical procedure in the manner of a plot. ' Contrasts ' is not a plot; it is only a design. A very good and original design, however, as we shall see presently.

' Quasi Rondo ' is hardly a good title for any musical piece whatsoever. Such a piece is either a rondo or it is not. This one is not. All that it can be said to do in the matter of approximating to the rondo form is that it begins and ends with an extensive section one may regard as the principal rondo subject, and that there is a good deal of broadly developed new matter in between that one may call a first and only episode. But the two statements standing first and last have a second theme which the first time appears in the key of the dominant and the second time in that of the tonic, like the two subjects in a perfectly regular sonata movement. ' Quasi sonata ' would thus have been as appropriate a description for this piece as that rather recklessly chosen by the composer. But what's in a name? What matters about this movement is that it has charm of manner, elegance of craftsmanship and a high entertainment value. The main theme has an indefinably Russian flavour and a quite unmistakable Tchaïkovskian touch—far more often the same thing than is readily admitted by those who wish to emphasise Tchaïkovsky's cosmopolitanism for all it is worth and for a good deal more than it matters. The tune is playfully developed, rather in a vein of fairy-tale ballet, with the solo part built into the fabric in a way that uses virtuosity to musical ends without displaying it conspicuously. In the second theme, however, the piano has the lion's share. It is a rich, singable melody luxuriously displayed in arpeggios.· This expository section ends with a very definite full close in the dominant (D major), the piano having shown in no uncertain manner that when it comes to hammering octaves it can be as pouncingly effective as the full orchestra—that, in fact, such octave passages are its own particular game.

The episodic middle section (lo stesso tempo ma molto capriccioso e rubato) begins with a long and elaborate solo passage treated in the rather swollen manner Tchaïkovsky sometimes adopts in his keyboard writing and working up by means of his characteristic stringendo device of tightening the rhythmic elements into shorter note-values. It employs two new melodic ideas, expansive in themselves and even more luxuriantly developed. The orchestra, which never comes in at all during the whole of this long interlude, re-enters for the recapitulation of the pretended rondo subject, which now proceeds much as it had done the first time, except for a new transition which ensures that the second subject should remain in the key of the tonic and, of course, lead to a tonic close.

Oddly enough, Tchaïkovsky added an optional coda of great brilliance and rather empty rhetorical showiness, which he wished to be played if the second movement of the Fantasia was to be omitted. This points to two interesting observations. In the first place, it shows that he had a keen sense of what was and what was not conclusive at the end of a display piece, even if he very rarely carried out a peroration tastefully. In the second, it proves that he had some doubt whether the 'Contrasts' movement would appeal to performers. As a matter of fact he had been uncertain about it from the first, for it had originally been intended to form the opening movement of the third orchestral Suite, Op. 55, but was discarded from it.

It is hard to see why this movement should have been even temporarily the object of that curious dislike which Tchaïkovsky, almost alone among composers, often conceived for this or that work immediately after its completion. 'Contrasts' is, in its way, an attractive as well as a characteristic piece, and it brilliantly solves a formal problem of a very uncommon kind. There are two main themes, apart from much incidental and ornamental matter: one slow, the other quick; and they are shown as contrasts not only one by one in the manner of first and second sonata subjects, but often simultaneously in various ways. As an achievement in neat thematic telescoping this piece may indeed be regarded as a *locus classicus*. The only fault one may perhaps find with it, considered as such a feat, is that the quick theme is in itself rather wanting in spontaneity. One has the feeling that it may have been adjusted to fit in with the slow one by trial and error before work on the composition began in real earnest.

It is important for the hearer to bear in mind that the counterpoint for the solo 'cello added to the slow tune, which had been introduced alone by the piano, is not the contrasting idea referred to in the title, but a mere episode. Neither is the quiet melody that follows over an accompaniment embodying one of those inner pedals which are so characteristic a trick of Tchaïkovsky's art— pedals consisting not of one single sustained note, but of a pattern of two alternating notes, which go on unchanged for some time while the surrounding harmony alters.[1] The first hint that something in an entirely new, quick rhythm is going to be set against the first theme occurs when the soloist plays rapid ascending scales to its re-statement by the oboe. These develop into even more rapid arpeggios, and then comes a very cunningly contrived transition where the arpeggios, as it were, act the part of mutual friends and introduce the two different rhythmic elements to each other in a passage which persuades them not only to meet but to overlap (Ex. 22).

The molto vivace has the character of an energetic Russian dance, not as Cossacks would know it—it is far too extensively developed for that—but as one would expect almost any nationalist composer from Glinka to early Stravinsky to have written it. The device of an unchanging figure which is harmonically wrenched this way and that by different discordant stabs is characteristic of the school to which Tchaïkovsky did not quite belong[2] (Ex. 23).

The Piano Concerto No. 3, in E flat (Op. 75) and the Andante and Finale for Piano and Orchestra (Op. 79) are best discussed together, for two reasons: they are both based on material sketched in the spring of 1892 and originally intended to become Tchaïkovsky's Sixth Symphony (in which case the *Pathétique* would have been the seventh); and they were discarded because they did not satisfy him as symphonic material, but afterwards the first movement was rewritten by him for a solo piano and orchestra. So far as we know, he did not go beyond shaping a Third Piano Concerto in one movement; the slow movement and finale were left in short score,

---

[1] Other instances of this may be found in the finale of the Fifth Symphony, where such a pedal introduces the second subject, and in the *Humoresque* for piano, Op. 10, No. 2.

[2] Cf., for example, the Dance of the Tumblers in Rimsky-Korsakov's *Snow Maiden*.

with no indication that they too were to be turned into concerto form. Since they originally formed part of the same work, it seemed reasonable, however, to assume that this was his intention. At any rate, after his death his former pupil, S. I. Taneev, did assume it and took it upon himself to rewrite the symphonic andante and finale for piano and orchestra in the same way; so that in Opp. 75 and 79 we now have a complete Third Concerto which, though unsatisfactory as a whole, may be thought to represent the after-thought arrived at by Tchaïkovsky, once he had decided that his material would not do for a symphony. It is true that even Taneev did not know for certain whether Tchaïkovsky, if he actually meant to turn out a full three-movement concerto, would not have pre-ferred to scrap the andante and finale altogether and to replace them by two entirely new movements; so if we decide that the finale at any rate is a poor piece of work, we must blame Taneev for preserving it rather than Tchaïkovsky for having conceived it. For we cannot even be sure how far the conception may have been carried out: indeed, as will be seen in a moment, there is reason to suspect that the finale, as it now exists, is only the design for structural key-points, not for a complete musical organism.

Whatever Tchaïkovsky may have changed his mind about in the matter of the orchestration of the first movement, however much material that would originally have been distributed over the orchestra he may have transferred to the solo piano, his scoring of Op. 75, apart from that instrument, is exactly like that of his last two symphonies, down to the piccolo alternating with a third flute, the three kettle-drums and the tuba, although the last is less essential to even a heavily scored piano concerto than to a symphony because the relatively small range of variety in bass tone commanded by the normal orchestra is admirably supplemented by the full and characteristic bass of the keyboard instrument.

It is difficult to imagine where the piano part actually takes over material previously intended to form part of the orchestral fabric and where it merely embroiders on it. Which is as good as to say that the adaptation is on the whole very well done. Only once—in the case of the long cadenza—is one conscious of a concession made to the soloist, and only once—in the final pages—is there any mere pad-ding and, indeed, sometimes just doubling of the orchestra in the piano part, as though Tchaïkovsky had suddenly grown tired of devising figuration intended to make the solo instrument stand out. Elsewhere the pianistic texture is often very congenial to the keyboard, as for instance in the rather Schumannesque second subject, which appears in the piano at its first statement in the unusually remote key of G major[1] (Ex. 24), and is recapitulated in an elaborated form, quite conventionally in the tonic key (Ex. 25).

Except for the cadenza the whole piece is an admirably knit symphonic first movement, and even that purely virtuosic feature, inserted no doubt as an afterthought, is structurally as satisfactory as possible, though as a feat of pianistic writing it suffers from the same kind of inflation as the cadenza in the B flat minor Concerto and hastens to a climax by that kind of tightening of more and more closely telescoped thematic features which is one of Tchaïkovsky's most obvious theatrical effects. What is good about the present cadenza is not its lay-out or its form, but its placing. It indulges in the usual elaboration of material already sufficiently developed elsewhere that makes most cadenzas appear supererogatory, if not impertinent; but it is wisely inserted into the working-out section, where developments have their proper sphere, not thrust upon the close of the recapitulation, where they come too late and merely delay the fall of the curtain needlessly, except in the most carefully calculated instances, and at worst disturbingly.

The material as a whole is admirable for a concerto, though it would not have been so for a symphony, or rather—let us be careful to qualify—for a Tchaïkovsky symphony. For it is on the whole decorative rather than dramatic material, and we must accept the fact that as a symphonist Tchaïkovsky was also a dramatist and did his best work when he frankly indulged that inclination. He may have felt that the planned E flat major Symphony was not going to turn out a dramatic work, but just a well-shaped, purely musical one: that in fact it would not be truly *his* sort of symphony. At the same time he must have been aware, as anyone even today who studies this work without preconceptions cannot fail to be, that this was music of far too fine a quality to be sacrificed merely because it would not turn into the kind of work it was first intended for; that indeed it was very good music for a concerto—vital, plastic and effective.

Why this concerto should never be performed passes comprehension, except perhaps that pianists feel that if they play Tchaïkovsky, they must at all costs do the B flat minor over and over

[1] It is curious to note that this seems to be a sort of compensation for what happened in the first movement of the Second Piano Concerto, where the first subject is in G and the second in E flat major.

again. But surely anybody not wedded exclusively to that work—
and monogamy is no virtue in concert-goers—would enjoy hearing
No. 3 for once in a way and as a curiosity with the other two reconstructed movements, and more frequently by itself as a particularly
attractive concert piece.

The first subject (Ex. 26) is the kind of thing that lends itself
admirably to a variety of symphonic treatment; and it gets plenty of
it, perhaps even a little too much, though all of it is very enticing.
The second subject has already been shown in two different forms.
There is also an abundance of subsidiary material, all equally
attractive and original. So, too, is the procedure of composition,
not perhaps all the time, but certainly at many points. The harmonic
short cut to the key for the second subject (E flat major switching
over to G major) is arresting (cf. Ex 27), and even more so is the
magical whole-tone scale modulation in the working-out (Ex. 28),
perhaps the best thing of the kind Tchaïkovsky had done since the
finale of the Second Symphony, and one of those poetic conceits
which, from Glinka's *Ruslan and Lyudmila* to Rimsky-Korsakov's
fairy-tales, had always stood for mirages and miracles in Russian
music.

We now come to Taneev's share in this resurrected and necessarily rather patchy concerto. Tchaïkovsky's disciple reduced the
orchestration to wood-wind, horns and strings for the slow movement,
but wisely resumed the scoring of the first movement for the finale,
though with the addition of side-drum and cymbals to enhance its
martial character. The orchestral lay-out often shows a deliberate
effort to match the Tchaïkovskian manner: elaborate horn-parts
' nourishing' the texture satisfyingly in the middle regions, the
prominent 'cello solo towards the end of the slow movement and the
little detached patches of rising scales near the beginning of the
finale are cases in point.

The andante is a simple lyrical movement in B flat major developed in Tchaïkovsky's characteristic manner, which includes a
great deal of pianistic embroidery of some technical interest but
no particular thematic significance and the ingenious introduction
of a counter-melody to enhance the effect of a tune at the very
moment when its repetition might possibly become tiresome—in
this case at the return of the main theme, the counterpoint being
the 'cello solo just mentioned. For a concerto the keyboard writing
here is not out-of-the-way difficult, but it shows how intimately
Taneev understood the peculiar Tchaïkovskian way of pianistic

treatment, even to its faults, which are thickness of texture (too many fistfuls of chords and too many octave doublings) and sometimes long stretches of repetition of accompaniment figures. As a symphonic movement this andante would have been rather mild and uneventful, but it does well enough for a concerto because the opposition of the solo instrument and the orchestra adds a certain tension and variety to it.

What does not do, either for a symphony or a concerto, unfortunately, is the finale, a vigorous, march-like allegro maestoso. It has energy in abundance—indeed, over-abundance—but no real vitality of invention. The material is dry and dead, nor does the extremely busy and strenuously athletic piano-part give any real life to it. There is plenty of bustle and very little enterprise.

The movement, which pounds away relentlessly, is mercifully short; but although that is an advantage because the quality of the music happens to be such that a little of it is all the better for not going a long way, it is impossible to feel that Tchaïkovsky would have been content with no more than that for the crowning movement of a symphony. One suspects that either this was originally meant to be a third movement preceding a finale (the Second and *Pathétique* Symphonies also contain middle movements in march-form) or that what is left here is only a preliminary linking-up of sketchy material. The very opening, for instance, does not give the impression of a first presentation of the theme so much as a development of it as it would appear in a working-out section. The sequences shown in bars 4 and 5 of Ex. 29 are not like a statement but like an argument on something said at an earlier stage.

A second theme, in G major, is very feeble, and the twiddling little figures that accompany it on the piano, whether by Tchaïkovsky or by Taneev, are nothing for either of them to be proud of, or for the player to enjoy, for they have not even the attraction of difficulty. Yet another theme, in C major, which comes after a re-statement of Ex. 29, like a second episode in a rondo, spells sheer bankruptcy of invention; and the very arid two-part writing in octaves for the orchestra that soon follows is not enlivened by the pianist's scale passages, which rush up and down fussily without adding the least interest to the musical goings-on. The second subject eventually returns in the tonic key, wrapped up in thick wads of arpeggios as though it were a precious object to be saved from breakage. Unfortunately it is nothing of the kind, and the presto peroration does not redeem a movement that can only be written down as one

of Tchaïkovsky's most lamentable failures. Yet we are bound to
remember that he must have known it to be that, since he never
intended it to be published.

Tchaïkovsky's single Violin Concerto, if not a profound work—
which in any case it was never meant to be—is a very well organised
one. Tchaïkovsky clearly took some trouble to build it up. He even
discarded the original slow movement because he felt it to be insufficient. We are able to judge that his instinct was right, for it
still exists in a version for violin and pianoforte: the *Meditation*
forming the first number in a set of three pieces, Op. 42, entitled
Souvenir d'un lieu cher, the remaining ones being a *Scherzo* and a
Melody. The *Meditation* is a shapely thing on a large scale,
but rather dull and mechanical. It lacks melodic distinction, a virtue
which the later slow concerto movement certainly possesses, for it
contains more than one tune that is strikingly memorable. Having
played or heard the *Meditation* once, one immediately forgets all
about it except for a general recollection of having listened rather
impatiently to its uneventful progress and its merely superficial
elaborations. The canzonetta in the concerto, on the other hand,
leaves the impression of a definite mood and of material that engages
one's affection. It is, moreover, better placed, so to speak. The
Meditation was in D minor, a key too near that of the work as a
whole, especially as it ended on a D major chord. The canzonetta
is in G minor, the subdominant minor, which makes a good contrast to the main key without being too alien to it.

The fact that the new slow movement was an afterthought,
conceived when the concluding movement had already been written,
gave Tchaïkovsky a chance to weave it closely into the work by
means of a transition leading straight into the finale. This is one
of those premonitory passages at which he was such an adept. The
join is made quite simply, but most effectively and with great
ingenuity—and simple things in art often require as much ingenuity
as the most complex. Near the end of the canzonetta Tchaïkovsky
brings in the little figure Ex. 30, in various ways quite naturally,
as though it were just part of the development; but presently we
learn that it was the harbinger of the phrase with which the solo
part begins the finale (Ex. 31), which in turn is the germ of
the principal theme (Ex. 32).

A matter of special interest arises here. We see how Tchaïkovsky
proceeded in one such case of thematic preparation, and although
we must not jump to the conclusion that he always worked in the

same way, it is permissible to suppose that an answer may be found here to' the question raised on p. 54 where a similar occurrence in the B flat minor Piano Concerto was discussed. In the Violin Concerto, at any rate, the invention of the finished theme came first and the transitional passage leading up to it was derived from it later.

The Concerto opens very simply, like a string quintet, and there is a deceptive appearance about the first-violin tune: it looks as though it were going to turn into an important thematic feature, but is actually nothing more than a formal opening sentence, like 'Once upon a time,' that sets the music going. After a very few bars things begin to happen: the orchestral introduction obviously works up to what *is* going to be a thematic feature, in fact the first subject, which soon appears in the solo part (cf. Ex. 33). It is oddly like a lyrical second subject, and certainly, if this were a symphony or a sonata, its mood and shape would be far too much like that of the actual second subject (Ex. 34). But this is a concerto and, what is more, a violin concerto. The violin is an instrument which makes its most striking impression with sustained melody, not with heroics or fire-works. True, it is capable of these too, but they are musically sub-ordinate, and Tchaïkovsky, realising this, properly lets them be so in this movement. Both the first and the second subjects give rise to plenty of rhetorical utterances and virtuosic elaborations, but these are developments, not the essence of the two themes. If the pro-cedure is not ideal from the point of view of concerto form con-sidered as an end in itself, we can only say that Tchaïkovsky had no interest in such academic abstractions and was concerned only with the creation of a form serving the particular end he had here in view. His Violin Concerto is none the worse for being specially devised for the violin and not as a text-book specimen of a pattern which no great master was ever content to use like a mould giving the same shape to everything that is poured into it.

The most elaborate and difficult passage-work, of which there is plenty in this movement, cannot help a single violin to produce much climax of tone-volume as distinct from climax of excitement. But such climaxes are quite simply obtained by the expedient of dropping the solo instrument now and again and carrying on with vigorous tutti passages This Tchaïkovsky does brilliantly, and he restores the balance by providing a climax of virtuosic excitement in a hair-raisingly difficult cadenza for the soloist.

We have already seen that the Canzonetta is linked up with the

69

finale. In a way it is also with the first movement, though there is a definite break after that. It certainly connects with it in the matter of key, for in spite of its being in G minor, it begins as the first movement ends, with a D major chord, from which the orchestra works through a delicately modulated transitional passage to the soloist's entry, where G minor for the first time firmly establishes itself. There is not a great deal of elaboration of the main tune or of the subsidiary material, but the piece is beautifully shaped and has that indefinable mood of gentle melancholy in which Tchaïkovsky is most individually expressive. Even in the first half-dozen bars alone he would be unmistakably recognisable. These bars recur later in the orchestra with decorations for the soloist, and so help to strengthen the coherence of the piece.

The finale again opens with an orchestral introduction obviously working up to some thematic event. It sounds rather like the entry of the chorus in an opera, preparatory to a great vocal outburst. What happens, however, is that suddenly the orchestra breaks off and leaves the soloist alone with a kind of preliminary cadenza beginning with Ex. 31. This leads to the initial statement of the dance-tune beginning with Ex. 32 and forming the subject of a rondo. The wild Cossack-dance measure is slightly relaxed for the appearance of an episode of more broadly melodic character, but the atmosphere of rustic Russian festivity is maintained, though for that moment it finds vent in folk-song rather than in folk-dance. Very soon afterwards an oboe-and-clarinet dialogue introduces an even more leisurely theme, which the soloist takes up over a light, syncopated string accompaniment with melodic echoes in the 'cellos. The fiddle's hankering after sustained melody having been satisfied, the main subject is resumed. The episodes eventually return in other keys and with different orchestral treatment, and the final statement of the subject leads to a very gay and dashing peroration.

The *Sérénade mélancolique* (Op. 26) and the *Valse-Scherzo* (Op. 34) for violin and orchestra antedate the Violin Concerto and may perhaps be regarded as exercises if not indeed as discarded sketches for it. The latter, at any rate, stands immediately in front of the Concerto, so far as the opus number indicates, and we are certainly justified in looking upon it as rejected material, for it has nothing but brilliance to recommend it. However, the brilliance is not merely the performer's concern, for it is inherent also in the polished workmanship of the composition as such. The piece is worth performing occasionally, if not by itself, at any rate with the

Sérénade mélancolique, which is considerably more valuable and highly characteristic of Tchaïkovsky's art in that vein of mingled sadness and graciousness in which he excelled when he felt things profoundly without being in too emotionally self-indulgent a mood: when he felt for others rather than for himself, we might say, as he does for example in the deeply touching but admirably restrained letter-scene for Tatyana in *Eugene Onegin*. Together these two concert pieces are capable of making an agreeable item, not perhaps for a soloist specially engaged, but for one of the orchestral artists to step out of the ranks to show what he can do individually.

The set of *Variations on a Rococo Theme*, for 'cello and orchestra (Op. 33) is the most familiar of Tchaïkovsky's concert pieces, as distinct from concertos. The theme has a graceful formality that may be regarded as owing something to the eighteenth century; but its flavour is peculiarly Tchaïkovskian, and it is obvious from the pastoral interlude in *The Queen of Spades*,[1] which contains some admirable imitation Mozart, that the composer could have come much nearer to a rococo colour as well as design if he had thought it important to do so in a work in which successful costumery clearly mattered less to him than good musical manners.

The manners here are perfect. The lightness of the music saves the 'cello from the temptation to whine, into which it falls notoriously easily. The theme is admirably suited to variation treatment: sufficiently simple in outline to bear elaboration and so clear in structure as to remain recognisable in disguise. It is introduced by the solo instrument after a brief, delicate, rather Schumannesque orchestral introduction. Eight of its sixteen bars, which amount to thirty-two with the repeats, are quoted as Ex. 35. It rather resembles in character another of Tchaïkovsky's themes for variations, that of the finale in the third orchestral Suite, in G major. Moreover, the graceful ritornello which links the 'cello variations together (Ex. 36) is very like the first variation in that movement in its gliding chromatic smoothness.

The ritornello is left to the orchestra except for a final clinching phrase in which the solo instrument takes part. This is most ingeniously devised in such a way as to finish with the two opening notes of the theme (marked *a* in Ex. 35), which thus form the upbeat for the theme to reappear in the first variation, where it is presented broken up into rapid triplets. The same procedure is followed between Variations I and II, but afterwards this link is dropped.

[1] See p. 177.

The second variation is a piquant exchange of swift phrases between soloist and orchestra, a good example of Tchaïkovsky's very individual way of scoring in differently coloured blocks set next to each other, examples of which may be found in many of his orchestral works.[1] The solo phrase at the end of the ritornello is now extended to make a modulation from the prevalent key of A major into C major for the third variation, where the time ·changes to 3/4, andante sostenuto. The ritornello, so far retained in its original form,. is now itself subject to new treatment. It leads quietly to a cadence in E major.

This, however, turns out to serve only as the dominant of A major, to which Variation IV returns. Here theme and ritornello are dovetailed, both appearing in new shapes. The fifth variation is in affair of shakes and brilliant cadential matter for the soloist, both the theme and the ritornello being left to the orchestra. The second cadenza turns the tonic (A) into the dominant of D minor, the key of the sixth variation. The seventh and last, marked *Coda,* returns to A major and develops the material extensively, with great vivacity and brilliance, and Tchaïkovsky exploits his ' mosaic ' manner to the full by breaking up the texture into minute fragments alternating between the solo instrument and the orchestra. The ritornello is again modified by the orchestra and accompanied by sweeping 'cello arpeggios. The instrument's abnormally, almost freakishly wide range is exploited to the full here, as indeed throughout the work. The 'cello has its drawbacks as a virtuosic solo instrument on account of the difficulty of making it audible above an orchestra in its lower ranges; but it is unique among all but keyboard instruments for its enormous, artificially enlarged compass.

Nearly the same range and similar technical resources are drawn upon for the *Pezzo capriccioso,* for 'cello and orchestra, Op. 62. It is not, as the title may seem to indicate, a kind of scherzo, but a slowish movement with a pale cast of melancholy in Tchaïkovsky's ' pathetic ' key of B minor. After an introductory page the main theme appears: a kind of song-without-words tune. It makes the most of the 'cello's sympathetic middle register without becoming too sentimental: it is too graceful for that in a wistful sort of way. Before long, interpolations in rapid triplets remind us that this is a piece for the display of skill as well as feeling; and when the key changes to D major, quick figure-work animates the solo part,

[1] E.g., March in the *Nutcracker* ballet, middle section; Fourth Symphony, finale; Sixth Symphony, third movement.

although the fundamental pace does not change. After a more ornate restatement of the main theme, this alternative section recurs with a deceptive turn into C major, which, however, reverts almost abruptly to B minor—the modulations as well as the material are capricious enough to justify the composer's title—for a final page of energetic buzzing that can be so effective on the 'cello, as Elgar has shown in the second movement of his Concerto.

4

Miscellaneous Orchestral Works

By

Ralph W. Wood

T CHAÏKOVSKY'S CONCEPTION of himself as above all a symphonist was hopelessly wrong. (No tenable definition of the word ' symphony ' seems to have found a place in his stock of ideas.) On the contrary, it is generally where the ' form ' is more or less rigidly prescribed from without that his music is most satisfactory; likewise in miniatures, where he felt no duty to spread himself and be grand and architectural. ' Sonata form,' the ' form ' used by a symphonist, so far from being rigid, is extremely loose; it leaves the composer innumerable choices in his task of building up a coherent movement that shall possess the fundamental characteristic of ' variety in unity ' and that, by the relationships of its successive thematic elements and the management of its transitions, shall have the appearance of a piece of organic growth. Faced with such choices, Tchaïkovsky was thoroughly uncomfortable.

As a matter of fact, as the letter quoted by Mr. Cooper on p. 26 shows, he all his life accused himself of weakness in respect of ' form.' From time to time throughout his career we find him expressing dissatisfaction with his own achievement, conscious of faults and anxious to overcome them; but ' form ' was the one factor that he actually named, and repeatedly named, in these outbursts. His well-known admiration—idolisation, indeed—of Mozart he more often than not elucidated as a recognition of Mozart's absolute mastery of ' form,' contrasting such clarity and ease with his own deficiencies. It was as a seasoned composer of forty-eight that he wrote:

> All my life I have been much troubled by my inability to grasp and manipulate form in music. I fought hard against this defect and can say with pride that I achieved some progress, but I shall end my days without ever having written anything that is perfect in form. What I write has always a mountain of padding: an experienced eye can detect the thread in my seams, and I can do nothing about it.

That indicates, of course—and it is not the only evidence—that he had duly achieved the realisation that design is the crucial factor in music, as indeed it is in every kind of artistic creation. And elsewhere we find proof that he had even grasped the fact that form and material must be interdependent, every piece of material carrying the implication of its own self-dictated form. But for some reason, probably not unconnected with his naïve and inveterate assumptions about emotion and music, and ' programme,' and so on, he never solved, or even actually squared up to, those form-cum-material problems of which he was so strongly but vaguely aware.

The large-scale orchestral works that principally occupied Tchaïkovsky's mind are as a rule divided into two categories—symphonies on the one hand and symphonic poems, programmatic overtures, etc., on the other. He himself differentiated them thus. They are differentiated thus in this present book. . . . But of the symphonies, No. 1 has a poetic sub-title, to No. 4 Tchaïkovsky gave a programme himself (in a letter to Nadezhda von Meck, the ' best friend ' of the dedication), for No. 6 he claimed a secret, undivulged programme.[1] And the overtures, etc., on the other hand, really have not—or rather, although they have, they do not actually in themselves make explicit—very individual programmes: they nearly all exploit more or less the same little group of emotional-cum-musical guiding lines. Case after case of confections he turned out; the labels were different, the flavourings were different, but the essences, and their rotation, were pretty much the same. The process of seeking, and with relieved joy eventually finding, a new subject to inspire him to serve up again, with every pretence of newness, just the same ingredients as before was an apparently necessary process of self-deception.

It follows that the ' form ' of the first movement of his symphonies and of most of the overtures, symphonic poems, and so on, with which we are to deal just now, is nearly always the same. Here it is. A—slow introduction; B—allegro with two main themes, strongly contrasted, the second usually in slower tempo, presented in the form: 1, development of 1, elaborate bridge, 2, development of 2, gradual return to 1, more or less complete recapitulation, usually finishing with material based on 1 after the re-statement of

[1] Probably a modification of the earlier one found among his papers for 1891 : ' The ultimate essence of the plan of the symphony is LIFE. First part—all impulsive passion, confidence, thirst for activity. Must be short. (Finale DEATH—result of collapse.) Second part love; third disappointments; fourth ends dying away (also short).'—ED.

the development of 2; C—coda, mainly slower tempo, re-stating the material of A or else giving a transformed version of one of the themes from B. Exceptions are sufficiently rare to be mentioned as they arise. Otherwise that ' form,' stereotyped, conventional, up to a point fundamentally effective, beyond that point fundamentally ineffective, may be understood to be the one Tchaïkovsky used.

So weak we're most of Tchaïkovsky's latest large orchestral works in the matter of design· that one is at first a little surprised to read his statement to the Grand Duke Constantine that he could ' say with pride ' that he had ' achieved some progress.' But when one inspects his earliest efforts in the genre one understands! We are concerned for the moment with eight compositions, which are just as appropriately to be considered together as are the six symphonies, and which, as has been hinted above, can be quite properly compared *to* the symphonies, though that will not to any extent be done here. They are:

> Overture to Ostrovsky's *The Storm*. Op. 76 (1864).
> *Fate*, Symphonic Poem. Op. 77 (1868).
> *Romeo and Juliet*, Overture-fantasia (1869).
> *The Tempest,* Fantasia. Op. 18 (1873).
> *Francesca da Rimini*, Fantasia. Op. 32 (1876).
> *Manfred*, Symphony. Op. 58 (1885).
> *Hamlet*, Overture-fantasia. Op. 67 (1888).
> *The Voevoda*, Symphonic Ballad. Op. 78 (1890–1).

We may as well dispose of *Fate* first; although not the earliest, it is distinctly the worst work on the list—so bad that one can only applaud the composer's action in destroying the score some ten years after it was written, and deplore the action of the publisher who reconstructed it from the orchestral parts and printed it shortly after the composer's death. One is hard put to it to say which is the more immature and feeble: the character of the themes or the type of uses to which they are put. The utter helplessness of the dead stops that mostly occur in place of transitions has to be seen or heard to be believed. Apart from the final bar, there are no fewer than eight ⌢ signs, seven of them over whole- or half-bar rests. The themes themselves would create for present-day audiences an unmistakable atmosphere of cinemas in the early days of silent films. The best one can say of the thing is that one or two of the modulations are highly effective (e.g., Ex. 37). And the most interesting point one can make about it is that it shows Tchaïkovsky already up to what were to become some of his favourite orchestral tricks, e.g., Exs. 38, 39 : the typical scale passage, pizzicato, and at N we find the characteristic singing of the melody—a melody afterwards used in *The Oprichnik* (Ex. 91)—by massed violins, violas and 'cellos (in three octaves), against accompaniment of wood-wind, harp and double-basses. The printed score is prefaced by some lines by one Batyushkov, but the truth is that those lines were only ever associated with the work because Nicholas Rubinstein, just before giving its première, decided that the title *Fate*, which was the only programmatic indication used by the composer himself, was insufficient. The lines were actually suggested by an enthusiastic and eccentric professor of botany, S. A. Rachinsky, merely on hearing the title of the work, not the work itself.

Like *Fate*, the Overture to Ostrovsky's drama *The Storm*,[1] owes its late opus number to the fact that it was published posthumously. Actually it was composed whilst Tchaïkovsky was still a student, being the holiday task that he presented to Anton Rubinstein at the St. Petersburg Conservatoire after the summer vacation of 1864. Ostrovsky's play had been a favourite with the now apprentice composer since its appearance in 1860; he had already toyed with the idea of turning it into an opera; in fact the idea was abandoned only because another composer, Kashperov, got in first. In a sketch-book he noted down the following programme for the overture:

> Introduction : adagio[2] (Katerina's childhood and all her life before marriage); allegro (hints of the storm); her longing for true happiness and love. Allegro appassionato (her spiritual conflict). Sudden change to the evening on the banks of the Volga; again conflict, but with traces of a sort of feverish joy. The coming of the storm (repetition of the motive after the adagio and its further development). The storm; the climax of her desperate conflict and death.

Such were the preliminaries to serious musical composition for Peter Ilyich Tchaïkovsky at the age of twenty-four, and such they remained till the day of his death. Indications of his typical form will be noticed, though there are obvious divergencies from it. When the overture was actually written it did not exactly follow the lines of the sketch. It is a fiery, intensely dramatic work, unlike what was to become typical Tchaïkovsky not only in its form but in much

---

[1] Constance Garnett's translation of the play was published by Duckworth in 1899.

[2] The broad melody for 'cellos and cor anglais introduced at but 23 of the andante misterioso which ultimately took the place of this adagio is the folk-song ' Iskhodila Mladen'ka,' another version of which was introduced by Mussorgsky in *Khovanshchina*.—ED.

of its material detail. It is original, interesting, forceful. Parts of it have an abandon only matched, if at all elsewhere in Tchaïkovsky's music, in *Romeo and Juliet*. One would like to hear it played once or twice, for it has somewhat the appearance of a masterpiece *manqué*. All the same one can understand why Anton Rubinstein was angrily contemptuous of it, not merely—one can assume—because of its composer's adventurousness but because of his crudity and callowness, particularly in construction. Anton's brother Nicholas, who could have produced and conducted it, took a similar view and pronounced a performance to be out of the question. (Even the inclusion of a brief fugal section had failed to placate them.) The last five bars, one only of the several passages that are, for Tchaïkovsky, unusual in their harmonic freedom, show —do we gather?— a 24-year-old's view of Death! (Ex. 40).

The orchestra employed is: piccolo, two flutes, two oboes, English horn, two clarinets, two bassoons, four horns, two trumpets, three trombones, tuba, plentiful percussion (including gong), harp and strings. Tchaïkovsky rarely wrote for less throughout his life, and not often for much more (though he very often added two cornets). The size of this orchestra, or rather the inclusion of such non-classical instruments as the cor anglais, harp and tuba, was one of the grounds of Rubinstein's censure, though Rubinstein himself used the tuba four years later in his ' musical picture' *Ivan the Terrible*. In an attempt to salvage at least part of *The Storm* Tchaïkovsky the following year wrote a Concert Overture in C minor of which the introductory andante is the andante misterioso of *The Storm* transposed from E minor and scored without the offending ' extras.' But Tchaïkovsky's friend, the critic Laroche, complained that the introduction without the cor anglais was ' like a woman robbed of her principal charm '; Rubinstein remained unappeased by the sacrifice; and the C minor Overture disappeared until 1922, when it was found among S. I. Taneev's papers. It had to wait till 1931 for its first performance.

From the *Storm* Overture and then *Fate* to *Romeo and Juliet*, a work with the inexplicable distinction of bearing no opus number, was an amazing jump. How Tchaïkovsky progressed so far between 1868 and 1869 is a mystery; or, rather, perhaps one should call it just an example of latent genius suddenly bursting through, and throwing off, the bonds of inadequate experience and immature technique. Of course, the fact that it was extensively altered in 1870, and not finally revised until ten years later still, has some bearing on its comparative excellence. When we review the whole of Tchaïkovsky's output in the perspective of the fifty years that have elapsed since his death, we find *Romeo and Juliet* one of his two or three very best compositions.

It is a pretty exact specimen of Tchaïkovsky's favourite formal scheme. If we compare it, as we are for several reasons tempted to do, with the overture *Hamlet* (both are based on mighty Shakespearean tragedies, both are called overture-fantasias, both are fine works— and almost exactly twenty years separated them), we find that it is a good deal more intricately constructed than the later piece, with more actual motives and more interchangings of them. We note, too, the much more elaborate coda section. *Hamlet* has, however, the same, normal Tchaïkovskian, outline. The orchestration of *Romeo and Juliet* is more varied, and not so preponderantly block-like; and it contains more of Tchaïkovsky's favourite antiphonal use of the families of instruments (cf. pp. 20–1, 55 and 62–3 of the Eulenburg miniature score.)

Romeo and Juliet has the fundamental characteristics without which it could not be accepted by us as actually from Tchaïkovsky's pen, and by the highest standards they must perhaps be reckoned as its limitations; that much given, it may be described as a master-piece—and as such it does continue to impress us despite its extreme hackneyedness. Yes, it is a magnificent piece of work; one that is absolutely Tchaïkovskian but that somehow just (when we think of the love-theme perhaps we must say ' only just ') misses giving the hints, or more than hints, of vulgarity found elsewhere; its impetuosity remains irresistible, and its certain passages of contemplative melancholy are not rhetorical but eloquent.

No musician can fail to be interested in *Romeo and Juliet*, one of the few compositions by Tchaïkovsky that are acceptable to every taste. (Directly we begin to think about him we are faced by the fact that he, who of all composers presents for the not-so-very-musical layman no problems whatever, is for the connoisseur a very perplexing figure indeed. And therefore an interesting one.) And interest in *Romeo and Juliet* must rightly focus much of its attention on the rather remarkable genesis of the work. The subject was suggested to Tchaïkovsky by Balakirev, more or less as a sequel to the latter's recently formed acquaintanceship with this young new-comer and a consequence of his belief that the newcomer had a future. Tchaïkovsky had the previous year dedicated *Fate* to Balakirev, who disliked the work, and said so, and why, but at the

79

same time expressed his gratification at the fact of the dedication. Balakirev not only offered Tchaïkovsky this Shakespeare tragedy as a subject but actually laid before him a detailed programme for the proposed composition, and the corresponding sketch of the musical form; he even named the series of tonalities he thought might well be used, and gave Tchaïkovsky a droll, but in fact quite reasonable, recipe for finding musical inspiration ('Take goloshes and walking-stick,' etc.). It is, of course, evident that Balakirev's notions about the relationship between literary subjects and musical compositions were exactly similar to those of the composer of the overture to *The Storm*. It is thus quite likely that, for instance, the fact that the material of the introductory andante non tanto quasi moderato of *Romeo and Juliet* undergoes an immediate re-statement a semitone lower was due to Balakirev. What actually occurs is that after the initial F sharp minor statement of what is usually referred to as Friar Laurence's theme[1] there is a succession of four thematic elements, in F sharp minor, D flat major, F minor and F minor, respectively; then the first theme is repeated, in a higher register instead of a low one, and accompanied by a pizzicato derivative from the last of the four thematic elements; after which the four thematic elements are repeated exactly as before, but now in F minor, C major, E minor, E minor. Semitonal relationships are common in the music of Balakirev and his circle (Borodin, the young Rimsky-Korsakov, etc.), but equally so in Tchaïkovsky's own subsequent works. The ubiquitous second subject, the slower 'love' theme,[2] from the main, allegro, section of *Romeo and Juliet* makes its first appearance in D flat, and has its eventual recapitulation in D. In the parallel main section of *Hamlet* the parallel 'love' theme is introduced in D, and recapitulated in D flat. The first two themes of the

[1] The original (1869) introduction was in E major and based on quite a different theme (Ex. 41). Balakirev objected to this as ' lacking in beauty and power and not even sketching the character of Friar Laurence. You need something there on the lines of Liszt's chorales (*Der Nächtliche Zug* F sharp major, *Hunnenschlacht* and *St. Elizabeth*) with an ancient Catholic character, something like the Orthodox, whereas your theme (E major) bears quite a different character—the character of Haydn's quartet themes, the genius of petty bourgeois music, awakening a strong thirst for beer ' (letter of December 1/13, 1869). In his revision of 1870 Tchaïkovsky substituted the introduction as we now know it (with which Balakirev expressed himself ' very satisfied ') and made the consequently necessary changes in the working-out and coda of the allegro (pp. 53–62 and 96, etc., of the Eulenburg miniature score). The further revision in 1880 lay largely in the addition of dynamic markings: e.g., the crescendo sign at bar 4 of the introduction and the poco più *f* marking at bar 5.—ED.

[2] Which Balakirev found ' simply *charming*,' which moved Stassov to tell the Handful ' there used to be five of you; now there are six,' and which Rimsky-Korsakov in later life considered ' one of the best themes in the whole of Russian music.'—ED.

symphonic ballad *The Voevoda* are announced in A minor and B minor respectively, and then immediately re-stated in B flat minor and C minor respectively. When, by the way, the ' love ' theme in Romeo and Juliet is re-stated, soon after its first appearance, in an extended form (following the delicious counter-subject), the *two* long notes with which it now starts, instead of the previous *one*, make it still more akin to, for instance, the *Hamlet* love-theme (see Ex. 44) and in fact a very typical Tchaïkovskian formula for that class of melody. A final comparison with *Hamlet* is forced in the third, coda, section; in each work this largely consists of a quasi-funeral-march (with an appropriate timpani ostinato) which in *Romeo and Juliet* is based on, and is a highly effective transformation of, the love-theme, whereas in *Hamlet* it is the first theme of the intro-ductory section that is used; and in *Romeo and Juliet* the coda *starts* with the quasi-funeral-march, whereas in *Hamlet* it only comes after a re-statement of the other, second theme from the introductory section. There are, as a matter of fact, more examples of genuine thematic development and transformation in *Romeo and Juliet* than in any other of Tchaïkovsky's works, and the coda is literally full of them.

The *Hamlet* overture is a work that has suffered a quite un-merited neglect in England, at least until Helpmann and the Sadler's Wells company based a ballet on it, a kind of popularisation that is not without its drawbacks. It is an interesting point that Helpmann was left comparatively free in his task of putting choreography to it by the fact that we have no record of the programme that the composer followed in writing it. Helpmann's interpretation, the scenario he devised, seems a very reasonable one, to say the least; but quite probably it is different from, and in subtlety far surpasses, Tchaïkovsky's own conception. That Tchaïkovsky did have a detailed literary scheme, on just the same lines as those of *Romeo and Juliet, The Tempest*, etc., is beyond doubt. The musical form of *Hamlet* is very similar to that of *Romeo and Juliet*, although less complex in detail, and closely approximates to what has been laid down above as Tchaïkovsky's norm in such matters. Its main departures from that norm, if they can be called departures, are that between the first theme of the allegro (Ex. 42) and what amounts to the love-theme (Ex. 44) another motive (Ex. 43) is stated, in both exposition and recapitulation, and that the opening theme of the slow introduction (Ex. 45) reappears towards the end of the allegro. The latter, especially, is a feature so often paralleled in other works of

Tchaïkovsky's that it ought almost to have been included in the norm. Another variation that hardly amounts to a variation is that there is a further new motive, introduced *after*, well after, the love-theme (Ex. 46). Like *Romeo and Juliet*, the *Hamlet* overture is in common time throughout. Even for Tchaïkovsky, the orchestration is remarkable in its block methods and the prevalence of a ' three-part-writing ' structure. One can only give here a single random quotation (Ex. 47). The three flutes are playing together in unison for the vastly greater proportion of their part.

Tchaïkovsky's other Shakespearian work (apart from the commissioned incidental music to *Hamlet*, dealt- with in Chapter VII) was the symphonic fantasia *The Tempest*. It was composed four years after *Romeo and Juliet*, seems to have made on the whole a considerably better impression on its first audience than that work, and was for a time well thought of by Tchaïkovsky himself. The adverse (and quite accurate) criticism of his friend Laroche, in 1873, the year of its production, wounded him deeply. It was when he heard it in Paris five or six years later that he decided, with surprise, that its form was ' diffuse ' and badly proportioned, that its orchestration was ineffective, and that in brief what ' I have hitherto regarded as one of my most brilliant works is in reality . . . unimportant.'

What Balakirev was to *Romeo and Juliet*, Vladimir Stassov was to *The Tempest*. Stassov suggested to Tchaïkovsky three possible subjects—*Ivanhoe* and Gogol's *Taras Bulba* being the other two. When Tchaïkovsky selected *The Tempest* Stassov produced a torrent of advice and a fully detailed programme which is printed in more concise form in the score : ' The sea. The magician Prospero sends his obedient spirit Ariel to raise a tempest, which wrecks the ship with Ferdinand on board. The magic island. First timid feelings of love between Miranda and Ferdinand. Ariel. Caliban. The lovers give themselves up to the delights of passion. Prospero renounces his magic power and leaves the island. The sea.' This is on the one hand very much what anyone acquainted with Shakespeare's masterpiece might expect, and on the other-quite enough to ruin any symphonic work. Tchaïkovsky followed it with sufficient exactness for very little to be left of his normal form; only, in fact, the return of the slow introduction at the end and the positions of the love theme. The place of the first theme of the allegro is filled by Prospero's motive, which however only returns *after* the recapitulation of the love-theme. Between it and the love-theme in what would normally be Tchaïkovsky's exposition-section the

' storm ' occurs, while Ariel and Caliban are depicted in the stretch that lies between the exposition and recapitulation treatments of the love-theme. Though nothing like so crude as *Fate*, *The Tempest* is far from technical perfection. It is in nearly every way a sort of half-way house between the almost incredible *gaucherie* of Tchaïkovsky's weakest works and the sometimes almost incredible bravura of his most assured ones. Its actual themes are moderately, but no more than moderately, expressive. The opening and closing material (identical), representing the sea, is reasonably effective; it includes some quite fine modulations, but is over-mechanical (Tchaïkovsky's everlasting fault). The love-theme (which undergoes, in its exposition, a series of small but pregnant modifications) has more than a touch of Tchaikovsky's eloquence, and more than a touch of his vulgarity. It can be appropriately compared with its counterpart in *Romeo and Juliet* (cf. Ex. 48 with pp. 83–4 of the Eulenburg score of *Romeo and Juliet*). (The orchestration of the *Romeo and Juliet* passage, by the way, is very nearly identical with the passage at N in *Fate*, referred to above). The storm itself realises, alas, our worst fears. It was rightly attacked by Laroche and Stassov. Like so much of *Francesca da Rimini*, it belongs to the old-time cinema. The ' sea ' sections employ a wash-background sort of scoring, with all the strings (except double-bass) ' div. in 3 ', that is very rare in Tchaïkovsky. Otherwise the orchestration is typical: lots of antiphonal stuff between the families and sub-families, plenty of syncopated-chord backgrounds, massings of strings, and so on.

After a gap of three years, which was most notably occupied by two string quartets, the notorious B flat minor Piano Concerto, a number of very delightful piano pieces, the Third Symphony and *Swan Lake*, Tchaïkovsky composed *Francesca da Rimini*. It was to have been an opera, and the libretto had been written—by one K. I. Zvantsev— to the composer's satisfaction. Zvantsev, however, a most fanatical devotee of Wagner's music and theories, stipulated that the proposed opera should be on Wagnerian lines. Naturally that did not suit Tchaïkovsky at all, and the project was abandoned. The subject, however, had thus taken root in his imagination, and the orchestral fantasia was duly, and with typical rapidity, composed.

Tchaïkovsky never had achieved, and never did achieve, a more completely controlled piece of work than in *Francesca*, and never showed, within certain immutable limitations, a more entire mastery of his material and realisation of his intentions. Notwithstanding his periodical self-indictments, the truth is that he did master ' form ' *as he actually understood it*, to a prodigious degree. What he called despairingly his 'mountains of padding' were simply inseparable from his basic conceptions, from the process of starting with an extra-musical programme and of deducing from that various musical motives of widely differing character and mood which had then somehow to be worked into one movement together. The alternative method, of allowing his second musical theme to arise, musically, after and in some sense *from* the first, or from developments of the first (and to hell with literary programmes, at least before the event!), probably never occurred to him. Probably *his* method never occurred to Mozart. Once again, let there be no mistake about it: Tchaïkovsky was incapable of the conception of absolute music, and it follows that one is correct in believing that there is no essential difference between his symphonies and his other big orchestral works and in sensing the same technical approach (e.g., to form) in both categories. For instance, à propos of the notorious programme for the Fourth Symphony that he outlined to Nadezhda von Meck, we have also the letter to Taneev already quoted by Mr. Cooper on p. 27.

The truth is that he often managed his 'mountains of padding' superlatively well—and never better than in *Francesca*. The fact that the work dates from just about the middle of his creative career (and that he had already done at least one equally good technical job years earlier, in *Romeo and Juliet*, gives a fair indication of the static nature of that career. In the preface to that rather amazing mixture of insight and sentimentality, *Beloved Friend*, Catherine Drinker Bowen writes: 'Rameau . . . once said of himself, " From day to day my taste improves. But I have lost all my genius." Peter Tchaïkovsky's musical taste improved very little during his fifty-three years—but he never lost his genius.' That is, possibly, true, (It all depends on where you consider his 'genius' to have lain.) But equally he never improved his genius. He certainly did not, to any extent worth mentioning, develop as a composer. He *thought* he did. See, for instance, the letter to Nadezhda von Meck dated December 30, 1879:

> To-day I set out to remodel my Second Symphony. It went so well that before lunch I made a rough draft of nearly half the first move-ment.[1] How I thank the fate that caused Bessel to fail in his contract and never print this score! How much seven years can mean when a man is striving for progress in his work! Is it possible that seven years hence I shall look upon what I write to-day as I look now at my music written in 1872?

[1] But cf. Taneev's comment in the footnote on p. 36.—ED.

Or, again, writing late in 1881 : '. . . I am much disposed towards writing music. I think . . . that I shall write better than I used to. . . . I have grown cold to my former music; all of it, without exception, seems immature, imperfect as to form, and empty. . . .' Of course, his real trouble was that although he was conscious of shortcomings and of striving after an unreached perfection his actual ideal never changed much; the problems to which he addressed himself were always the same ones. Study of his music can hardly fail to uncover that fact, and that fact is a very simple proof that he never really grew or matured. In absolute artistic achievement, so far at any rate as these ambitious orchestral works of his are concerned, he reached—or it would be more accurate to say that he abruptly shot up to—a momentary zenith in 1885. In technical mastery, in solution of the only problems he can be believed to have envisaged, he never surpassed the *Francesca da Rimini* of 1876. It is significant that most of his critics from that day to this seem to regard it as among his best works. Yet *Francesca*, despite the assurance of its technical management in every aspect, is really a very low-grade piece of music.

The score is prefaced by a 22-line quotation from Dante (*Inferno* V), beneath a short prose précis to the effect that ' This is from Dante, the second circle of Hell. There you see chastised the sensual whose punishment is to be tormented continuously by the cruellest hurricanes in deep darkness. Among those tortured people we recognise Francesca da Rimini, who tells her story.' In form it is different from all Tchaïkovsky's other works. It does open with an andante lugubre, but neither this section's material nor any slow section at all is found at the close. The andante lugubre is followed by a più mosso-moderato, which leads presently to a short reference to the opening motive. Then, broadly, we have a simple lay-out of allegro vivo—andante cantabile non troppo—allegro vivo. The second allegro section is identical with the first but for (*a*) omitting a certain rather long pedal-bass passage, (*b*) eventually rushing into a brief coda, poco più mosso. Up to and including the andante cantabile, the listener could imagine that this was going to be like any of the movements that were Tchaïkovsky's idea of sonata form; but neither the andante cantabile nor even the smallest particle of its contents recurs after the return of the allegro. Of course, that is in accordance with the programme; Francesca does not tell her story twice; for once Tchaïkovsky's preliminary extra-musical scheme has to an extent hindered, instead of helped, his innate tendency towards musical disunity. Thus we have two slices of the stormy allegro vivo with an entirely unrelated slow movement sandwiched between them. The necessary elaborate transitions are effected with Tchaikovsky's customary skill, that art which never conceals art. When it is said that the oft-repeated main theme of the slow movement is one of Tchaïkovsky's loveliest the reservation has, of course, to be made that Tchaïkovsky's loveliest is still, emphatically, Tchaïkovsky's; never, surely, was there a composer who so constantly—above all in his best passages—makes the listener reflect, if reflection comes at all, that silk purse just cannot be made out of sow's ear. (All the more astonishing, therefore, is that one exceptional ' zenith' work.) The material of the allegro vivo must be the very worst that ever came from Tchaïkovsky's pen; beside it, *1812* seems attractively made of good, solid, honest, academic bread-and-butter. It is just empty blood-and-thunder, and its only appropriate context would be a storm, or cowboys chasing Red Indians, on the old silent screen. It is over-full, just—and ' just means everything—goes beyond the limit, of diminished sevenths and of Tchaïkovsky's relentless, immaculate, ineluctable sequences and repetitions.

The opening motive has something to be said for it, and it also deserves mention as being, out of the many occasions on which Tchaïkovsky used cornets, one of the comparatively few when their presence is both noticeable and effective (Ex. 49). The chromatic-scale rantings that so largely occupy the allegro vivo are really not worth quoting and Ex. 50, which comes towards the climax of the interminable hectic ' working-up,' is cited not because of its intrinsic merit but because it is so very typical. The re-statement of the opening motive (Ex. 49) into which (after the climbing down from that climax) the music proceeds, is rather felicitous. Already, by then, the basses are preparing for the lead-in of the unforgettable first (clarinet and pizzicato) statement of the andante cantabile theme. That theme, by the way, has a counter-theme answering it, very much after the pattern of the love-music in *Romeo and Juliet*—but perhaps more notable as an indication that Borodin, say (*vide* the first theme proper, No. 17, letter A, in the Polovtsian dances of *Prince Igor*, and innumerable others), and Tchaïkovsky were, after all, of the same race (Ex. 51). One finds this chromatic sliding above a dominant or tonic pedal here, there and everywhere in the music of the Mighty Handful: it is not so common in Tchaïkovsky, but the example we have just noted is not the only one. Rather more interesting is the relationship between the soft horn-fanfares that occur at the dying-down of this section, just before the return to the allegro vivo, and one of the *Hamlet* motives (see Ex.ˑ 46). The actual opening notes of the recapitulation of the allegro take one back to *Romeo and Juliet* (Ex. 52). The brief coda, poco più mosso, is a piece of *extremely* mechanical and conventional fireworks, though the final series of chords is striking in its way. The orchestration throughout is typical (cf. Ex. 53). It is interesting to compare the two bars after O with a passage in the finale in the Second Symphony (Ex. 54).

Of all Tchaïkovsky's large-scale works for orchestra (excluding the suites) there are only two that do not open in slow tempo: the First Symphony and the symphonic ballad *The Voevoda*. The latter has no connection with the early opera of the same name. The score is prefaced by Pushkin's translation of Mickiewicz's ballad *The Voevoda* : a poem about a voevoda (a Polish big-wig) who returns from war to find his young wife dallying with her former suitor. The voevoda and his servant have their guns ready to shoot the couple, but somehow the servant's ball kills his master instead of the lover. The musical design is a kind of inversion of Tchaïkovsky's norm, slow and fast sections being interchanged; but not *exactly* so, either in the disposition of some of the motives or in the general proportions; the key cycle, too, is planned differently in places, though the semitonal changes are characteristic. The full plan is as follows:

Allegro vivacissimo	Theme	1	A minor
	„	2	B minor
	„	1	B flat minor
	„	2	C minor
	„	1	C minor—D minor
			Development
Moderato—Più mosso	Theme	3	E flat major
Moderato	„	4	E minor
	„	3	D major
	„	4	E minor
			Bridge
Allegro moderato	Theme	5	E minor
Moderato con moto	„	3	E flat major
Allegro giusto			Development
Allegro vivacissimo	Theme	1	Various keys—conclusion in A major

It is in 3/4 (or 9/8) throughout.

The Voevoda seems a rather uninspired work. Pedal-points are used over-much, and there are plenty of the merciless Tchaïkovskian repetitions. For once there are no notable themes, and needless to say there is nothing that might compensate us for their absence. The return of the first motive has no dramatic, and not much musical, justification. (The appearance of the E flat major theme brings us an astonishing specimen of Tchaïkovskian superlatives—rubatissimo). On the other hand, this piece has a certain quiet integrity; there is a certain emerging of control and basic earnestness and eloquence, in place of Tchaïkovskian rhetoric (rubatissimo or no rubatissimo), that makes it well worth an occasional performance.

Tchaïkovsky more than once categorically and elaborately stated to Nadezhda von Meck that composition and orchestration were not, for him, separate processes.[1] All, however, that he really meant was that he never composed in the abstract, no musical idea came to him without being in terms of this or that instrumental colour. The fact remains that from the beginning to the end of his career 'composing' a work and 'orchestrating' it were two distinct operations. Obviously he composed into a draft on a couple or so of staves, with broad indications of the scoring written in, and it was the transcription of that draft into the full score (a separate job often started upon months after the composing of the work) that was the 'orchestration' so frequently referred to in his letters. *The Voevoda*, for instance, was 'composed' towards the end of 1890, but its 'orchestration' seems to have lasted from the spring of 1891, through the summer (when Tchaïkovsky visited Paris and discovered the celesta, a then brand-new instrument, which he at once resolved to employ in the symphonic ballad and in his new ballet, *Nutcracker*) and on until late October.

What makes the question of the 'orchestration' process particularly interesting in the case of *The Voevoda* is that this work is, as it happens, orchestrated in a very remarkable manner—and in a manner, moreover, that makes it rather difficult to imagine a previous draft on a couple or so of staves. The opening, as a piece of scoring, and—above all—as scoring that seems inseparable from its material, is unlike Tchaïkovsky; it reminds one, even, of Sibelius (Ex. 55). Later on the side-drum has thirty-two bars of that timpani rhythm. Note the horn writing at G (Ex. 56). It goes on like that for sixteen bars (with second and fourth horns naturally taking turn and turn about with first and third). Ex. 57 is something else that could have come from Sibelius. Not only the celesta but the harp is prominent and important. In places we find an impression-

[1] Cf. p. 28 and 32.

istic background technique that, once more, is very unusual in Tchaïkovsky. That, of course, is the kind of thing we find rather in French scores, from Debussy onwards, but equally in Sibelius. Sibelius is, first and last, the man to whom anyone, seeing this score without its title-page, would attribute it (cf. Exs. 58 and 59). In Ex. 58 the doubling in unison of first oboe and first clarinet, while the second oboe is omitted, is very noteworthy indeed—one of the points that make us wonder whether indeed this score can have been actually written by Tchaïkovsky. One other uncharacteristic feature is the continual ' long-term ' dividing of the strings. The orchestra employed is three flutes, two oboes, English horn, two clarinets, bass clarinet, two bassoons, four horns, two trumpets, three trombones, tuba, timpani, side-drum, harp, celesta, strings. It is only when we turn our attention from the instrumental build of the score, and the lay-out and interrelations of its textures, to the actual notes the instruments play, that the Sibelius illusion is destroyed.

It remains to discuss both the longest and the greatest of Tchaïkovsky's symphonic poems. In October 1882 Balakirev—again Balakirev!—had written to Tchaïkovsky: ' Forgive me for having left your last letter so long unanswered. I wanted to answer you at length and in perfect peace and quiet. I first offered the subject I hinted to you about to Berlioz, who declined it on account of age and ill-health.' (That was in September 1868, no less than fourteen years earlier, when Berlioz was sixty-five and Balakirev thirty-two.)[1] 'Your *Francesca* gave me the idea that you could work out this subject brilliantly, provided you *took great pains*, subjected your work to stringent self-criticism, let your imagination fully ripen, and didn't hurry to finish anything. This magnificent subject is no use to me, as it doesn't harmonise with my intimate moods; but it fits you like a glove. It is Byron's *Manfred*.' Following which the worthy Balakirev instructs Tchaïkovsky that the work must have an *idée fixe* (*à la Symphonie fantastique*) that occurs in all the movements, and proceeds to give in great detail the programme, movement by movement, even providing the key scheme. ' Isn't it a splendid programme? I'm sure that if you exert yourself this will be your *chef d'œuvre*.' In 1884 he returned to the charge, sending Tchaïkovsky a copy of the programme originally proposed to Berlioz, with a fresh key-scheme suggested in the margin. (He had not

[1] The actual letter to Berlioz is printed in *Perepiska M. A. Balakireva s V. V. Stasovim*, Vol I (Moscow, 1935).—ED.

ventured to dictate the choice of keys to Berlioz!) It is interesting to observe how Tchaïkovsky's own key-cycle when he actually composed *Manfred* in 1885 was modified from the suggested ones; it will be observed that he interchanged the tempi and programmes of the two middle movements. The three schemes are:

BALAKIREV (1882)	BALAKIREV (1884)	TCHAÏKOVSKY (1885)
(I) F sharp minor (second subject in D major)	(I) B flat minor (second subject in D major)	(I) Tonality ambiguous (only establishing B minor more than halfway through the movement) (second subject in D major)
(II) A major (slow movement)	(II) G flat major (slow movement)	(II) B minor, D major, B minor (scherzo)
(III) D major (scherzo)	(III) D major (scherzo)	(III) G major (slow movement)
(IV) F sharp minor (appearance of Astarte in D flat)	(IV) B flat minor (appearance of Astarte in D flat); coda—B flat major	(IV) B minor (appearance of Astarte in D flat); coda in B major

Tchaïkovsky's programme, prefaced to the movements in the score, runs as follows:

(I) Manfred wanders in the Alps. Weary of the fatal questions of existence, tormented by hopeless longings and the memory of past crimes, he suffers cruel spiritual pangs. He has plunged into the occult sciences and commands the mighty powers of darkness, but neither they nor anything in *this* world can give him the *forgetfulness* to which alone he vainly aspires. The memory of the lost Astarte, once passionately loved by him, gnaws his heart and there is neither limit nor end to Manfred's despair.

(II) The Alpine fairy[1] appears before Manfred in the rainbow from the spray of a waterfall.

(III) A picture of the bare, simple, free life of the mountain folk.

(IV) The subterranean palace of Arimanes. Infernal orgy. Appearance of Manfred in the middle of the bacchanal. Evocation and appearance of the shade of Astarte. He is pardoned. Manfred's death.

So far as the first movement is concerned, it varies from Balakirev's prescriptions in the details of the wording but in gist is much the same. The second (third in Balakirev) is identical. The third (Balakirev's second) is much less detailed than Balakirev's. Balakirev had talked of Alpine 'hunters,' and finished : 'Naturally at the beginning you'll have to have a little hunting music, only here you'll have to be *specially careful not to collapse into triviality*. God preserve you from rubbish in the way of German fanfares and *Jägermusik*.' Tchaïkovsky played safe and cut out hunting and

[1] *Sic.* Byron had called her the 'witch of the Alps.'

its music altogether. The finale is practically the same in both schemes, but here a very interesting *musical* divergence occurs. Balakirev had written (1882) : ' A contrast to this infernal orgy will be provided by the *evocation and appearance* of Astarte's shade (D flat major, the same music that in the first movement was heard in D major, only there this thought was brief, a sort of reminiscence, and was immediately drowned in Manfred's mood of suffering; here the same idea can be developed in a full and complete form . . .).' Tchaïkovsky does nothing of the sort. The theme (Ex. 62) does reappear indeed, and in D flat (as against D in the first movement) —which is a literal acceptance of Balakirev's idea, though of course it forms a different relationship with the rest of the work (in which Tchaïkovsky's keys are a fourth above Balakirev's original ones), but, so far from being extended, the theme makes a rather briefer appearance in the fourth than in the first movement, and certainly undergoes no kind of development. What it does undergo is a very elaborate, repetitious and sequential, fragmentary preparation (based on what were sequelæ to it in the first movement), before Tchaïkovsky manages really to bring it in, duly in D flat. Having achieved that objective, he rushes it and its allegro non troppo sequel (identical with a passage to which it *eventually* proceeded in the first movement) off in a mere sixteen bars, and we find we have said good-bye to it for ever. The preparation had occupied thirty-three bars!

There are several points about *Manfred* that make it markedly different from all Tchaïkovsky's other works. Firstly, it is his only work in the *nominal* programme category that is in more than one movement. Secondly, the first two movements do not re-capitulate their middle sections. Thirdly, the whole composition not only is vastly long—it plays something like an hour and a quarter —but is *designed* with the utmost spaciousness; nothing quite like the long-breathed deliberation of the third movement, or, in the second, the practically verbatim recapitulation of the whole huge variegated first section after the equally huge middle section, is to be found elsewhere in his output. Its heroic, but perfectly judged, proportions make one think rather of *Ein Heldenleben*. The form of the first movement, in itself, is different from that of any other Tchaïkovsky movement. After an opening section in which a long stretch of material is quite characteristically at once repeated in another key (or, rather, sequence of keys), we have a series of sections each bringing new themes and none of them recapitulated later. Only half-way through, as has already been noted, does the movement assume even the signature of the key in which it ends and the main key of the whole work. The very beginning is in a rather ambiguous A minor. Both that ambiguity and the actual build of the opening theme remind us definitely of the same part of the *Hamlet* overture (Ex. 60). Exs. 61, 62 and 63 are other salient motives; the last is, of course, based on Ex. 60, but actually sails in with every possible assumption of newness. Nevertheless the movement is completely satisfactory as a piece of design, and in that respect almost unique among its composer's large movements.

The scherzo consists of a broad ABA structure. A is a vivace con spirito that contains a number of short thematic elements, closely related and strung very neatly together, with meticulous Tchaïkovskian repetitions verbatim that the speed saves from being wearisome. B is l'istesso tempo but quite different in character (Ex. 64). The harmony through most of this section reminds us of Balakirev and his school in the same way as that *Francesca* passage cited above (Ex. 51). Half-way through it Tchaïkovsky tricks us into thinking that he is making a neat return to A, instead of which he twists back to reiterations of the B subject in surprising new tonalities and textures. Into a recapitulation *in extenso* of A the music eventually does run quite neatly and naturally, and that in its turn runs with equal naturalness into a simple but spun-out coda of an exquisite ethereal, crystalline quality.

The pastoral third movement is a long-drawn, sustained stretch of quiet rapture, exactly reproducing the spirit of its literary heading. Apparently Tchaïkovsky thoroughly believed in the idealistic state referred to, which may be a ludicrous and even contemptible fact philosophically speaking but is fortunate musically. Nowhere else has he given us a movement remotely like this one, and this one is exceedingly beautiful. The opening theme (Ex. 65) is, perhaps faintly, but indisputably, of a Berliozian cast. (And Tchaïkovsky had always so misunderstood and underrated Berlioz!) The fact is that this movement, though not of course in the same class, does succeed in making us compare it to the ' Scène aux champs ' in the *Symphonie fantastique*; by quite different means it gives something of the same ineffable feeling of simple and spacious serenity.

The fourth is perhaps the least admirable movement, but nevertheless quite passably good. After two brisk subjects have been dealt with in the opening allegro con fuoco there is a short lento passage, followed by an extract from the first part of the first movement. Tempo I returns, actually, with a brief fugal treatment of the first subject, from which Tchaïkovsky proceeds into a developmental section in which the first two subjects are combined contrapuntally. After a considerable climax we are led into some more of the opening material of the first movement, which is interspersed with references to the first subject of the finale. After another climax, which is worth quoting because it shows the composer indulging in a—for him—remarkable modernism, we reach an adagio with change of metre and some more material from the first movement (Ex. 66). We are now into the fantasia-like preparation for the beautiful andante 'Astarte' theme from the first movement. The remainder of the finale is rather like a condensed recapitulation of the last half of the first movement, though there are also entirely new elements, principally the grandiose passage in which the harmonium is added to the orchestra, and the succeeding B major coda. One or two other pieces of harmonic daring are worth quoting (cf. Exs. 67 and 68).

Manfred is scored for three flutes (third alternating with piccolo), two oboes, English horn, two clarinets, bass clarinet, three bassoons, four horns, two trumpets, two cornets, three trombones, tuba, three timpani, cymbals, bell, tambourine, triangle, bass drum, gong, two harps, harmonium, and strings—perhaps the largest purely orchestral force Tchaïkovsky ever employed. There are several signs that his mood during the orchestration was one of exceptional care and elaborateness; for instance, the direction to the second bassoon to play a certain passage an octave higher if the *piano* on the lowest B — A sharp is impracticable, the directions to horns to play *pavillon en l'air* (though that does also occur in *The Tempest*), and the direction to strings to play with the full length of the bow (just after O). It is interesting to note that in a chromatic scale played in successive upward rushes of bassoons, clarinets and flutes he does not bother to overlap them; it is true that they are doubled by strings, but the strings too are not properly overlapped (cf. the orthodox treatment in *Romeo and Juliet*, pp. 20–1 of the miniature score). The bell has a small but salient part; the composer remarks: 'The bell must be of medium size and it would be good to place it in an adjacent room, not in the concert hall itself.' The effect just after O (Ex. 63) when all the strings enter *senza sord.* in unison, having been muted all through the previous section even in *fff* tuttis, is terrific. This is one of the passages that occur in both first and fourth movements; the melodic line also includes a highly idealistic *ffff* assignment for the three flutes—in their lowest register, and even including the low B which is not on the instrument. In one respect at any rate just like so many others of his scores, this one makes us wonder if ever there has been another composer so fond as Tchaïkovsky of using all his strings (apart from double-bass) in unison or octaves. The two harps are used very well, *as* two, with a wealth of varied effects, including (in the finale) alternating glissandi in slightly different tunings. Although much is just characteristic Tchaïkovskian scoring, there is also much that shows him doing what he really so seldom did—*thinking* and *searching* and *finding*, instead of just repeating, however industriously and enthusiastically, effects that had long been sheer routine. Several passages in *Manfred* (such as, to give only one example, the dovetailed

octaves— —for 'cellos and also bassoons on p. 231 of the

full score) in their various ways enable us to understand, after all, the quasi-Sibelian orchestration of *The Voevoda* more easily than we can understand the contrary, backward-looking character of most of the rest of Tchaïkovsky's post-1885 orchestral work.

Balakirev was right. *Manfred* was Tchaïkovsky's *chef-d'œuvre*. It is devoid of vulgarisms and of most of his other weaknesses, and in their place possesses several virtues found nowhere else in his music. It is a masterpiece, and its neglect is quite lamentable —though its length and difficulty may to an extent account for that neglect.

In addition to those already mentioned Tchaïkovsky wrote in the course of his career three other 'overtures'—one in F major dating from 1865–66, a *Festival Overture on the Danish National Hymn* (Op. 15), and—*1812.*

All that need be said of the Overture in F is that it was originally written for small orchestra and some six months afterwards, at Rubinstein's request, re-scored for full orchestra. It was a product of his very earliest days.

Only a very short time before his death Tchaïkovsky wrote with approval to Jurgenson of the 'Danish overture,' which he said he believed, so far as he could remember it, to be 'effective and, from a musical standpoint, far superior to *1812.*' He also gave the opinion that it might become 'a popular concert work.' The second view, at least, we know now to be incorrect, and a perusal of the score suffices to assure most of us that the first was equally so. An early work, Tchaïkovsky composed it, at Nicholas Rubinstein's request, to celebrate the impending marriage of the Tsarevich with Princess Dagmar of Denmark. It is an elaborate piece, far from devoid of interest to a student of his development. But by absolute standards it must be called merely laborious (which is needless to say, seeing who wrote it), conventional, empty, in places crude—quite valueless as music. The seventh of its ' subjects ' is the old Tsarist national hymn (Lvov's ' God Preserve the Tsar ').

The overture *1812* (Op. 49) was also the fruit of a request from Nicholas Rubinstein. He suggested a *pièce d'occasion* for the All Russian Art and Industrial Exhibition to be held in Moscow; he was chairman of the music section of the Exhibition and it was his design to organise symphony concerts, as well as concerts of a lighter kind, including some specially written works (cf. his letter of September 18/30, 1880, the last he ever wrote to Tchaïkovsky). Tchaïkovsky took his cue from the fact that the new Cathedral of the Redeemer, built in Moscow to commemorate the events of 1812, was nearing completion and that its consecration was expected to coincide with the Exhibition. *1812* must be one of the most dreary and repulsive works in the whole of music. What, however, we must note is that not its programme, nor the fact that it was a commissioned work, nor even its preposterous array of performers (full orchestra with plenty of percussion, cannons, bells—and military band *ad lib.*) is responsible for its obnoxiousness. Nor is its design, which is elaborate, workmanlike, and quite close to Tchaïkovsky's norm for large-scale orchestral works (but—formally an advantage—minus a love-theme). What makes us unable to call it anything but noisy, vulgar, and empty, is just the actual material used : a hotchpotch of a Russian liturgical theme (bravely demoded from Locrian to diatonic major), a Russian folk-tune, the Marseillaise, ' God Preserve the Tsar, as well as some of the composer's own. In every other respect it is, in no derogatory sense, perfectly characteristic Tchaïkovsky.

His orchestral output includes three other commissioned pieces that may properly be disposed of here. They are marches, and all three, like the Danish overture and *1812*, quote ' God Preserve the Tsar.' The well-known *Slavonic March*, Op. 31, was composed in 1877 for a concert in aid of the soldiers wounded in the war between Turkey and Serbia, and it was for some time known as the *Russo-Serbian March*. It is an elaborate work in its genre, with five sections and half a dozen themes. Few listeners, perhaps, would guess that the composer has marked the tempo—for the first three sections, the whole of the B flat minor portion of the work—Moderato in modo di marcia funebre. It is an expert, in a superficial way extremely stirring, piece of work—conventional in essence but with a veneer of striking originalities. It is worth remembering that the themes employed, for what good and for what bad they are, are not Tchaïkovsky's own but Serbian national airs (plus the Russian anthem as already mentioned); but it is also worth noting that they really could very well have been his own, so far as their character is concerned. Very little, in the way of general criticism, is to be said of the *Slavonic March* that cannot be said of the larger part of Tchaïkovsky's orchestral output, and to regard it, just because it is a *pièce d'occasion* and because it is very popular, as outside the main and estimable stream of his work is a mistake. The chance— if we can call the fact of a composer's mind working in the same way on two separate occasions ' chance '—the chance resemblance between a passage in it and a passage in *Francesca* is symbolic. It is by no means another *1812*, nor in any real sense related to the two other marches: the *Coronation March* for the coronation of Alexander III in 1883 and the *Jurists' March* written in 1885 for the jubilee of the Petersburg School of Jurisprudence, where the composer had been educated. Both are in D and in translation both are entitled on the score *Marche solennelle*. Both are quite empty and valueless compositions.[1]

We have now dealt with what one type of admirer would name as Tchaïkovsky's most important class of work and also with some productions that everybody would probably agree to be his very worst. It is time for us to look at what another type of admirer (at any rate in the present neglected and unknown condition of *Manfred*) would almost certainly name as being among his most worthwhile music.

From Rome in February 1880 Tchaïkovsky announced to Nadezhda von Meck that he had ' during the past few days sketched the rough draft of an *Italian Capriccio* based on popular melodies. I think it has a bright future; it will be effective because of the wonderful melodies I happened to pick up, partly from published collections, and partly out in the streets with my own ears.' Incidentally, it was a cavalry bugle-call, which he heard every evening while staying at an hotel that was next to the barracks of the Royal

[1] The two other marches sometimes described as orchestral works—*The Russian Volunteer Fleet* (which Modest Tchaïkovsky called the *Skobelev March*) and a military march for the 98th Yureysky Infantry Regiment—were written only for piano.

Cuirasseurs, that he used to open the work. It is just a question of taste, and a crucial test of one's attitude to Tchaïkovsky, whether one prefers that opening to the opening of the Fourth Symphony. Or whether one can stomach the vulgarity of the oboes in thirds (on p. 12 of the Boosey and Hawkes miniature score) better than the vulgarity of the andante second subject of the first movement of the *Pathétique* Symphony.

The *Italian Capriccio* is an excellent sample of Tchaïkovsky's spacious, grand manner—in the matter of page-to-page construction. In all-over form it is an unashamed string of unrelated, contrasted movements, with only the occasional recurrences of a passage from the opening section (p. 4 of the miniature score) by way of architecture. If, as in the *Slavonic March*, the tunes are not the composer's own, he has at any rate treated them with far more originality than those in the March. It is a light work, in a literal sense a vulgar (i.e., popular) one; but one at which surely no musician ought to turn up his nose—least of all, any of those who have no qualms over the slobbering vulgarities (in the other sense) of, say, the last two symphonies. The orchestration is daring, original, hugely effective—and much of it unlike Tchaïkovsky's usual methods. One would welcome space to quote extensively, but a single reference— surely one of the happiest scoring inspirations, within this genre, of Tchaïkovsky or anyone else—must suffice : the lay-out of the accompanying chords when the cornets take over the melody from the oboes at the bottom of p. 12 of the miniature score. The orchestra employed is a large one: third flute (alternating piccolo), English horn, two cornets, bells, glockenspiel, triangle, tambourine and harp in addition to the standard complement.

It is an odd fact, though very far from unparalleled in musical history, that one of Tchaïkovsky's most successful works, pleasing alike to both the main classes of his admirers, was written—as he put it in a letter to Jurgenson—' accidentally.' He had made sketches for something that hovered, in his conception, between a symphony and a string quartet! Then came the characteristic quick flare-up of industry and invention. From Kamenka he wrote to Nadezhda von Meck on October 10/22, 1880 : ' My muse has been so kind that in a short time I have got through two long works: a big festival overture for the Exhibition, and a serenade for string orchestra in four movements. I am busy orchestrating them both.' The overture was *1812*; the Serenade (Op. 48) was the crystallisation of the symphony/quartet project. An endearing note at the beginning of the printed score of the Serenade announces that the larger the string orchestra employed the better the composer's wishes will be met. The first movement is on the whole true to its title, *Pezzo in forma di sonatina,* though very characteristic Tchaïkovskian features of its form are that there is a slower introduction-section which returns at the end, and that each of the subjects of the main allegro is developed, to the small extent that each *is* developed, after its own statement, instead of there being any general, central development-section in which both themes would be used. It is quite a nice piece of music, not very typical Tchaïkovsky as to its material—and perhaps none the worse for that. The writing for the string-orchestra medium is excellent. The second movement, a valse, is delightful and, for all its simplicity, memorable. Its themes stick. As in so many of Tchaïkovsky's valses, the first of them starts with a scale passage, in this case upwards.

The third movement is a very beautiful little Elegy and, again though simple, of striking originality. Needs anyone to be reminded of the opening? We have to stomach, of course, the typical B flat passing note in the first violins at bar 30. The whole piece is very pure Tchaïkovsky, akin to the best, the delightful best, of his piano miniatures with its quiet elegance, its sincere feeling, its exquisitely polished academic procedures, its memorable and simple melodies.

The finale is the worst movement. It is founded on one of those tiresome moto perpetuo Russian tunes—and Tchaïkovsky had the audacity to make the movement into what at any rate was *his* usual idea of sonata form, complete with slow introduction (which is also based on a folk-tune, a hauling song from the Volga). Instead of bringing back that introduction as a coda (which, in any case, its character would have precluded) he breaks a little before the end into a re-statement of the opening material of the *Pezzo in forma di sonatina,* and then works out of it again in very trite, perfunctory, schoolboy manner into a boisterous close concerned with the ' merry-go-round ' tune.

The writing for the medium is splendid throughout the Serenade. The prevalence of three-part writing, and even two-part, would be astonishing were it by any other composer of the period. Two of the parts are often in octaves and sometimes another two at the same time (cf. the return of the main valse theme on p. 25 of the Eulenburg miniature score and the passage beginning at bar 108 of the finale, p. 42 of the score).

Tchaïkovsky left one other composition for string orchestra, an entr'acte written in 1884 for the jubilee of the actor I. V. Samarin and published after the latter's death as an *Elegy* dedicated to his memory. It is often referred to as a ' little ' work, but is not particularly short. It is, in fact, definitely too long for its material. The main theme, of which we hear too much in its course and whose salient rhythmic phrase is also overworked, is rather dreary though not entirely without charm. The piece contains the rhetorical pauses and the cadenzas that Tchaïkovsky found it so difficult to exclude from even his least ambitious products. This was one of the compositions subsequently used in the *Hamlet* incidental music.

Perhaps the clearest proof that, after opera, the only kind of composing in which Tchaïkovsky was really interested was for the orchestra lies in his attitude to his four orchestral suites: Op. 43 (1878–9), Op. 53 (1883), Op. 55 (1884) and Op. 61 (*Mozartiana*) (1887). For the simple truth is that if the fifteen pieces that make up the first three orchestral suites were arranged for piano solo and then mixed up with all Tchaïkovsky's authentic piano compositions the student not already acquainted with them would be hard put to it to pick them out (unless perhaps by the nature of the lay-out for the instrument). Now Tchaïkovsky never professed to place the least value, seriously speaking, on most of his piano pieces. Yet upon fifteen precisely similar musical conceptions, designed for the orchestral medium, he lavished all the care, endured from them all the anxiety and anguish, took in them all the pride, that he took, endured, lavished in the case of his operas, symphonies and overtures. And if further evidence be desired, look at his idea in *Mozartiana*, where he took three piano pieces of Mozart's and thought by putting them into orchestral guise to further their popularity and increase their just appreciation both among the general public and among musicians.

One could write at considerable length of the genesis, the vicissitudes and the ultimate fates of these suites. They came from the more worldly-successful half of Tchaïkovsky's career and figured very largely in that success. But the music is simply not worth detailed study; with the exception of the variations from No. 3 the suites are pretty thoroughly out of the repertoire now, and the most suitable treatment is to indicate as briefly as may be how far such oblivion is a satisfactory and how far an unsatisfactory state of affairs. We are certainly not facing a matter of lamentable neglect, by which the musical world is heavily the poorer, as in the case of *Manfred*.

The First Suite, the outcome of an idea for an orchestral scherzo, was composed at intervals and at a good many different places over a long period.. It consists of Introduzione e fuga (D minor), Divertimento (B flat), Intermezzo (D minor), Miniature March (A), Scherzo (B flat), Gavotte (D). The fugue is the essence of worthy conventionality and could more or less have been written by anyone from Bach to Mendelssohn. That said (and it is true, after all, of most nineteenth-century fugues), one may add that it is within its limits quite a pleasant affair. In a letter Tchaïkovsky referred to the Divertimento as a ' minuet,' but it has a good deal of valse blood in it and the title it bears has at least an appropriate lack of definition. It is quite a nice little piece, if rather undistinguished. With the Intermezzo we recognise with certainty our surroundings; we are unmistakably in the region of the salon pieces for piano. It is a specimen that has the basic virtues of Tchaïkovsky in that mood though by no means at his most inspired or charming. Characteristically the piece rises to a tremendous-looking climax, with *fff* tremolando chords alternating with helter-skelter downward rushes, before its quiet last statement of the opening subject and its *p-pp-ppp* codetta. The Miniature March is a trivial, undistinguished ' musical-box ' piece; one could imagine it to have been from the pen of Cui or Lyadov or Glazunov or, indeed, anyone of the cohorts of even less eminent Russian composers of the nineteenth century. Shall we bother to note how the opening of this March and a salient phrase in the Scherzo both recall the middle section of the well-known Romance in F minor for piano, Op. 5? But nothing at all in this suite has the allure or distinction of that piano piece The fifth movement is not a typical scherzo and not altogether typical Tchaïkovsky. In its middle section it achieves almost incredible longueurs. It is, indeed, a choice specimen of what Tchaïkovsky's relentless patterning could come to when no spark of inspiration was present. And the finale is no more a typical gavotte, nor any more inspired. The orchestra used varies from number to number. Trombones are absent throughout. The Miniature March is scored for piccolo, two flutes, two oboes, two clarinets, glockenspiel, triangle and violins. However, what most strikes one about the orchestration is that the question is not so much how far piano arrangements of the pieces would betray themselves by being unpianistic as how far, in fact, they do as they stand have the appearance (even more than much of Tchaïkovsky's other music) of piano pieces transcribed for orchestra. Not *badly* transcribed, of course; far from it. On the contrary, bristling with academic competence. Perhaps that obvious and rather stereotyped workmanlikeness is just the trouble. Anything intrinsically, essentially, exclusively, spontaneously orchestral seems far to seek.

The Second Suite comprises (1) *Play of Sounds*, (2) Valse, (3) *Burlesque Scherzo*, (4) *A Child's Dreams* and (5) *Grotesque Dance* (*in Dargomïzhsky's style*). This suite, which is sub-titled ' characteristic,' is of very mixed quality. The *Play of Sounds* is a very elaborately constructed piece, including as one element a fugue. It is quite pleasant music, employing a full orchestra (with English horn but no cornets). The waltz, on the other hand, is one of the worst Tchaïkovsky ever wrote, quite unattractive—even though trumpets and trombones have an all-too-rare *tacet*. The Burlesque Scherzo, which uses not only the full orchestra but four accordeons, *ad lib.*, is (perhaps contrary to one's initial fears) an original, energetic piece, well worth hearing occasionally, accordeons or no accordeons. With *A Child's Dreams* we swing back once more, at least as far as ' neutral '; this is a pleasant conventional berceuse, not very original and not very distinguished, conscientious and tasteful—but for a bizarre and extravagant section in the middle, which, merely in its aspect as a page or so of scoring, looks much more like Stravinsky than Tchaïkovsky. The part one may assign such a section in a child's dream is too obvious to need naming. Once more horns are the only brass instruments; harp is added for the first time. The *Grotesque Dance,* which goes back to the normal full orchestra, is a very typical example of the more obvious Russian style with which Westerners have become so very, very familiar, full for them of the atmosphere of knee-boots, beards and frog-dancing. One might find it an exhilarating piece of music if one were in an indulgent mood. One of the main themes (Ex. 69) deserves quotation for its unusual tonal implications. For some not at all obvious reason the composer twice in this suite writes for clarinets in C.

It was, according to Tchaïkovsky's diary, in ' trying to lay the foundations of a symphony ' that he eventually teased out the germ of the Third Suite. It is all very characteristic light, conscientious Tchaïkovsky: bordering on triviality, bordering on dullness, but just managing to keep clear of both. The two outer movements, a comparatively very light Elegy and the well-known Theme and Variations, are in G major; the two inner ones, a very nice *Valse mélancolique* and a Scherzo, in E minor. As in the other suites, the orchestral force varies from piece to piece. The Scherzo is exceptional in Tchaïkovsky, by using trombones but no tuba. The Theme and Variations that from the beginning to the present day have taken so comparatively large a share in Tchaïkovsky's popularity. Well, it is quite a pleasant little theme. After its statement, mostly *pp*, we have the following variations : (1) The same key, tempo and metre (andante con moto 2/4), theme in octaves, pizzicato, as bass with flowing and quick-moving counterpoints high above; (2) Ditto. Somewhat more harmonic and melodic disguise of the theme, and spiccato demisemiquavers ceaselessly buzzing on top; (3) Ditto. Undisguised theme on top, triplets introduced in middle parts; (4) pochissimo meno animato, B minor; (5) Allegro vivo, 3/4, G Major; (6) Allegro vivace, 6/8, G major; (7) L'istesso tempo, 2/4, G major (something of an imitation chorale, under airy-fairy upper parts); (8) Adagio, 3/4, A minor (E major close) (tune, cantabile e molto espressivo); (9) Allegro molto vivace, 2/4, A major (*à la danse Russe*, the merry-go-round type, with even a hint of hurdy-gurdy accompaniment)—modulating at end with F sharp major chord and a large-gesturing cadenza; (10) Allegro vivo e un poco rubato, 3/8, B minor—a rather longer section, mostly very light, ending with another, briefer cadenza; (11) Moderato mosso, 4/4, B major, tonic pedal sustained throughout until last few bars, which elaborate a modulation into G major already embarked upon; (12) (Finale) Polacca—Moderato maestoso e brillante, 3/4, G major—a long, fully-extended movement in itself. . . . A meaningless string of words, you say? No more meaningless, as a whole, than the string of bits and pieces that the composition itself is. If, on the other hand, the string of words is not quite meaningless, if it conveys anything (say to an experienced reader of programme-notes), it will convey—that résumé—a pretty good idea of what the thing is like. For those who enjoy such things this is a fair-to-average specimen, making up in verve and brightness what it lacks in profundity or subtlety. It is a good deal less than Tchaïkovsky at his best, whichever view one happens to take of what *is* Tchaïkovsky's best.

> A large number of Mozart's most admirable small works are, incomprehensibly, very little known not only to the public but even to the majority of musicians. The author of this suite, *Mozartiana*, wished to give a new impulse to the performance of those little masterpieces, whose succinct form contains some incomparable beauties (Moscow : 5/10/1887).

Thus Tchaïkovsky, two years after *Manfred* and one before the Fifth Symphony. The first two pieces are fairly close transcriptions of the Gigue in G (K. 574)—not very characteristic, or at any rate essential, Mozart, but rather like an exercise in chromaticism and in Bachian counterpoint—and the Minuet in D (K. 355); piano pieces both. For the Gigue Tchaïkovsky uses two flutes, two oboes, two clarinets, two bassoons, two horns, two trumpets, two kettle-drums, strings; for the Minuet double wood-wind, two horns, strings. The third number, for double wood-wind, four horns, one kettle-drum, harp, strings, is called *Preghiera (d'après une transscription de F. Liszt)* and is based, on the whole only remotely, on the motet *Ave verum corpus* (K. 618). There is very little Mozart left in it. Why take Liszt's rubbishy transcription, anyway? Just because, possessing a harmonium, Tchaïkovsky happened to possess that too? Look at it how you will, the thing is indefensible, not to say inexplicable. For the Theme and Variations, once again from a piano solo, Mozart's variations on ' Unser dummer Pöbel meint,' from Gluck's *Pilgrims of Mecca* (K. 455), the orchestral apparatus is the same as for the Gigue, plus cymbals and glockenspiel. Tchaïkovsky uses the cymbals, among other things, for a loud thump at the end of Variation 3 on a beat that Mozart left silent. That, however, is almost the only actual excrescence of which he is guilty. What *is* strange is that he, whose own orchestral writing is so predominantly three-part—a thing he may well have learnt from Mozart—is so little content to leave Mozart's two or three parts alone, without ' filling-in,' in this transcription. A profounder mystery is how a man who did recognise Mozart's absolute pre-eminence among composers, who went so far as to call him ' the Christ of music,' was capable of such an act, an act so utterly misguided and insensitive, as the writing of *Mozartiana*.

5

The Chamber Music

By

Colin Mason

O F TCHAÏKOVSKY'S WHOLE output chamber music forms a
very small proportion. Except a number of student-exercises,
mostly unpublished, it consists only of three string quartets, a Piano
Trio, and a String Sextet, in that chronological order, plus the three
pieces for violin and piano mentioned by Mr. Blom on p. 68, the
sole interest of which is that one was originally intended for the slow
movement of the Violin Concerto.

Tchaïkovsky was not at first attracted to chamber music as a
medium of expression, and this, when we think of his musical
personality, is not surprising. What is surprising is that his first
full-length work for string quartet, the one in D major, Op. 11, shows
such mastery of the quartet technique, mastery which he never
surpassed. In fact, this quartet is, as a whole, the most satisfactory
of all his chamber works in its consistency of style and its artistic
interest, despite its feeble but popular slow movement.

The quartet opens with an effective syncopated figure in 9/8 time,
which persists throughout the first subject. This is very strongly
rooted in D major, and is used for some bars over simultaneous tonic
and dominant pedals. At the beginning of the transition the composer relaxes the block-chord progression, in a contrapuntal interlude, with a B minor—F sharp minor flavour, but soon resumes
it, keeping one part always flowing in undulating ornamental
semiquavers, carrying the music through much dominant preparation to the second subject in A major. This is smooth music, the
first section of which is based largely on a plain arpeggio figure,
the second a step-wise movement more floridly accompanied. The
first half then recurs, also with semiquaver movement in another
part, and passes into a transition similar in style to the earlier one,
which leads us to the development with a newly syncopated rhythmic
flourish.

The development reverts to the opening figure, with the first violin making much of the sort of thing quoted in Ex. 70, and the accompanying parts persisting with the syncopation, with interludes of imitative counterpoint based on the first part of the second subject. After the second of these interludes, the music becomes more complex and more eloquent, and Tchaïkovsky ingeniously brings all his thematic material together; the syncopated quavers, the semiquavers, and both sections of subject two. However, he quickly heightens the dramatic effect, and reduces the complexity, by cutting out subject two and introducing the semiquaver rhythmic figure with brusque vigour into the syncopated accompaniment. A repetition of this procedure, after another reversion to the very contrapuntal passage, leads towards the recapitulation, by means of a gradual subduing of the dramatic element. The three accompanying parts resume the undisturbed syncopation, with the tonic-dominant pedal as before, and the semiquaver first-violin figure assumes a less bold and more sinuous quality. Except for this the recapitulation says nothing fresh, closely following the lines of the exposition and leading with another flourish into the faster coda. Here too, all the material is alluded to, though with less poetry than in the development.

The second movement, andante cantabile, is less interesting, though the quartet's popular fame rests on it. The first theme is a Great Russian folk-song, a beautiful tune with ludicrous words ('Vanya sat drinking; as he drank he thought of his sweetheart,' etc.). But Tchaïkovsky wastes it. First he presents it with a simple yet saccharine harmonisation. Then he introduces a second tune of his own over an ostinato figure; next presents the folk-tune again, at first with first and second violins and violas all playing *unisono*, and then returns to the second melody ' on the G string ' accompanied by dry pizzicato chords. This is a brief coda—and that is all.

The scherzo is better. It is in D minor, and makes the same use of alternate tonic and dominant chords over the double-pedal as the first movement. It has a certain charm and a delightful quartet texture. Formally it is divisible into A—B—A, of which B—A (but not the first A) is marked to be repeated. Ex. 71 shows three fragments, two from A and one from B, from which it will be seen that, after many classical models, A_2 is the germ of B. The trio is in B flat, and soon shows Tchaïkovsky's affection for pedalpoints by a long decorated tonic pedal in the cello part.

The sonata-rondo finale is of the same quality as the first movement, but more vigorous (without being, like too many finales, *only* vigorous). The style of its thematic material gives the impression that it might easily have lapsed into fugality, but fortunately Tchaïkovsky had the good sense to resist the temptation; as a writer of imitative counterpoint he is excellent, but as a fugue-writer his judgment, if not his technique, is less sound. Ex. 72 is a fragment which illustrates the vein of the whole movement, where we find real part-writing and attractive counterpoint.

The tonic-dominant pedal crops up again, in the second violin and 'cello, while viola and first violin repeat the opening theme canonically *ff*, a fine bit of vigorous and sonorous quartet-scoring. The second principal theme (Ex. 73) played by the viola, largamente, is a very typical Tchaïkovskian ' second-subject-of-finale ' melody (cf. the Second Symphony, Serenade for strings, etc.). Another point illustrating Tchaïkovsky's technical competence and technical imagination is the return of the first subject after the development : on the second violin, surrounded by pseudo-imitations, and *passing to the first violin* at bar 4 (Ex. 74).

This is perhaps the least ambitious quartet of the three and, possibly for that reason, the best. It lacks the idiomatic freshness of Borodin or Dvořák; but it is consistently good chamber music throughout, and consistently interesting nearly throughout. In the two later quartets, Tchaïkovsky is not so consistent, trying to say things which are not good Tchaïkovsky, not often good chamber music, and occasionally not worth saying at all. Both works, however, have interesting sections, particularly the last in E flat minor.

The F major, Op. 22, opens with a curious slow introduction full of intensely dissonant (for the period) appoggiatura harmonies and free cadenza-like passages for the first violin; this has little aesthetic value of its own and no relationship to the rest of the movement. Having cleared his throat, however, Tchaïkovsky gives us something more interesting. The first violin still takes the lead with a winding tune, underneath which, at the fourth bar, Tchaïkovsky introduces an ornamented pedal C, with the tune above much syncopated, returning soon to the figuration of the first bars. Then come two pages in which one senses extreme poverty of invention. Tchaïkovsky writes figures harking back to the syncopated section of the subject mentioned above, often repeating and inverting them, with mechanical syncopation and a mechanical accompaniment. There is no masterly transformation here; nothing but square, mechanically-produced tunes running about aimlessly. The activity grows, semiquavers and demisemiquavers drawing more attention to the nothing they are achieving so desperately, until with a first-violin flourish like those of the introduction, the composer opens the development with a return to the first half of the first subject. The development at last offers us some music of interest : for instance a striking canon at the seventh for 'cello and first violin (with terrific quasi-orchestral demisemiquaver rushes on the viola) near the end. The beginning of the recapitulation is again neat, the end of the development leading naturally into the *fifth* bar of the first subject.

The scherzo which follows is more attractive. It has not much to say, but its simplicity, its skipping 6/8—6/8—9/8 rhythm, and the contrast of the piquantly scored trio (which might almost have been written by Borodin), give it charm. There is nothing in it that calls for analysis, but one notes violent harmonic clashes which the naïve exuberance carries over unobjectionably, almost unobserved.

It is the slow movement which is the best of the work, though it contains neither learned music nor any sweetly luscious melody to earn it the popularity of the andante cantabile of the D major Quartet. Yet the movement is simply enchanting. The chief motive is a falling fourth, in the rhythm of the opening of the *Fidelio* overture, which is kept going almost throughout the first page, with an accompaniment which, though it gains importance, never approaches any intricacy harmonically or contrapuntally, though the part-writing is always in true quartet-style. That cannot be said of the middle section, pochissimo più mosso—or at any rate, of its *fff* climax where the composer makes four solo strings attempt what only a symphony orchestra could achieve. After this, with a transition of diminishing excitement, he leads us back to a more intricate presentation of the simple opening, now more delightful than before, and so concludes.

The finale unfortunately soon dispels the good impression this movement can create. It is brisk and little else, with a texture based mainly on this figure, on repeated notes : It contains no deft harmonic touches or rhythmically subtle figuration, but it does contain one typical Tchaïkovskian tune in D flat, of the same type as that which occupies precisely the same position in the finale of the B flat minor Piano Concerto (which dates from the same period). Although there is a contrapuntal episode, for which one longs, it is neither interesting nor apt. Like the fugato passage in the finale of Schumann's Piano Quintet (where after the absurd parallel lines of figuration for all the instruments, one feels the need for part-writing), it comes, not as a welcome relief, but as a forced and uninspired incongruity. It continues like this, through a three-part contrapuntal passage over a pedal C, running through a semi-quaver flurry of octaves into a section which is as maddeningly orchestral as the already mentioned passage in the andante. The first violin and viola playing the ' typical Tchaïkovskian tune ' (now in the tonic key), have to take the normal role of the full string orchestra in the average Tchaïkovskian *ff* tutti, while the second violin, reiterating the rhythmic figure quoted above, acts as an *ersatz*-brass section. This Second Quartet as a whole, though a favourite with the composer himself, is the least satisfying of the three. Although it touches higher spots that the First or the Third, the general level of interest is lower than theirs, and the style less fine and well balanced.

No. 3, in E flat minor, Op. 30, has one bad movement and one magnificent one, with the middle two of fair quality : a balance which places it on the same level as the D major, except that here the bad movement is perhaps the most important one, the finale. This quartet opens, like the Second, with a lengthy introduction, in B flat major, rather chromatic and diminished-seventh-ish, and perhaps not quite as passionate as Tchaïkovsky thought, but stylistically and technically appropriate; the middle section consists of a first-violin melody, cantabile e molto espressivo, accompanied by plain pizzicato chords. The main part of the movement, allegro moderato, begins very like the introduction, with first violin and 'cello moving in contrary motion. From the start, it is rhythmically interesting. Tchaïkovsky presents separately three or four rhythmic patterns : a dactyl, quaver triplets, a dotted figure. Then he shortens the intervals between his changes of rhythmic figuration and eventually combines them all. Finally he separates them again, reducing the moving part always to triplets, ready for the return to the violin melody of the introduction. Occasionally this rhythmic complexity is complex only on paper; there is, for instance, a passage in the second subject, with quavers, triplets and semiquavers all going together, which in performance is merely a confused ' washed-in ' background.

The first section of the movement scarcely does more than present these rhythmic motives, and all except the first are used in progression by step; in the triplets, both the accented and the auxiliary notes move conjunctly. This gives a curiously static effect to the whole section. The second theme is in B flat, and opens over a long tonic pedal, followed immediately after by one on A. Here the melodic movement is more free, and one could almost say that it is only here that the movement really begins, for the first section of the allegro is completely absorbed into this new section, and seems to be treated as a second introduction. Melodically it said almost nothing, and both its chief rhythmic characteristics are used in the second part. Ex. 75 shows the main figure, of which the opening major third is sometimes extended downwards to an augmented fourth. By syncopation and the constant use of the rhythmic pattern ♪♪♪ ♩ ♪ ♪♪♪ | ♩ Tchaikovsky gives an effect of 2/4 time to many passages of the second subject, particularly at the end, where sustained chords with an ornamented bass in the rhythm just quoted lead into the development.

The development, technically so-called, though fairly long, is hampered by the fact that, as so often in Dvořák, there has already been so much development in the exposition. And it is overshadowed in interest by the recapitulation which, after the first subject, introduces a completely new idea: a cantabile melody, again with a suggestion of 2/4, first for 'cello, then on first violin (both times in A major) and finally on the inner instruments in octaves accompanied by simultaneous 3/4 and 9/8 figures (B flat major). Only then does Tchaikovsky recapitulate his second subject in the tonic major, adding an extensive coda based on it and restoring the minor mode, plus an epilogue reverting to the cantabile melody of the slow introduction. Such structural novelties, which in no way arise from the logic of the music, inevitably suggest some sort of concealed programme: perhaps some allusion to the violinist Laub, to whose memory the Quartet is dedicated.

Of the second movement it is impossible to write substantially, because there is no substance to write about. It is in A—B—A form, based on two contrasted figures; but nothing very interesting happens to either. The movement is in fact nothing more than an airy, gracious intermezzo.

The third movement, andante funebre, is the most direct tribute to Laub. The first part consists mainly of 'sobbing' block chords, con sordino, and violin declamation, the second of one of Tchaikovsky's most characteristic melodies (Ex. 76). The A section then recurs, with a pattern of ornamental semiquavers in the first

violin, returning to an enlarged version of B, this time in B major
instead of G flat, the music going back finally, through a passage
based on the recitative parts of A, to A itself.

The finale is in a vigorous, almost boisterous mood, but has little
to say despite its volubility.

That was Tchaïkovsky's last essay in quartet form. Technically
it shows no advance on the D major, though artistically perhaps the
first movement of No. 3 stands out above the rest of his quartet
music. Its curious form is interesting; the slow prologue and epilogue remind one of the prologues and epilogues to Restoration
plays, which are related to the matter which they enclose but could
be dispensed with, without any loss of coherence or artistic com-
pleteness. It is a pity that Tchaïkovsky's inspiration petered out so
lamely in the finale, spoiling an otherwise good quartet.

Tchaïkovsky's next chamber work was another memorial composition, the Trio written in memory of Nicholas Rubinstein—which
accounts for the undue prominence of the piano part. The work
is in two real movements, the second being a big set of variations,
including a fugue, concluding with a long summing-up variation
which constitutes the equivalent of a third movement. The rather
heavy-handed first movement—its piano part almost suggesting the
solo in a concerto rather than chamber music, while violin and 'cello
do their best to act as a full orchestra—calls for little comment; the
only point of special interest is the opening of the recapitulation
where the first theme, originally moderato assai, returns at nearly
half speed, adagio con duolo e ben sostenuto, and continues for 22
bars before the return of the original tempo.

The second movement is a set of variations—in the Tchaïkovskian, not the classical sense—on a very simple theme, presented
first by the piano solo, and repeated by the first violin as Var. I,
and by the 'cello as Var. II, this time however rather neatly transformed into 3/4 instead of 4/4 time. Var. III is faster, a scherzoso
in which the strings play pizzicato chords, and the piano dashes
along, whispering to itself with delicate humour, as if at some
secret joke. (Each variation is said to be connected with some incident in Rubinstein's life.) In Var. IV the theme crops up again
almost ' in the raw,' but in C sharp minor and treated contrapuntally, with a two-part invention flavour, which is however disappointing because the counterpoint seems more forced than felt.
Var. V (C sharp major) consists of another period of piano solo
activity, a musical-box effect at the top of the keyboard. This is

followed by a valse in A major, quite a long one, where, as usual in this dance-form, Tchaïkovsky is completely at home; this is charming, polished, salon-music; the valse-melody is a counterpoint to the theme—as appears after some 50 bars. Var. VII (E major again) is practically a piano solo, with little but interjectory ' slashes ' on the strings; again the effect is essentially orchestral—the heavy piano chords ineffectually suggesting brass or wood-wind and brass. Var. VIII is a three-part fugue, the piano running about in octaves all through; it is an ineffective fugue[1] and the composer himself suggested it as an *ad lib*. cut.

In Var. IX (C sharp minor) Tchaïkovsky begins to look as if he might make something of his theme, but everything is in the first page; the muted melodic line of the violin, with its long-held notes, soon palls, and the rippling piano figure becomes tiresome, while no daring harmonic touch gives life to the monotonous figuration. Once again, this is not true concerted music; violin and 'cello alternate with the melody or even double each other, while the piano accompanies. Var. X conversely is a mazurka in A flat virtually for piano solo; like most of Tchaïkovsky's variations, here and elsewhere, it is not a variation at all in the classical sense but a genre-piece based on a melodic transformation of the theme or its opening motive (Ex. 77). In Var. XI the theme reappears in its original form and key, with a new accompaniment.

The third movement, Variazione finale e coda, is in full sonata-form,.with the theme of the variations as second subject. (The finale being in A major, the ' theme ' naturally appears first in its own original key of E major.) Recognising that he had put more strain on his material than it, or the average listener, will bear, Tchaïkovsky allowed a cut from p. 86 to p. 102 (of the Eulenburg miniature score). In other words one can begin with the recapitulation. These pages contain a few interesting moments and many dull ones, of which the composer repeats all except the good ones, before coming to his coda, which reverts to the opening of the first movement and finally dies away, lugubre, in the manner of a funeral march.

The last chamber work, the *Souvenir de Florence* for string sextet, is more interesting than the Trio, better music intrinsically and better written. There is a certain similarity to, if not imitation of, Brahms in the frequent use of the second violin and violas in

---

[1] Less ineffective if Taneev's suggestions, cf. *Sovetskaya Muzika* (1936, No. 6) are acted on.—ED.

moving, but purely harmonic passages, identically figured, creating a unifying inner web. Compare, for instance, the texture of the opening of the Sextet with that of Brahms's G major Quintet. Another similarity to the quality of some of Brahms's string music is that, despite the essentially right string texture, the music is easily and satisfactorily translatable on the piano.

The first subject consists of several motives, some of which seem to be incidental but crop up later in the development. Of these, the more particularly striking are the first falling theme against a rising bass (A_1 in Ex. 78, which shows only the melodic-harmonic skeleton, not the figuration), and C, a rising theme against a falling bass. B is an incidental pattern which acquires importance later. After C, A returns, leading to D, a tranquillo passage with a faint taste of C in it, and to a transition based on A_2 and C, bringing us only now to the second subject, which is also divided into several sections, the first a very long one, consisting of a sustained, still Italianate melody containing a curving figure in 2/4 time against the 3/4 accompaniment. The second motive is based on rising fourths and falling fifths with a sequential counterpoint beneath it. This lovely section leads us imperceptibly to the development. This section of the movement is theoretically and contrapuntally very ingenious; much more important, it has artistic value as well as technical interest. Even if it had not, one could not help admiring Tchaïkovsky's use together of A_1 and A_2, the rising and falling basses, the curving 2/4 figure, the second-subject idea with its little counterpoint, and D; all fit in with the mosaic-like neatness of the Flemish contrapuntists. But they make here a very lovely section, which is always in keeping with the clear lines of the exposition. One of the most interesting points of the movement is the opening of the recapitulation: a sudden pianissimo with a long crescendo reaching its climax with Ex. 78 A *fff* and sonorously scored.

The adagio second movement opens with an introduction not unlike the opening of the first movement. Then comes a long-drawn singing melody, first played by the leader with pizzicato triplet accompaniment. But the most remarkable part of the movement is the moderato middle section, where Tchaïkovsky, always the orchestrator at heart, rejects as thoroughly as possible the means of melody, harmony, figuration and even rhythm, and evolves 30 bars of chamber music solely from shades of monochrome and from dynamics. All the strings play together practically throughout: block chords reiterated in semiquaver triplets *a punta d'arco*. There are incessant alternations of *mf* and *pp*, quick crescendos from *ppp* to *ff* and equally quick diminuendos. As an essay in sheer sound-effect, without the least musical content whatever, the thing is astounding. It is probably unique in the whole range of chamber music.

The third movement is a trifle, but a very pleasing one. It has no obvious qualities one can pin down and no solid substance to describe; just a vague, carefree quickness and gaiety which are irresistible, but no more susceptible of description than a breath of air. The finale, too, is a movement with negligible thematic substance. It is largely based on a pentatonic theme, which might well be a folk-dance, perhaps a pipe-tune from the Caucasus or even further east. Its treatment is brilliant but semi-orchestral.

That is the total chamber music. And it is not a very distinguished total. Despite the technical and stylistic excellence of the D major Quartet, there is little that can be singled out as *essentially* chamber music. One might sum up that Tchaïkovsky had a thorough, academic knowledge of the medium, but no special appreciation of its finer subtleties.

6

The Piano Music

By

A. E. F. Dickinson

THE PIANO IS a peculiar instrument. Its habitual relation to the rest of the instrumental family may be described as motherly. A harp still, it excels as the background of that fascinating social figure, vocal melody, and it can also replace that figure by a very fair imitation of the vocal graces. Verbally inarticulate, it can yet suggest the dramatic contrasts and absorbing moods of stage music, and while it naturally presides over any actual dancing that calls for precision, it can convey pressing invitations to the valse without a ballroom in view. But the piano has won most personal distinction through housework; that is, in preludes and fantasias and studies, where the composer has explored and spring-cleaned the mass of chordal sequence and figural movement which constant impromptu provision for his workshop has accumulated. In this way Chopin unlocked a new kind of personality in music: in the first Prelude and B flat minor Scherzo, for example. Apart from stray anticipations in Bach and Scarlatti, such adumbrated melody or flying chords or vivid accompaniment had not been felt before. In the Scherzo, moreover, two main moods are expanded so resourcefully that the displacement of the second by the first is, so to speak, a personal matter. Beethoven had been blunter in instrumental approach, but his sonatas and bagatelles reveal many intimacies and resolve some titanic conflicts, so echoing French rather than Italian opera. Finally, Liszt's Sonata maintained a memorable, quasi-personal *idée fixe* through the divers stresses of successive movements, thus brilliantly executing in the large and in pure music what Schumann had often done in miniature and over an undercurrent of literary or autobiographical suggestion.

All these gained their freedom of expression through contact with the piano as a special and—for their purposes—novel invention. Here they learnt to vie with the varied colour and rich life of the opera on which most of the public attention was centred, with their own multiple virtuosity as the prime resource. On the piano, too, they developed their style. This is specially true of Beethoven's first period of composition, but in a more elusive manner it explains Schumann's early preoccupation with the piano.

No such progress or predominant interest illuminated the writings of Tchaïkovsky for piano solo. Most of them consist of stray collections of *morceaux*—valses and scherzos and trifles with pretty titles —and their general quality is of flimsy material sewn together in a trite pattern, often with incredibly literal repetition. Even the mature Sonata in G, Op. 37 (1878), shows no obvious advance on the student Sonata in C sharp minor (1865). It must be admitted that in Tchaïkovsky's hands the piano reverted, to a considerable degree, to the more commonplace matronly occupations, simulating songs of nocturnal solitude or (in the wider Elizabethan sense) humorous dances. The composer's attention was plainly fastened on opera, ballet, symphony, symphonic poem and other orchestral work. Even his Piano Concerto in B flat minor owes its force to certain haunting themes and to an adroit treatment of the orchestra in conjunction with the soloist rather than to the cheerful Lisztian swagger (but not Lisztian accomplishment) of the piano rhetoric. After all, when the piano *enters* with nothing more than loud reiterations of the tonic chord (and a false tonic at that), one experiences emptiness rather than *élan*; and there is a good deal more pianistic vanity to live down. A verdict on the Piano Concerto as a whole is not my concern here, but if its original contribution to pianistic development is in question, the burden of proof lies undoubtedly with the Concerto's admirers.

We must now attempt to gather the fragments and form a coherent impression. Tchaïkovsky's Op. 1, No. 1, was a *Scherzo à la Russe* for piano. It is based on an Ukrainian folk-song which the composer had used in the discarded string quartet Allegro in B flat, but this, if it means anything, merely points to the misty nationalism that was abroad at the time. The style is no more national than *Nutcracker*, and the *muzhïk*, who at the outset sounds reasonably happy in his arty surroundings, has to go pompous and massive in the end, with unfortunate consequences. The companion Impromptu concentrates on this heavy furioso style, with a surfeit of octaves in each hand. In the same year—1865—Tchaïkovsky wrote his first sonata, which will be considered at the end of this essay. Two years later—no less—the three pieces of Op. 2 formed a souvenir of a pleasant holiday in the country. The third of these is the well-known *Chant sans paroles* in F. Here the main theme is slight but unpretentious and still fragrant, and its treatment is discreet : an adroit reminiscence at the end avoids the bathos of a formal re-statement. A blemish is the repeat of the pointed eleven-bar phrase in the second episode : such precise stress cannot stand literal recurrence. The piece is not particularly pianistic, but its brittle glitter suits it, and not the cloying vibrato and effeminate pizzicato texture of popular transcriptions. Its neat shape shows up the preceding Scherzo, whose main features lose their appeal in too exact repetition. *The Castle Ruins*, the first piece of the set, presents insistent phrases of unusual six-bar length with a compensating final compactness, but if we compare Mussorgsky's parallel picture, *Il vecchio Castello*, or even the starkly impressionistic *Catacombæ* (in *Pictures from an Exhibition*), we become aware at once of a much more penetrating sense of the characteristic. A year later came the Romance in F minor, dedicated to Désirée Artôt, an opera-singer to whom the composer was seriously attached for a time. If it is a declaration, it is a poor one. The first theme is weak Chopin diluted, whose restatement later needs something more than an undercurrent of passing imitation to justify it. The middle energico episode begins with one of those jejune phrases it is difficult to understand any serious composer bothering to write down, and its return ' to conclude ' is positively irritating.

In the next seven years Tchaïkovsky produced the score of pieces that make Opp. 7, 8, 9, 10, 19 and 21. Op. 7, a Valse Scherzo on the usual ABA plan, evades positive statement with some facility, and thus the repeat of A and further hint of B are not transparent enough to sound otiose. Op. 8, called *Caprice*, also capers successfully from theme to theme in an ' arch ' pattern (ABCBA), though episode C soon palls with the overstatement of its opening phrase. The *whole Salon Polka*, Op. 9. No. 2, suffers from precise overstatement, quite unsuited to its frail and wayward material, and unredeemed by a final hackneyed bravura of double octaves and German sixths. The Mazurka in the same set is cast in the same afflicting mould except for a receding finish. The Nocturne in F, Op. 10, No. 1, recalls the Romance in tone and structure : here the return of the middle section makes a reasonable epilogue. The Humoresque following (Op. 10, No. 2) is the composer at his most indiscreetly repetitious, both in the ' humorous ' opening and in the inevitable and somewhat precious interlude. These pieces make little pretence at concealing any joins. The ABA which suits an actual dance or dance-piece—dance, interlude, dance—is too often used as a mass-production mould, and each main section is frequently as palpably ternary in itself.

The *Evening Reverie*, No. 1,of Op. 19, begins and ends with a pretty exhibition of *Sehnsucht*, interspersed with a major section whose ungainliness suggests a rude awakening ('But I'm married to James!') rather than the usual optative mood presumably intended. The *Humorous Scherzo*, Op. 19, No. 2, is vivacious, and the final jollying up of the delicate middle theme over a relevant pedal figure makes an agreeable finish. The Nocturne in C sharp minor, No. 4, begins and resumes sensitively, with a commonplace interlude. In the Capriccioso, No. 5, light as it is, invention is rather more sustained.[1] The Theme and Variations, the last number of the set, are altogether on a different level, however. The square-cut theme makes an immediate appeal, and while its shapely melodic line (see Ex 79) readily persists in nearly every one of the dozen variations, the relative lengths of the four successive phrases are nicely varied from time to time, and there is considerable rhythmic and harmonic renovation. The result is a series of reasonably engaging contrasts, pianistically interesting apart from a pretentious coda, and creatively an advance on the technically resourceful set of variations in A minor (Op. posth.) which Tchaïkovsky had written in 1863-4. The work is thus a preparation for the more characteristic variations of the Piano Trio, Op. 51. The conventional kaleidoscopic pattern gave the composer the jog he needed to make him cultivate phrase-distinction for its own sake. As the thematic treatment is essentially melodic, the quotations in Ex 79 give a fair idea of the changing character.

The *Six Pieces* of Op. 21 are all based on the same theme, all but the final Scherzo being in the minor. The stately but unpianistic Prelude, a song without words, develops from its initial text, and so inevitably does the Fugue, No. 2, a competent piece of academic writing in the vocal style, with tightened texture to add strength to the subject and its rising seventh. The other four pieces are furnished with a middle section to keep the ball rolling. The Funeral March has character, but the incessant repetition of the initial bar-rhythm is not assisted by its unpianistic quality, and the flashy rhetoric of the episode is decidedly laboured. The Scherzo, No. 6, is the most interesting number, with a piquant 6/8 ♩♪♪ ♫♫ rhythm to begin

[1] It is based on the sketch for the opening of a Symphony in B flat (cf. the composer's diary, June 11/23, 1873)—ED.

with, but again the interlude is disappointing and the complete da capo after it unfortunate. In view of the formal nature of the common melodic factor, which is little more than a rising fourth with a preliminary turn, the transformations of theme in this set are not striking, nor are the rhythmic changes hard to devise. Some are more, some less, effective amplifications of the common formula, and little more can be said.

Tchaïkovsky's next essays at the piano were made during 1875–76 : the well-known set of *Seasons* published month by month throughout 1876 in the journal *Nuvellist*. They were pot-boilers and it cannot be said that the numbers are particulary seasonable or characteristic. The texture is heavy, the thought commonplace and the design conventional. In eleven cases there is a resort to a palpable ABA pattern, and in most instances there is much unnecessary repetition. The only piece of any interest is *March*, a rhapsodic tone-picture of the lark's song. The popular *November* (*In the Troyka*) ends with a pretty fall of snow over its yearning tune, but has not much else to say for it. *December*, a Christmas piece, is a valse in Tchaïkovsky's slickest, sickliest style.

The twenty-four pieces of the *Children's Album*, Op. 39, are nearly all commendably brief. None is as sensitive as the best of Schumann's companion album, and a good percentage are definitely insipid, but the witty examples are not given space to grow tedious. The *March of the Wooden Soldiers, New Doll, Polka, Baba-Yaga* and *Song of the Lark* are pleasant trifles, as might be expected, and *In Church* and *Doll's Funeral* are the opposite. The *Twelve Pieces of moderate difficulty* of Op. 40 include some tried favourites, such as the monotonous but compact *Chanson triste* and the Valse in A flat, of which the main section harps unpleasingly on chromatic chords, and the interlude is deadly. The Funeral March maintains solemnity in its first and not too congruent third section, but the intervening major section is nugatory, though not so offensive as the main melody of the *Interrupted Rêverie* (No. 12), after which it is refreshing to turn back to the busy dexterity of the opening colourful (i.e., chromatic) Etude, even if the final plain octaves are strip-tease by any Chopin standard. The ' interruption ' appears in shorter form as *The Organ-grinder Sings* in the *Children's Album*.[1]

---

[1] The ' offensive ' melody is a Venetian popular song, and its interruption of the composer's ' rêverie ' in Op. 40, No. 12, is a sort of diary entry. The whole story is told in a letter from Milan to Nadezhda von Meck (December 16/28, 1877). After telling her how in Florence he had heard a boy of ten or eleven singing in the street (the boy from whom he afterwards acquired the melody used for the song ' Pimpinella,'

The *Six Pieces* of Op. 51 are mostly light dance movements. No. 1, another Valse in A flat, contains passable material spoilt by repetition. The *Dumka*, Op. 59, was written in 1885. It is on the whole a pleasantly written fantasia on folk-themes, varied enough to make the final reappearance of the opening tune an event.

The *Eighteen Pieces* of Op. 72 were finished in 1893. Each has a separate title, but scarcely any breaks new ground, and the early tendency towards mechanical and literal re-statement persists, a tendency which no programme interest can remedy. This is most obvious in the dance-pieces—the *Characteristic Dance*, Mazurka, *Valse à cinq temps* and *Un poco di Chopin*, another Mazurka, with reminiscences of Chopin's Valse in the same key, C sharp minor; but the ternary shadow also dogs the opening Impromptu and other miscellaneous sketches. In these Tchaïkovsky almost defies himself to make the habitual and expected fascinating. The *Characteristic Dance* cannot maintain its initial vigour or the Valse its piquant metre in a complete recurrence, and the weaker pieces show a tedious overstatement. Amongst the latter may be placed *Un poco di Schumann*. A 'Schumann' variation, such as the composer had introduced into the variations of Op. 19, is a reasonable proposition (Schumann had himself taken off his hat to Chopin in this way in *Carnival*), but a whole piece must either carry a mannerism too far or use it as a base for indicating fresh angles in a new orbit, and this Tchaïkovsky fails to do. The *Concert Polonaise*, No. 7, is more successful: it acquires virtuosity just when its grand polonaise stride threatens to stiffen with over-use at the return stage. The long *Scherzo-Fantasia* also develops its plastic phrases and sinuous harmony sufficiently at the outset and conclusion to warrant a full recapitulation; the interlude, like many other episodes in Tchaïkovsky, relies overmuch on ringing facile changes over a uniform bass pedal. The *Cradle Song* exhibits the same facility with more appropriate material but none the less *ad nauseam*. No. 18, *Invitation to the Trepak*, is a fairly resourceful expansion of a salient phrase. Altogether the most satisfactory sketch is the *Rustic Echo*, somewhat akin to Debussy's *Minstrels* in its alternation of a folkish tune with

Op. 38, No. 6, and for part of the valse in the Fifth Symphony), he goes on: ' A certain street-singer with a little daughter used to appear sometimes in the evening before our hotel in Venice, and one of their songs pleases me very much.' (Here he quotes the song almost exactly as it appears in No. 23 of the *Children's Album*, only in 3/8 time and with an eight-bar prelude marked ' guitar.') ' It's true this street-artist has a very pretty voice and the *rhythmic sense* innate in all Italians. This last quality of the Italians interests me very much, as it is something quite opposite to our folk-songs and our way of singing them.'—ED.

a musical-box effect, the tune being varied each time and the musical box the last time.

It is a relief to turn from these trifles, each dedicated to a different person and produced, one suspects, in response to some quite external prompting, to the two piano works which apart from the variation sets are the only ones to show any constructive ambition. The Sonata in C sharp minor, published posthumously as Op. 80— it is not even listed in *Grove's Dictionary*—was written in 1865, the year in which Tchaïkovsky left the Petersburg Conservatoire as a student. It has a certain youthful brusqueness which ultimately gives an impression of sectional composition—at least to those who look for it, knowing the cut-and-dried sequel—but there are many good features, amongst others a frequent spontaneity. There are four movements. The first is the strongest, with Ex. 80 as the chief theme and Ex. 81 as the basis of an orthodox, Brahms-like second subject. This second thematic group is drawn out too long for its material, but the subsequent development is reasonably interesting and re-statement is freshened by new detail. The sequent andante is thin : it consists of four or five variations, rather ordinary in both harmonic and pianistic texture. The scherzo makes a good thing of its opening restlessness, but the trio, short as it is, cannot make much of its material. An adagio epilogue, of interest in its hint both of the strained mood of the composer's final style (a strain significantly absent from the off-hand moods of Op. 72) and also of the abrupt and sinuous chromaticism of Franck, prepares portentously for a dashing finale. This is an unequal movement. The first theme is forceful and pianistic, and so is the development, which incidentally contains an interlude (Ex. 82) remarkably like Franck in harmonic framework. The second subject, however, presents Ex. 83 on a confident tonic pedal and resists no impulse to mark the ascent of the stately curve at *x* or to explore other avenues leading in the same direction. If we wish to learn the dependence of form on rhythm and even more on mere measure, we can compare with Tchaïkovsky's slapdash melodic craftsmanship Humperdinck's dramatic reservation of the expansion of an almost identical phrase for the *final* appearance of the tune that contains it, after that tune has faced disintegrating elements of the most menacing kind (overture to *Hänsel und Gretel*). Tchaïkovsky's re-statement can but cross all the t's he has already crossed (in the tonic major), and he crosses a couple more in a trite chromatic sequence; but the final development of the initial phrase, compressed to half its normal space and brought into conjunction with the syncopated figure of the first subject, is not only vigorous but a distinct compensation for the previous emphasis of a foregone conclusion. And so to a thumping finish. Surely with this in his desk young Tchaïkovsky would in time show a more comprehensive and sustained musical thought, dynamic, lyrical and technically effective?

According to the present survey this development did not materialise. There remains for consideration the Sonata in G, Op. 37, written in 1878 in the comparative tranquillity that followed the year of mental storm and stress. There is no more hint of neurosis in this sonata than there is in Beethoven's Second Symphony. There is a somewhat parallel conscious exultation in the world of sound-relationship (Ex. 84). Moreover, this not particularly original thought forms with its companion phrase of insistent descending thirds not only first subject but quasi-orchestral refrain, as in a concerto. It returns in full just before the second subject, heralds the development pomposo, dodges formal re-statement at first but returns midway as before (with fresh appendages for purposes of the usual key-disturbance) and finally takes charge of the coda. This assumption of privilege leaves the second subject somewhat in the shade, and in any case the latter is of small significance except its unusual keys (E minor and G major, G minor and B flat major) and the usefulness of its two phrases in development and coda (bass). The movement ends in a climax, but it is not a climax of close thought. The slow movement develops a short and sensitive main theme in E minor in contrast with two episodes, the second of poorish quality, on the plan $aba^1/c/ab^1a$. In this scheme a^1 is marked by a move towards a sensational chord (E flat), followed by a pronounced silence, sufficient to interrupt the rhythm. In re-statement the incident is keyed up by an insistent rhythmic figure. This is almost grotesque. Here is an elaborate movement damned by a lack of what we may call personal musicianship; redeemed, perhaps, by the final transformation of c into the original 9/8 and E minor. The scherzo is one of those elusive trifles which we have met elsewhere under the same title and which are doubly unconvincing in a sonata. The finale relies, like the first movement, on a chordal sequence in a pronounced rhythm—here, plain syncopation—for the prime refrain in its sonata-rondo pattern, but it is confined within normal bounds, and there are distinct first and second episodes. The latter greets us with hands outspread as only Tchaïkovsky can (Ex. 85), and bestows a lingering look in the coda, in the manner of an old

school friend who knows our necessities before we ask. It thus anticipates the obsessional style of the last two symphonies. The fact is
that sonata-rondo is designed to balance pivotal themes with extem-
porary episodes and if the latter start posing as *idées fixes*, the release
of rondo is replaced by a counter-stress for which there is not, as in
opera or symphonic poem, a dramatic ground. Common sense cries
with Orsino, ' Enough! no more : 'tis not so sweet now as it was
before.' The Sonata must be judged, then, as a disappointment. No
movement is quite satisfactory as a whole, though the first and last
may claim to carry the listener over awkward transitions by the
appeal of their salient rhythms and dominant moods. Disbeliefs
arise equally over corroborative details.

So much time is already given by public and private pianists to
established figures of musical history, especially of the nineteenth
century, that contemporary comment is almost bound to point to
neglected contemporary work, first and foremost. Revival needs
justification, rather than any attention to new paths. In the case of
Tchaïkovsky we must be satisfied that he meets a general need or
reminds the twentieth century of what it lacks. It must be admitted
that the evidence of our survey is barely in his favour. There is no
call for old trifles unless there is about them at least some exquisite
craftsmanship or unusual inwardness, and no call for old sonatas
unless they are organic or at least comprehensive wholes or embody
structural types that were new in their time and retain something
of their former freshness. One cannot avoid the conclusion that
Tchaïkovsky was not really interested in the piano or its artistic
future. The study of his piano music has its critical interest in the
exposure of the difficulties of maintaining a characteristic style
throughout a purely instrumental work, but the products of analysis,
by which our appreciation may be enriched, are negative rather than
positive, a document in weeds rather than flowers to hand on to
future gardeners.

———————

Editorial Note : Mr. Dickinson has not mentioned the collection
of *Fifty Russian Folk Songs* arranged for piano duet. It is true they
originated as pot-boilers—the first twenty-five (1868) being taken
entirely from Villebois' collection, and all but one of the second
twenty-five (1869) from Balakirev's, often preserving traces of Balakirev's harmonisations as well—and are not all irreproachable as
essays in folk-song arrangement. But many are charming miniatures,

easy and delightful to play, and (the most interesting point) we meet most of them in Tchaïkovsky's other works. No. 1 had already been used in the *Storm* overture and C minor overture; No. 2 reappears as No. 11 of the *Children's Album*; Nos. 10, 17, 29, 32 and 34 were used in the *Oprichnik* dances; No. 6 in the second movement of the Second Symphony; Nos. 14, 26 and 36 in *Snow Maiden*; Nos. 23, 24 and 25 in both the *The Voevoda* and *The Oprichnik*; Nos. 28 and 42 in the finale of the Serenade for strings; No. 47—the only one of the fifty collected by Tchaïkovsky himself—in the andante cantabile of the First String Quartet; and No. 48 in *1812*. No. 49 is the most famous of all the Volga hauling-songs; it is odd that Tchaïkovsky's arrangement of it—one of the earliest—is almost completely unknown.

7

Operas and Incidental Music

By

Gerald Abraham

IT WOULD CERTAINLY be inaccurate to speak of Tchaïkovsky as an operatic composer who wrote symphonies and other instrumental music in his spare time. Yet that view of his work as a whole would be no more badly out of focus than the popular one: that he was an instrumental composer who wrote an opera or two. Tchaïkovsky wrote six symphonies—seven if you count *Manfred*—but ten operas, and if the non-symphonic instrumental works are thrown into one of the scales we can still put the incidental music for Ostrovsky's *Snow Maiden* and for *Hamlet* (to say nothing of the three ballets) into the other. Even some of the instrumental works, e.g. *Francesca da Rimini*, originated in opera-projects. 'To refrain from writing operas is, in its way, heroism,' wrote Tchaïkovsky in 1885. 'I don't possess this heroism, and the stage with all its tawdry brilliance none the less attracts me.' From July 1854, when, barely fourteen, he wrote to the now almost forgotten poet, V. I. Olkhovsky, about a libretto for a one-act comic-lyric opera, *Hyperbole*—a work which he was certainly quite incapable of composing at that age[1]— to his death nearly forty years later, when he was considering the operatic possibilities of one of George Eliot's *Scenes of Clerical Life* (*The Sad Fortunes of the Rev. Amos Barton*), the spell of the stage was never broken, the longing to succeed on it never stilled. In addition to the ten libretti which he actually set, he began or at least considered no fewer than twenty others. And although of the ten operas he completed some failed to satisfy even himself and only two have won much success in the world, they embody an enormous mass of music far too beautiful and too interesting to be passed heedlessly by. Moreover, Tchaïkovsky's search for subjects, his views on their nature and treatment, his work on libretti, throw penetrating light on his creative personality.

[1] There is extant a letter in which the would-be composer tells the poet that his libretto ' completely corresponds to his wishes: there is only one thing—there are too many arias and recitatives, but very few doets [*sic*], trios, etc.

124

The early fascination of the stage is easily accounted for. In the years of Tchaïkovsky's impressionable boyhood opera—and Italian opera at that—was the only kind of music that flourished in St. Petersburg. The sole chance of hearing symphonic music was at the Sunday afternoon University concerts, where a mainly amateur band sight-read its way through classical scores. Even the Russian Opera was in a poor state, and the boy went there only to hear his favourite *Life for the Tsar*, itself more Italian than some of our history-book accounts would lead us to believe. But it was the Italian Opera that fascinated him; it was only there, his brother Modest tells us, that he could hear ' a good orchestra, good choral singing and first-rate soloists '; it was there that he deepened his early love for *Don Giovanni* and *Der Freischütz* and made the exciting acquaintance of Meyerbeer, Rossini, Donizetti, Bellini and Verdi. And these Italian sympathies were considerably strengthened by the influence of the Neapolitan singing-master Piccioli, who acknowledged no music but that of the last four of those masters and held Beethoven and Glinka in equal contempt. Modest does his best to minimise Piccioli's influence but has to admit it as one of the reasons why ' Peter Ilyich at that time preferred operatic music to symphonic and not only took little interest in the latter but even regarded it somewhat disdainfully.' In considering Tchaïkovsky's career as an opera-composer all this must be kept well in mind. He began it— and ended it—as a follower of the traditions of Verdi and Meyerbeer and Glinka. Though more than a quarter of a century younger than Wagner, he was—apart from his general dislike of Wagner's music—not interested in ' music drama ' or operatic reform. Though a contemporary and companion of Dargomïzhsky and Mussorgsky, he had no use for operatic realism : ' If the quest for realism in opera is carried to its ultimate conclusion, then you will inevitably arrive at a complete negation of opera,' he said, apropos of Dargomïzhsky's *Stone Guest*. He was content to take, and leave, the conventions of Victorian opera as he found them.

He once stated his very simple aesthetics of opera to Nadezhda von Meck (letter of November 27, 1879) :

> In composing an opera, the author must constantly think of the stage, i.e., not forget that the theatre needs not only melodies and harmonies but action to hold the attention of the theatre-goer who has come to hear *and see*—finally, that the style of theatre music must correspond to the style of scene-painting : simple, clear and colourful. Just as a picture by Meissonier would lose all its charm if it were put on the

stage, so would rich music, full of harmonic subtleties, lose a great deal in the theatre, for there the listener needs sharply drawn melodies against a transparent harmonic background. In my *Voevoda*, however, I was mainly concerned with filigree-work and quite forgot the stage.

And he went on to state yet another reason for his persistent pursuit of operatic success :

The stage often paralyses the composer's musical inspiration, so that symphonic and chamber music stand far higher than operatic music. A symphony or sonata imposes on me no limitations; on the other hand opera possesses the advantage that it gives the possibility to speak in the musical language of the masses. An opera may be given forty times in one season, a symphony perhaps once in ten years.

At the same time, ' despite all the seductions of opera, I write a symphony, sonata or quartet with infinitely greater pleasure.' Again, writing on the same theme to the same correspondent six years later (letter of September 27, 1885), he says :

I am *pleased* by your supercilious attitude to opera. You are right in disapproving this really *false type of art*. But there is something irrepressible that attracts all composers to opera : it is that it alone gives you the means to communicate with the *masses* of the public. My *Manfred* will be played once or twice, then laid aside for Heaven knows how long, and no one but the handful of connoisseurs who go to symphony concerts will know it. Opera, and opera alone, makes you friends with people, makes your music familiar to the real public, makes you the property not merely of separate little circles but—with luck—of the whole nation. I don't think there is anything reprehensible in striving for this, i.e., it wasn't vanity that guided Schumann when he wrote *Genoveva* or Beethoven when he composed his *Fidelio*, but a natural impulse to broaden the circle of their hearers, to act on the hearts of the greatest possible number of people. It isn't just a matter of pursuing external effects, but of choosing subjects of artistic value, interesting and touching the quick.

' Touching the quick ' : that was Tchaïkovsky's vital test for an opera subject. It must be concerned with strong human emotions. Twice in his early days (1869) he toyed with fantastic subjects, *Undine* and a *Mandragora* of which we know very little, but he never returned to them. In the summer of 1891 he was offered a fantastic and exotic libretto, *Vatanabe*, by Karl Waltz, the principal machinist and scene-painter of the Bolshoy Theatre, Moscow,[1] and a letter to Waltz expresses his views on a genre that has been cultivated with great success by other Russian masters :

[1] Author of a fascinating book of reminiscences, *Sixty-five Years in the Theatre* (Moscow and Leningrad, 1928).

I have read *Vatanabe* with the liveliest satisfaction. The subject is charming, in the highest degree poetic, and at the same time effective. I am ready to write music for it with the greatest pleasure, but on the following conditions. *Vatanabe* will be a *fairy ballet,* not an *opera ballet.*[1] I absolutely refuse to acknowledge that indefinite and unsympathetic form of art known as *opera ballet.* For one thing: either my characters will *sing* or they will *mime.* That they should do both is absolutely unthinkable. As an opera *Vatanabe* is not a suitable subject for me, since I tolerate a fantastic element in opera only in so far as it doesn't get in the way of the doings of real, simple people with their simple human sufferings and feelings. But make the *Sun Prince* sing I emphatically cannot. Only human beings can sing—or, if you like, angels and demons mixing with humans on the human plane. Moreover, *Vatanabe and Ga-tani and Nao-Shik* are for me essentially beings outside the real world, and I should find it decidedly difficult to depict them properly by other than *symphonic* means. However, I regard *Vatanabe* as an excellent *ballet* subject and I am prepared to write music for this unusually well-chosen idea to the best of my ability. . . .

Again, to A. F. Fedotov, who offered him a *Prisoner of Chillon* libretto in February 1892, he wrote:

I cannot write music with love and enthusiasm for any subject, however effective, if the characters do not compel my lively sympathy, if I do not love them, *pity* them, as living people love and *pity.* . . .

And one other interesting point:

Finally, it is no slight objection that in general I avoid foreign subjects, since I know and embrace only the Russian man, the Russian girl or woman. Medieval dukes and knights and ladies captivate my imagination but not my *heart,* and where the heart is not touched—there can't be any music.[2]

Hence his rejection of such subjects as S. A. Rachinsky's *Raimond Lully,* de Vigny's *Cinq-Mars* and Constantine Shilovsky's *Ephraim;* hence his failure with *Die Jungfrau von Orleans.*

Deep human emotion, then, was the first requisite, and *Romeo and Juliet* delighted him, ' for in it is love, love, love . . . .' Not that love was the only emotion he recognised as suitable: ' I need,' he wrote to Stassov rejecting the latter's suggestion of an opera based on *Cinq-Mars,* 'a subject in which a single dramatic motive pre-

---

[1] A hybrid genre, of which Rimsky-Korsakov's *Mlada,* which in 1891 had been finished but not yet produced, is the outstanding example.

[2] Compare his judgments on *Aïda* and *Parsifal* respectively: ' I must have people, not dolls. The feelings of an Egyptian princess, a Pharaoh and some crazy Nubian girl are outside my knowledge and comprehension ' (letter to S. I. Taneev, January 2, 1878). ' Lord, how boring and—despite the genius and mastery—how false—*nonsens* —all this miraculous stuff is!' (letter to his brother Modest, September 11, 1884).

dominates, for example, love (whether maternal or sexual makes no difference), jealousy, ambition, patriotism . . .' (letter of April 8, 1877). At the same time he recognised that, while operatic subjects and characters must be broad and simple in conception, the simplicity must not be extreme. Among his reasons for turning down the idea of an opera on Pushkin's short novel, *The Captain's Daughter*, was that ' the heroine, Mariya Ivanovna, is lacking in interest and character; she is a faultlessly good and honest girl and nothing else, and that isn't enough for music.' Again : ' I was tempted above all by the last-century setting and by the contrast between the gentry in European costumes on one side and Pugachev and his wild rabble on the other. But a single contrast isn't much for an opera subject : one must have living characters, touching situations.' On the other hand, he found the subject as a whole ' too broken up and demanding too many conversations, explanations and actions unsuited to musical treatment.'

Operatic action must be not only clear-cut but strong and swift. ' In the ordinary drama it is always possible to keep the interest alive by little scenes of social habits (*bitovïmi stsenkami*) or by brilliant dialogue—in opera (where this holds good only to a certain extent) speed and conciseness of action are indispensable, or the composer will never have the power to write—or the audience to listen to the end.' he wrote to Shpazhinsky, the librettist of his *Sorceress*. Musset's *Lorenzaccio, André del Sarto* and *Les Caprices de Marianne*, though the subjects had attracted him, were finally turned down on the grounds of ' absence of dramatic action ' and ' profusion of philosophising.' One must go straight into action. He asks Stassov, who was rather unwillingly preparing an *Othello* libretto for him (Stassov considered the subject ' decidedly unsuited ' to Tchaïkovsky's talents and character), to cut out the first two street scenes and start the action straight away in the council-chamber : ' Brabantio rushes in and announces Desdemona's disappearance.' Again : ' It seems to me that the mutual relations of the characters must be made clear to the spectator down to the smallest details in the very first act, in Venice.' Superfluous characters must be done away with and essential points in the action simplified and underlined : ' Cannot Bianca be dispensed with in Act IV and the handkerchief scene be arranged without her; for instance, couldn't Iago bring in the handkerchief? Is such a departure from Shakespeare possible? . . . I should be glad if Bianca didn't exist.' And the whole business of the handkerchief ' ought to be made much more noticeable and in stronger relief.' In the case of Shpazhinsky's *Sorceress* Tchaïkovsky had peculiar difficulties, for Shpazhinsky was not merely the librettist but the author of the original drama and tended to cling rather determinedly to unessential lines and scenes. The composer has to tell him, for instance, that ' after the Third Act, i.e., the scene of " Kuma " and the young Prince, where the drama has reached its culminating point and is ripe for the catastrophe, it is impossible to drag out two more whole vast acts, at any rate it's impossible in opera.' Considering that Tchaïkovsky was such a sound theorist on operatic technique, it is surprising—though a cynic might say it is not surprising—that he was not more successful in its practice.

It is possible that Tchaïkovsky's first essay in opera was inspired by Pushkin's *Boris Godunov*; at any rate we know from a letter of Laroche's, written in January 1866, that he had composed a ' scene from *Boris*.' (It was the scene between the Pretender and Marina by the fountain.) But his first completed operatic score was based on a drama by A. N. Ostrovsky (1823–86), the founder of Russian realistic drama. Ostrovsky's famous *Storm* was Tchaïkovsky's favourite Russian play; as Mr. Wood has already told, it inspired one of his earliest orchestral overtures and roused the desire to write an opera on it; when he went to Moscow in January 1866, as a young professor at the Conservatoire, he made Ostrovsky's acquaintance and actually persuaded the dramatist to prepare a libretto from his play *The Voevoda*, also known as *A Dream on the Volga*.[1] But a part or the whole of this libretto was mislaid; Ostrovsky seems to have lost interest or patience after partly re-writing it from memory, and ultimately the words of only Act I and part of Act II came from his experienced hand; the rest were the composer's. Moreover, in his anxiety to cut out everything inessential to the action Tchaïkovsky sacrificed just those ' little scenes of social habits ' which are the flesh and blood of nearly all Ostrovsky's plays, leaving only the bare bones of a commonplace melodrama :

Act I. Enter Praskovya Vlasyevnà, the bride of the old *voevoda* (governor of the province), with her sister Mariya, their nurse Nedwiga and their maids. When the latter depart, enter Bastryukov, who is in love with Mariya (love-duet). The *voevoda*, having seen Mariya, falls in love with her and demands her in place of her sister. Bastryukov tries in vain to save his beloved.

[1] Mussorgsky had already in 1865 set the lullaby in *The Voevoda*; years later Arensky based an opera on the play.

I

Act II. Scene 1 : Bastryukov's servants await his return from a hunt. He enters, followed by Dubrovin, who announces that the *voevoda* has carried off his wife, Olena. The two young men agree to break into his castle and rescue the girls.

Scene 2 : Mariya bewails her fate, in a song about the nightingale. Enter Olena, who tells her that Bastryukov will be waiting for her in the garden at night. The duet is interrupted by the appearance of Nedwiga and the maids, who try to comfort Mariya with song and dance.

Act III. Bastryukov and Dubrovin enter the *voevoda's* garden at night; Mariya and Olena appear. Quartet interrupted by the *voevoda*, who, mad with jealousy, tries to stab Mariya. Enter as *deus ex machina* the Tsar's emissary with the new *voevoda* sent to supersede the old scoundrel whose crimes have become known to the Government.

The composer then proceeded to cover these bones with music which he admitted in later years to be quite unsuited to the theatre : symphonic, full of ' filigree-work,' and ' too massively orchestrated.' The composition occupied him during the greater part of 1867, and the orchestration was completed in Paris the following summer, though one of the most successful numbers, the ' Maid's Dance ', had been written—perhaps as an independent orchestral piece, perhaps for the projected *Storm* opera—as early as the spring of 1865, long before the present opera had been thought of; and part of the music of Act I (the *voevoda's* meeting with Mariya Vlasyevna, his love arioso and his dialogue with her) is based on the second subject and a transition passage from the Concert Overture in C minor also composed in 1865. *The Voevoda* was produced at the Bolshoy Theatre, Moscow, on January 30/February 11, 1869, but disappeared from the repertoire after five performances.

It is, unfortunately, impossible to discuss the music of *The Voevoda* at length, for Tchaïkovsky, recognising its deficiencies, afterwards used some of the best passages in his third opera, *The Oprichnik*, and then destroyed the original score (with the exception of the overture, the already mentioned ' Dance ' and an entr'acte published as Op. 3).[1] The orchestral and chorus parts, and six of the less important solo parts, remained in the archives of the Bolshoy Theatre, and from these S. Popov was able some twenty years ago to reconstruct practically the whole score with the help of the following additional materials :

[1] I have also discovered a piano potpourri ' on motives from Tchaïkovsky's *Voevoda* ' by ' H. Cramer ' (pseudonym of Tchaïkovsky himself) which has proved useful in identifying themes.

(1) Two volumes of sketches for two acts of the opera, found in 1925 after the death of Tchaïkovsky's former servant, A. I. Sofronov.

(2) The printed libretto.

(3) An unfinished copy of the vocal score of the third act with composer's corrections.

Olena's narrative in the second scene of Act II and part of the ensuing duet[1] were composed, on Tchaïkovsky's materials, by Boris Asafiev (better known as the critic ' Igor Glebov ').

I have been unable to procure this reconstructed score or Popov's description of the work,[2] but some idea of the music can be gathered from the published fragments and the passages transferred to *The Oprichnik*. The main point that strikes one is the intensely national idiom, so characteristic of Tchaïkovsky's early works. Consider the two tunes from the ' Maids' Dance ' quoted in Ex. 86; the first motive of (*b*) is very characteristic of Russian folk music. Both the opening chorus of girls and the chorus of girls that closes the second act are actual folk-songs—the words as well as the music[3]—and the clarinet melody that accompanies the entrance of Bastryukov and Dubrovin at the beginning of Act III, if not itself a folk-tune, is marked by melodic characteristics commonly found in Russian folk-melodies. Mariya's ' nightingale ' song, ' The nightingale in the grove loudly sings ' (Ex. 87), the most immediately popular thing in the opera, is definitely a folk-melody[4] and Kashkin also speaks of a successful tenor aria in the pentatonic mode.[5]

If *The Voevoda* had had luck, its successor *Undine* had worse; for it never even reached the stage. After toying for a while with a Græco-Babylonian subject from the time of Alexander the Great, offered him by Ostrovsky, Tchaïkovsky came across a ready-made libretto on the subject of La Motte Fouqué's *Undine*. Zhukovsky's beautiful translation of Fouqué's story had long been a favourite

---

[1] Tchaïkovsky himself afterwards used the theme of this duet as material for the first two numbers of Act IV of *Swan Lake*.

[2] In the Moscow journal *Kultura teatra*, Nos. 5–6, 1921, of which the only known copies in this country were destroyed in the bombing of the British Museum.

[3] Nos. 23 and 25 of Tchaïkovsky's *Fifty Russian Folk-Songs* for piano duet.

[4] Cf. No. 24 of the *Fifty Russian Folk-Songs*.

[5] Tchaïkovsky returned to Ostrovsky's play many years later when at the dramatist's request he wrote an orchestra' ' melodrama ' to accompany the monologue of the Domovoy (or ' house-goblin '), a character he had excluded from his operatic version, at the end of Act II. The music was used for a production of the play at the Maly Theatre, Moscow, on January 19/31, 1885, but was long believed lost. In 1932 it was discovered in the Central Music Library of the State Academic Theatres in Leningrad; it consists of 45 bars of lyrical music in G minor, scored for two flutes, oboe, clarinet, bassoon, harp and strings.

with Tchaïkovsky, and it was long believed that this libretto, made by Count F. A. Sollogub for Lvov, the composer of the Tsarist national anthem, was based on Zhukovsky; according to Alfred Loewenberg, however, Sollogub's version is a translation of a French text by the well-known libretto-monger Vernoy de Saint-Georges.[1] The action differs in some details from that of the *Undine* operas of E. T. A. Hoffmann and Albert Lortzing; for instance the striking figure of the water-spirit Kühleborn has disappeared :

> *Act* I. Undine's foster-parents, the fisherman and his wife, in their hut. Enter the knight, Huldbrand (tenor), who tells them of his adventures in the wood. Enter Undine (soprano), with whom he falls in love, forgetting his betrothed, Berthalda. The lovers embrace and go out together into the stormy night.
>
> *Act* II. The Duke, Berthalda's father, is naturally enraged with Huldbrand, but the knight has now returned to his first love and appears at her birthday festivities. Undine also appears and, having interrupted the rejoicings with a ballad revealing that Berthalda is really the daughter of the fisherfolk, leaps into the Danube.
>
> *Act* III. Huldbrand, once more in love with Undine, bewails her loss as he waits before his marriage to Berthalda. The bridal procession is interrupted first by the Duke, then by the fisherman, each of whom has been visited by Undine's spirit and persuaded to forbid the marriage. Berthalda insists on going on with it, but Undine herself rises from a well and effectually disperses the procession. Final love-duet for Undine and the knight, after which he dies and she is transformed into a spring.

Tchaïkovsky set this farrago of romantic nonsense with tremendous enthusiasm; he began the composition in January 1869, finished it in April and completed the orchestration in July of the same year. The score was hurriedly despatched to St. Petersburg, where it was shelved for nearly a year on one pretext after another and then rejected by the opera committee of the Imperial Theatre, the same committee which a few months later also rejected the original version of Mussorgsky's *Boris*. As with *The Voevoda*, Tchaïkovsky afterwards used some of the best numbers in other works—thus the fateful bridal procession of Act III became the andantino marziale of the Second Symphony, while one of the love-duets for Undine and Huldbrand (probably that in the last Act) is now familiar to everyone as Odette's adagio in Act II of *Swan Lake*—and then burned the score. Thanks to the circumstance that five numbers from Act I were given a concert performance in Moscow in March 1870, and so

---

[1] *Annals of Opera* (Heffer, 1943). Dr. Loewenberg tells us that Lvov's *Undine.* was produced in St. Petersburg in 1848.

were preserved in the archives of the Bolshoy Theatre, we still know something of the *Undine* music in its original form. These five numbers were:

(1) Introduction to the opera;
(2) Undine's aria, ' Streamlet, my brother ';
(3) Mixed chorus (allegro): ' Help, help! Our stream is raging ';
(4) Duet for Undine and Huldbrand: ' O happiness, O blessed moment ';
(5) Finale for soloists and mixed chorus: ' O hours of death.'

The last three had been forgotten till Popov unearthed them in 1920; he also found that the Introduction had been used unchanged as the Introduction to Ostrovsky's *Snow Maiden* when Tchaïkovsky wrote his incidental music to that play and that Undine's aria, re-orchestrated and somewhat altered, had been turned to account for Lel's first song in the same play. (In *Undine* Tchaïkovsky had made novel and effective use of the piano as an orchestral instrument in the accompaniment to this aria.)

Undiscouraged by this failure with a fantastic-romantic subject, Tchaïkovsky turned to a curiously parallel one in S. A. Rachinsky's *Mandragora*, a story of a knight who finds the magic plant in his castle garden, uproots it and finds it transformed into a lovely girl.' She follows him, dressed as a page; he falls in love with another woman; and Mandragora is changed back again into a flower. Again a knight who falls in love with a faëry being, is unfaithful to her, and drives her back to her native element! Indeed, the parallel is so close that one wonders whether Tchaïkovsky was not already playing with the idea of putting some of the *Undine* music to fresh use. But the only fresh music composed for *Mandragora* was a ' chorus of flowers and insects ' bearing the date ' December 27, 1869,' and orchestrated during the first fortnight of 1870; this chorus was afterwards performed several times as a concert-piece[1] and won the praise of critics as opposed as Balakirev and Laroche. Long before this, however, Tchaïkovsky had, on Kashkin's advice, abandoned the idea of the opera. In January 1870 Rachinsky began another libretto for him, *Raimond Lully*, but by February his choice had definitely fallen on a tragedy, *The Oprichnik*, by a well-known historical novelist, Ivan Ivanovich Lazhechnikov (1792–1868), and he proceeded to work out his own libretto. Yet, the choice once

[1] The full score was then lost, though Glazunov made an orchestral version from the piano score in 1898, but the original full score was discovered among Nicholas Rubinstein's papers in the Moscow Conservatoire in 1912.

made, little further was done for a whole year; the non-performance of *Undine* seems to have damped Tchaïkovsky's interest in his new opera and he does not appear to have worked at it much till nearly the end of 1870; it was not finished till April 1872.

The Oprichnik was luckier than *Undine*. After seven months' delay it was unanimously accepted by the opera committee and produced at the Maryinsky Theatre, St. Petersburg, on April 12–24, 1874. And although the composer at once felt a profound dislike for the work and would gladly have suppressed it,[1] it is interesting as the earliest opera of Tchaïkovsky's that we possess complete.

The 'oprichniks' were the dreaded bodyguard of Ioann IV, popularly known as Ivan the Terrible—aristocratic rakes and ruffians in the dress of monks—and Lazhechnikov's play is just such another drama of the reign of that unpleasant monarch as Mey's *Maid of Pskov* which Rimsky-Korsakov had just turned into an opera (produced in 1873) and his *Tsar's Bride* which attracted the same composer a quarter of a century later:

> *Act* I. Prince Zhemchuzhny (bass) is in his garden, entertaining his friend, the elderly Molchan Mitkov (bass), to whom he promises his daughter Natalya in marriage; exeunt. Enter Natalya (soprano) with the old nurse Zakharyena (soprano) and maids; she bemoans her fate; exeunt. Enter, roughly breaking down the fence, Natalya's true love, Andrey Morozov (tenor) and his friend, the Tsar's favourite, Basmanov (alto) with oprichniks. It appears that Zhemchuzhny has robbed Andrey and his mother of their fortune and driven them from their home; Andrey decides to join the ranks of the oprichniks in order to get his revenge; exeunt. Re-enter Natalya, mourning for her lost lover. Re-enter Zakharyevna with the maids, who sing and dance to distract her.
>
> *Act* II. Scene 1: Andrey's mother, the Boyarïnya Morozova (mezzo-soprano), alone, brooding over her wrongs. Her heart is not lightened when Andrey enters and tells her of his friendship with Basmanov, whom she regards as his evil genius.
> Scene 2: Andrey, before the assembled oprichniks, takes the most solemn oath to become one of their number, renouncing everything else in the world, however dear. As he does so, he sheds bitter tears—to the joy of Prince Vyazminsky (baritone), his father's old enemy.[2]

---

[1] In later years he tried to forbid its performance but was unable to do so, having parted with all his rights to the publisher Bessel. At the time of his death he was thinking of ' re-composing two-thirds of *The Oprichnik*.'

[2] Vyazminsky had to be introduced in the opera in place of the Tsar himself, whose representation was forbidden by the censor. (The censor also took out some lines from Basmanov's part in Act I, describing the oprichniks' nocturnal amusements.) Oddly enough, Ivan had been allowed to appear and sing the year before in *The Maid of Pskov*; in *The Tsar's Bride* he was allowed to appear, but only as a mute character.

Act III. A square in Moscow; the populace complain of the doings of the oprichniks, and the old Boyarinya is hooted after by boys who call her ' bitch ' and ' she-oprichnik.' In rushes Natalya, who has run away from father and bridegroom, and throws herself into the old lady's arms. Enter Zhemchuzhny with servants in pursuit; he is about to carry off his daughter when Andrey and Basmanov appear, with a band of oprichniks. The women are rescued but are horrified to find Andrey has become an oprichnik; his mother disowns him; Basmanov suggests that the Tsar may release him from his oath.

Act IV. Wedding festivities in the Tsar's palace. Andrey is to be released from his oath and to marry Natalya; but till midnight he is still an oprichnik. Vyazminsky interrupts the festivities, with malicious joy, with the announcement that the Tsar wishes to see the bride—alone. Andrey is beside himself; in trying to save Natalya he breaks his oath. The oprichniks lead Natalya to the Tsar and Andrey to execution. The stage is empty for some time. Vyazminsky leads in the old Boyarinya, who demands to be taken to her son; from the window the Prince shows her the scene of execution; she falls dead.

In justice to Lazhcchnikov it should be said that his play, however melodramatic, is marked not only by subtler character-drawing—for instance, Molchan Mitkov is shown as a noble and sympathetic figure, who renounces Natalya and even pleads for Andrey—but by a more clearly motivated action. For the weaknesses of the libretto Tchaïkovsky was himself to blame, for he had the extraordinary idea of transferring to *The Oprichnik* not only a good deal of the music of *The Voevoda* but its original text as well. Up to a point there was little harm in this. One heroine lamenting her fate is very like another, one chorus of servants trying to cheer up their mistress with song and dance is like any other chorus of servants trying to cheer up their mistress with song and dance; so Mariya's song about the nightingale in Act II of *The Voevoda* (Ex. 87) quite harmlessly became Natalya's song about the nightingale in Act I of *The Oprichnik*, and the folk-song choruses at the beginning of Act I and the end of Act II of *The Voevoda* could be easily and naturally transplanted into the first act of *The Oprichnik*. But it was disastrous to use the conversation of the two young heroes at the beginning of Act IV of *The Voevoda* for the conversation of the old villain Zhemchuzhny and his friend in the opening scene of the later opera. And because Tchaïkovsky wanted to use the music of Bastryukov's entrance in Act I again for Andrey's entrance in Act I (the parallel being that each is a young lover breaking into a nasty old man's garden), Andrey is made to break in violently with his violent friends instead of creeping in alone and unobtrusively as in Lazhechnikov's play. Of the sixty-two pages of Act I in the vocal score of *The Oprichnik* only thirteen were new music: Basmanov's recitative and arioso, with Andrey's reply, and Natalya's fine arioso in G flat, 'O wild wind, carry to my love the tale of my bitter sorrow,' one of those rich, passionately singing melodies that bear the unmistakable mark of Tchaïkovsky's invention (Ex. 88). Yet if unmistakably Tchaïkovskian, it is not altogether unrelated to a famous passage in the same key in the fourth act of *Les Huguenots*, Raoul's 'Tu l'as dit; oui, tu m'aimes.' That places *The Oprichnik* pretty accurately; it is Meyerbeer translated into Russian. The subject—the crude drama with one 'strong' situation after another—would have delighted Meyerbeer. And the operatic convention that Tchaïkovsky adopted to clothe it in music is not very different from the convention of, say, *Le Prophète*: a 'number' opera with the numbers partly broken down and linked with ariosos and the like, and the whole texture given a semblance of unity by the use of one or two reminiscence-themes (more than in Meyerbeer but hardly enough to claim comparison with Wagnerian leitmotives). The two most important of these recurring themes are contrasted in the short orchestral introduction which takes the place of an overture; one is the menacing theme of the oprichniks (Ex. 89), the other the melody in which the old Boyarinya pleads 'Dear son, thou wilt not leave me lonely in my bitter lot,' in the first scene of Act II (Ex. 90), (The introduction is laid out sectionally: (*a*) conventional stormy figures and 'oprichniks' theme, D minor, (*b*) Ex. 90 in A major, with Ex. 89 breaking in, pizzicato, (*c*) the aria from the second scene of Act II, in which Andrey tells the assembled oprichniks why he wishes to become one of them, F major, (*d*) Ex. 90 in F, with Ex. 89 breaking in as before, (*e*) the music of the execution scene, Ex. 90 distorted and in diminution, (*f*) Ex. 89 transformed into D major and thundered out triumphantly). The 'oprichniks' theme in both its minor and its major forms, and in various transformations, plays an important part throughout the last three acts. In the dramatic pause while the stage remains empty before the final catastrophe Exs. 89 and 90 are effectively combined.[1]

I have said that *The Oprichnik* is Meyerbeer translated into Russian. I must emphasise that it is very thoroughly translated. Not

[1] Perhaps this is the place to mention that the short orchestral prelude to Act II was composed and orchestrated by Tchaïkovsky's pupil, Vladimir Shilovsky.

only are the passages transferred from *The Voevoda* almost entirely folkish[1]; not only are a number of actual folk-melodies introduced[2]; but many pages of the score are saturated with Russian folk and ecclesiastical idioms (e.g., the old Boyarinya's great monologue at the beginning of Act II, which emphatically deserves rescue from oblivion, the various choruses of the oprichniks,[3] the wedding chorus that opens Act IV). Sometimes Tchaïkovsky spoils the intensely national flavour of his melodic line by commonplace or text-book harmonisation, at others—for instance, the beautiful B flat minor passage for Andrey, echoed by the chorus,[4] in the scene immediately following the oprichniks' dance in the last act—the matching of Russian melody with Russian harmony is perfect and any expert might be pardoned for attributing the music to Rimsky-Korsakov or even Mussorgsky. In *The Voevoda* and *The Oprichnik*, indeed Tchaïkovsky stands very close to his colleagues of the 'Mighty Handful.' Some of the girls' choruses in Act I might easily be transferred to *May Night*; just before the end of the act Zakháryevna, telling the girls to sing and dance, speaks with the musical accent of the nurse in *Boris* (the passage originated with Nedwiga in *The Voevoda*); as in the finale of the Second Symphony, written at about the same time, there are experiments with the whole-tone scale (cf. the passage some forty bars before the end of Act III); orchestral motives, sometimes from a previous number, are used to hold together recitative dialogue or even a vocal solo (cf. the scene between Andrey and his mother, following her monologue in Act II, and Natalya's arioso when she pleads with her father in Act III). Even the long stretches of rather watery and colourless lyricism do not finally stamp the opera as something that could not possibly have been written by one of the 'Handful.' It is in Tchaïkovsky's conventional handling of the chorus that one feels the difference most: above all in the

[1] Mrs. Newmarch's remark in *The Russian Opera* about Tchaïkovsky's 'grafting upon *The Oprichnik*, with its crying need for national colour and special treatment, a portion of the pretty Italianised music of *The Voevoda*' is so preposterous that I can only suppose she had never seen the score; as I have shown, two of these 'almost Italian' graftings were based on Russian folk-melodies.

[2] Those in the 'Dance of the Oprichniks and Women' in the last act include Nos. 10, 17, 29, 32 and 34 of the *Fifty Russian Folk-Songs* for piano duet.

[4] Their first devout modal chorus in Act II, scene 2, has a close affinity with the introduction to the *Romeo and Juliet* overture, an affinity that is emphasised when the theme is taken up by the orchestra with a pizzicato bass moving in quavers.

[4] Yet another borrowing from. *The Voevoda*, and a passage that Tchaïkovsky recalled almost note for note, and in the same key, not only in the accompaniment to Frost's monologue in his *Snow Maiden* music but, very slightly altered and still in B flat minor, in the 'Cygnets' Dance' in Act IV of *Swan Lake*.

choral crowd-scene that opens Act III, which stands immeasurably below not only Mussorgsky in dramatic quality but Rimsky-Korsakov in colour and raciness. The last part (cantabile e con grandezza) of the penultimate scene of the opera is hopelessly weak, and uncharacteristic—particularly Vyazminsky's part.

On the other hand the 'watery and colourless lyricism' is always liable to colour and thicken into that type of cantilena which is absolutely and peculiarly Tchaïkovskian. I have already quoted from Natalya's first arioso (Ex. 88). Andrey's aria in the second scene of Act II, used in the introduction to the opera, is similar but less striking. And unfortunately most of these patches of lyrical charm occur in contexts from which they could hardly be detached for concert performance, the outstanding case being the crown of the love-duet in the last act, 'Thou art my life and light, my joy and rest,' where Tchaïkovsky salvages a theme from the (temporarily) destroyed symphonic poem *Fate* (Ex. 91). In the same way, the G minor andante portion of the already mentioned penultimate scene stands out as truly Tchaïkovskian; and even such a comparatively weak passage as the andante espressivo of Natalya's arioso in the third act foreshadows one of the most memorable melodies in *Eugene Onegin* (cf. Ex. 99).

Tchaïkovsky's next stage work was not an opera but the already mentioned incidental music to his favourite Ostrovsky's 'spring tale' *Snegurochka (Snow Maiden)*, familiar to every lover of Russian music through Rimsky-Korsakov's operatic setting (composed 1880–1 and produced early in 1882). This poetic play, packed with symbolism and Slavonic mythology and folk-lore, concerned with characters some of whom are human, some personified forces of nature, and set in the fantastic never-never kingdom of the Berendeys, is strikingly different from the prose dramas of the Moscow bourgeoisie with which Ostrovsky's name is generally associated—though there were fantastic elements in the original *Voevoda* play. For the third time Tchaïkovsky had as his subject the unhappy love of a non-mortal girl for a mortal and her final dissolution into her native element. *Snow Maiden* was a commissioned work for both poet and composer; the Bolshoy Theatre urgently needed a 'show'—a spectacle combining opera, play and ballet—just as the Maryinsky Theatre in Petersburg had needed a 'show' the previous year and thus given birth (or, rather, miscarriage) to the famous collective *Mlada* of Cui, Mussorgsky, Rimsky-Korsakov and Borodin. According to Kashkin, the whole score—nineteen numbers—was completed in three weeks during March and April 1873 (for the production on May 11/23).

Now nineteen real numbers, not mere fanfares and the like, represent a considerable quantity of music for one play, and although the only singing characters are the shepherd Lel and the chorus (plus a monologue that is almost a monotone for Frost, and a song for the young peasant Brusilo, who has disappeared altogether from Korsakov's version) it would not have needed an enormous amount of extra work to turn the whole thing into an opera, and, according to his brother, Tchaïkovsky had some idea of doing this but was forestalled, to his intense annoyance, by Rimsky-Korsakov. But the circumstance that the same subject was set by these two masters at so nearly the same period does give the critic a chance to make some piquantly odious comparisons, the more easily as Korsakov's prologue and four acts correspond exactly to Ostrovsky's, his alterations being limited to simplifications and cuts (such as the excision of 'the fair Helen' who appears as Bermyata's wife!)

Of the five numbers Tchaïkovsky provided for the Prologue, the introduction is (as I have already told) simply the not very interesting introduction to *Undine*. But the dances and chorus of the shivering birds, Frost's monologue, the chorus of Berendeys dragging in the *maslyanitsa* (the carnival effigy), and the melodrama accompanying the *maslyanitsa's* lines, are well worth looking at—and hearing. One is almost at once plunged into the same folk-melodic ambience as in Korsakov's opera: the bird chorus, the accompaniment to the monologue, and the melodies of the carnival chorus (one of which also provides the basis of the melodrama) are all either directly borrowed or closely imitated from folk-music. And one also notes with amusement that Rimsky-Korsakov in the accompaniment to *his* bird chorus saw fit to adopt precisely the same acciaccatura 'twittering' effect as that with which Tchaïkovsky had begun his dances, that he likewise cast his bird music in naïve 2/4 rhythms, and that his *maslyanitsa* monotones pretty much as Tchaïkovsky's Frost does. And if Rimsky-Korsakov's seven-bar patterns (2 + 2 + 3) have a peculiar charm, Tchaïkovsky's bird dances (Ex. 92) are not altogether conventional either.

Tchaïkovsky then opens the first act with a delicious little pastoral duet, still folkish in flavour, for two clarinets over quiet string chords; Korsakov opens it with pastoral calls for solo horn and solo oboe. As regards Lel's first two songs the honours are even, for if Tchaïkovsky's adaptation of the rather feeble aria from *Undine* cannot compare with his rival's beautiful, almost unaccompanied, modal setting of the berry-gathering song, his treatment of the second song, ' The shepherd sings as the forest murmurs,' is decidedly the more attractive. Oddly enough, it has the melodic *naïveté*, and is orchestrated in the bright, transparent, primary colours, that one associates with Rimsky-Korsakov (cf. Ex. 93). Indeed, it seems to have exercised some slight influence on Korsakov's A major bird chorus in the Prologue.

Neglecting Tchaïkovsy's not very interesting prelude to Act II and the melodrama for muted strings accompanying Kupava's complaint to the Tsar, based on part of the same music, we reach a particularly interesting series of parallels. First the chorus of blind gusli-players in praise of Tsar Berendey that opens the second act: Tchaïkovsky wrote this[1] in E minor, Aeolian, and Rimsky-Korsakov was content to do the same, though his melody has a finer spread and his use of Glinka's harp-and-piano convention to represent the guslis is more picturesque than Tchaïkovsky's simple pizzicato chords (Ex. 94). Tchaïkovsky's chorus of people and courtiers, though not without folkish touches, sounds square-cut and conventional beside Rimsky-Korsakov's striking unaccompanied version, but it is difficult to choose between the two introductions and opening choruses of Act III although the music is in both cases founded, in accordance with Ostrovsky's direction, on the folk-tune, 'Ay, vo pole lipon'ka ' (' In the fields stands a lime tree '). It is perhaps characteristic of the two musicians that Tchaïkovsky chose a version of the tune in normal A major and harmonised it with modal cadences, while Korsakov's version is in A Mixolydian (i.e., A major with G natural). But it would be a nice point to determine which is the more authentic—and which the more ' Russian ' treatment of it.

The dance of the *skomorokhi* (clowns or tumblers) presents no such problem; Rimsky-Korsakov's familiar piece has won general popularity, while Tchaïkovsky's—noisy and commonplace—has been not unjustly forgotten. Nor can either of Tchaïkovsky's settings of Lel's third song (an entirely new one was published posthumously) seriously challenge Rimsky-Korsakov's, though here again the latter has taken a hint from his predecessor in introducing the song with some capers on a solo clarinet. Brusilo's song about the beaver, which Korsakov transferred to the old peasant Bakula and placed earlier in the act, does not amount to much, and the short orchestral piece

---

[1] Or, rather, extended it from a folk-tune; the original will be found in his *Fifty Russian Folk-Songs* (No. 14).

which Tchaïkovsky wrote for the scene where Mizgir in the enchanted wood is led astray by the Wood Spirit, though adequate, demonstrates his marked inferiority to Rimsky-Korsakov in grotesque and fantastic conceptions. But the purely lyrical music for the Spring Fairy's granting of her daughter's wish and the chorus of flowers—Tchaïkovsky uses the same music for the prelude to Act IV—restores the balance; this is Tchaïkovsky's ground rather than his rival's; indeed, his rival's music (9/8, A major, andante) seems to be slightly indebted tó his own (6/8, A major, andantino) and one of the motives of Korsakov's Spring Fairy is a modified echo of a little bass motive in Tchaïkovsky.

The two remaining numbers of Tchaïkovsky's *Snow Maiden* music are 'Tsar Berendey's March and Chorus' and the final hymn to the sun-god Yarilo. The march corresponds not to Korsakov's 'Tsar Berendey's March' (which belongs to the second act) but to the opening of his finale, one of his most striking and charming pages; Tchaïkovsky's music has its own, if less original, piquancy and his tiny folk-tune trio[1] is deliciously naïve. In both cases the processional music leads without a break into the millet-sowing ritual and both composers have necessarily based their choruses on the traditional tunes associated with the words[2]; both settings are extremely effective. The two settings of the hymn to Yarilo, however, are completely different in conception; Tchaïkovsky took yet another folk-tune, 'Vo gornitse, vo svetlitse,'[3] which happened to fit Ostrovsky's words, and evolved from it a most brilliant finale which has nothing in common with Rimsky-Korsakov's novel setting in 11/4 time.

To sum up: if Tchaïkovsky's *Snow Maiden* music is inferior to Rimsky-Korsakov's delightful opera, it still by no means deserves oblivion. Few of his early works are more deserving of resuscitation, and though it will obviously never be heard again in the theatre nothing would be easier than to prepare a concert suite of the best numbers.

Oddly enough, Tchaïkovsky's next opera, *Vakula the Smith*, was also challenged by a later Rimsky-Korsakov work on the same subject, though in this case the younger man, aware of the other's feelings on the subject of *Snow Maiden*, tactfully waited for his death to 'release' the subject (Gogol's story *Christmas Eve*). But the

[1] The tune is No. 24 in Balakirev's collection, No. 36 in Tchaïkovsky's.
[2] Rimsky-Korsakov introduces both the variants given by Balakirev (Nos. 8 and 9 of his collection); Tchaïkovsky uses No. 8 only and in a slightly altered form: cf. also No. 26 of his *Fifty Russian Folk-Songs*.
[3] Cf. No. 96 of Rimsky-Korsakov's *Hundred Russian Folk-Songs*.

parallels between *Vakula* and Korsakov's *Christmas Eve*, though interesting, are less so than the *Snow Maiden* parallels since Korsakov wrote his own libretto while Tchaïkovsky's opera was a setting of a ' book ' prepared by the poet Polonsky for Alexander Serov and then made the subject of a competition in which Tchaïkovsky, after (though not as the result of) some discreditable manœuvring, was successful. The original version of Tchaïkovsky's opera was composed and orchestrated in less than three months (early June to August 21/September 2, 1874) and produced on the Maryinsky stage, Petersburg, on November 24/December 6, 1876. I say ' the original version ' for although *Vakula* was a favourite work of Tchaïkovsky's he recognised its shortcomings; it was ' overfilled with details, too thick in scoring, insufficiently effective from the point of view of the singers . . . too musical and not theatrical enough, the harmony too chromatic. *C'est un menu surchargé de mets épicés . . .* too symphonic, or even like chamber-music'; accordingly in February and March 1885 he undertook a drastic revision of the score—' writing completely new scenes, taking out the bad, leaving in the good, lightening the weight of the harmony,' as he wrote to the singer Emiliya Pavlovskaya—and the new version was produced at the Bolshoy Theatre, Moscow, on January 19/31, 1887, with a new title, *Cherevichki* (*The Slippers*), so odd to Western ears and so unpromising in translation that it is generally known outside Russia as *Les Caprices d'Oxane* or *Die goldene Schuhe*. The original ' comic opera in three acts ' had become a ' comic-fantastic opera in four acts '— though the new fourth act is simply the last scene of the original third act; of the 484 pages of the new full score, 112 were fresh music.[1]

---

[1] The passages inserted or completely re-written in 1885 are:

In the overture: 7 bars in the allegro giusto.

In Act I: The last four pages (in the vocal score) of the duet for Solokha and the devil; the dialogue of Chub and Panas in the snowstorm scene (some 25 bars were cut from the snowstorm music itself); the 45-bar allegro non troppo leading to Vakula's arioso; and the greater part of the music following this arioso (i.e., practically the whole of Nos. 5, 6 and 7).

In Act II: The schoolmaster's little song, with the recitative passages preceding and following it; all but the first 24 bars of Solokha's scene with Chub; the quintet; 26 bars in the chorus at the beginning of the second scene (from the entry of the first group of youths and maids, bearing a star); the last 21 bars of this chorus; the 21-bar dialogue before Oksana's song (cf. Ex. 96*b*) in the next number; 14 bars of choral exclamations and recitative for Vakula a little later. and minor interpolations in Oksana's part (including the brief molto più lento with its coloratura cadenza, and the trills at the very end of the number).

In Act III: Vakula's recitative (with echo) when he first appears with the devil in the sack; His Highness's couplets; all the music after exit of the Master of Ceremonies.

In Act IV: The allegro vivace chorus of peasant lads (except the first 8 bars).

The action is as follows:

Act I. Scene 1: Moonlit, snow-covered Ukrainian village. Comic love scene between the witch Solokha (mezzo-soprano) and a devil (baritone), who has a grudge against Solokha's son, the smith Vakula (tenor). As he flies off with Solokha the devil causes a snowstorm and steals the moon so as to interfere with the young man's courtship of Oksana (soprano), daughter of the old Cossack, Chub (bass). Chub and his crony Panas (tenor) are seen blundering about in the darkness.

Scene 2: Chub's hut. The coquettish Oksana mocks at Vakula's love-making. Enter Chub, so covered with snow that Vakula doesn't recognise him and throws him out. Oksana in turn drives Vakula away—and then regrets him. Enter village girls singing Christmas carols.

Act II. Scene 1: Solokha's hut. She and the devil flirting and dancing. A knock; the devil hides in a sack; enter another of Solokha's lovers, the *golova* or headman (bass). Another knock; the *golova* hides in another sack. The scene is repeated with the schoolmaster (tenor) and with Chub. Last of all enters Vakula, who carries the sacks away to his smithy to make more room in the hut for the Christmas festivities.

Scene 2: Carollers, among them Oksana who mockingly tells Vakula she will marry him—if he will give her the Tsaritsa's slippers. He goes off absent-mindedly with only one of the sacks, the one with the devil inside. The carollers find the other sacks—and their contents.

Act III. Scene 1: River-bank. The *rusalkas* (water-spirits) tempt the melancholy Vakula to leap into the water. The devil creeps out of the sack and nearly gets Vakula in his power, but the smith gets the better of him, leaps on his back and orders him to fly to the Tsaritsa.

Scene 2: Antechamber of a palace. Vakula flies in on the devil's back. His appearance coincides with the entrance of a band of Zaporozhtsy Cossacks who are to have audience of the Tsaritsa.

Scene 3: The throne-room. Vakula and the Zaporozhtsy are received by 'His Serene Highness' (bass).[1] Vakula plucks up courage to ask for the Empress's shoes; the boon is granted; amid the general festivities (dances by the Cossacks and ladies of the Court) Vakula summons the devil and rides away on his back unnoticed.

[1] The censorship would not tolerate the representation of even an anonymous Tsaritsa on the opera stage. (Through Gogol's story she could be identified as Catherine the Great.) Rimsky-Korsakov got permission for a ' Tsaritsa ' and wrote the part for a mezzo, but members of the Imperial family raised a storm at the *répétition générale* and a baritone ' Highness ' had to be substituted at the first performance, as in Tchaïkovsky's opera.

> *Act* IV. Christmas morning in the village. Solokha and Oksana are
> bewailing the supposed loss of son and lover. Vakula appears with
> the slippers; Oksana admits that she wants him more than the
> slippers. General rejoicing.

The music with which Tchaïkovsky clothed this typically Gogo-
lian tale ranks among the best he ever wrote.[1] In fineness of workmanship the score ranks high above that of *The Oprichnik* and its
lyrical inspiration is purer and far less uneven. Melodically *Vakula*
is saturated with the characteristics of Ukrainian folk-music; I have
not been able to identify a number of complete folk-tunes as in *The
Oprichnik*—my acquaintance with Ukrainian folk-melodies is a good
deal more limited than with Russian ones—but I can testify (and
could easily show with music-type examples if space permitted) that
the score is full of typical Ukrainian and Russian folk-motives.
Perhaps the most obvious, and least attractive, Ukrainian feature is
the short-breathed hopak-type tune in 2/4 time, of which there are
numerous examples in *Vakula* : Solokha's sparkling duet with the
devil in the first scene (which also provides the music for Vakula's
aerial ride), her dance with him in Act II, most of the scene with the
golova in Act II, the song for the schoolmaster inserted in the revised
score, the Russian dance and the dance of the Zaporozhtsy in the
court scene, the ' drink ' chorus of the young peasants in the final
scene, among others. Even the recitative is often nationally coloured,
as in the passage where Oksana laments that her father has gone out
and left her alone on Christmas Eve, of which a fragment is shown
in Ex. 95. And I can give no better indication of the charm of
Oksana's musical portrait than by quoting first the opening of
the aria which immediately follows that ('An apple-tree bloomed
in the garden ' : Ex. 96*a*) and then the melody to which she proposes
the bargain with the Empress's slippers (Ex. 96*b*). Rimsky-Korsakov's Oksana is colder and harder; the big ' mirror aria,' which corresponds in his *Christmas Eve* to the scena in which Exs. 95 and 96*a*
occur, more successfully hits off the character of Gogol's coquette.
But Tchaïkovsky's Oksana is easier to fall in love with.

There is an interesting parallel a little later when Vakula enters,
thanks to the fact that both librettists kept closely to an actual phrase
of Gogol's (cf. Ex. 97). Tchaïkovsky's setting has the more lyrical
impetus and the almost-identity of the second bars of each melody

---

[1] That was also his own opinion. As late as 1890 he told Jurgenson that he
' considered it, so far as the music is concerned, almost my best opera ' (letter of
July 2/14).

suggests that some dim—and doubtless unconscious—recollection of it helped to control Korsakov's inspiration twenty years later. Otherwise the score of *Vakula* had little or no influence on that of *Christmas Eve*, though oddly enough I suspect that it may have had some on Korsakov's already mentioned *Snow Maiden*. Such passages as the accompaniment to the devil's whisperings just before he creeps into the sack and the scene where Oksana is drawn on in a sledge towards the end of Act II are thoroughly characteristic of Rimsky-Korsakov's *Snow Maiden* style; and the Russian and Zaporozhtsy dances in the court scene have something more in common with the popular dance of the *skomorokhi* in Korsakov's *Snow Maiden* than a slight common debt to Dargomïzhsky's *Kazachok*. As Rimsky-Korsakov himself freely admitted, he was always extremely susceptible to influences. Yet period and environment—and common indebtedness to Glinka, in particular—account for much. Tchaïkovsky harmonises Exs. 96a and 97a with transparent, diatonic chords absolutely in Glinka's style, that same ' Glinka's style ' which we recognise so often in Borodin and the more lyrical pages of Mussorgsky and Rimsky-Korsakov. The simple variations on the theme of the Zaporozhtsy, when they first appear in the second scene of Act III, are pure Glinka (cf. Finn's ballad in *Ruslan*). As one turns the pages of the score of *Vakula* one is struck, even more forcibly than in *The Oprichnik*, by the younger Tchaïkovsky's affinity with the ' Handful.' The magnificent broad melody in B major in which the devil evokes the snowstorm in the first act might have been written by Borodin, and though the snowstorm is musically rather conventional there are some novel harmonic effects of seconds and ninths[1] as Chub and Panas stumble about in the dark, and the scene concludes not only with descending whole-tone passages in the bass but with whole-tone harmonies[2] that are hardly perceptibly resolved on the last bass crotchet (Ex. 98). The augmented and diminished intervals of the music that follows the first knock which interrupts the devil's dance with Solokha, the entire texture of the music to which the disconsolate Vakula appears on the river-bank, carrying the devil in the sack, the chorus of

---

[1] They occur in one of the additions of 1885.

[2] Tchaïkovsky also used descending whole-tone scales, though not whole-tone harmonies, many years later in scenes 5 and 7 of *The Queen of Spades* to mark the appearances of the old Countess's avenging ghost to Hermann. Its employment here was probably suggested by the recollection of Dargomïzhsky's use of whole-tone music in *The Stone Guest* to mark the appearance of the Commander's avenging ghost to Don Juan.

rusalkas just before, with its alternation of 3/4 and 5/4 measures : all these stand in the direct line which stretches from the fantastic and supernatural music of Glinka's *Ruslan* to the fantastic and supernatural music that Rimsky-Korsakov was writing more than half a century after *Ruslan*. The opening of the choral scene at the beginning of the second scene of Act II, with its double pedals, is pure Glinka—though, as usual with Tchaïkovsky, the Glinka of *Life for the Tsar* rather than the Glinka of *Ruslan and Lyudmila* (with the ' Mighty Handful,' it was the reverse : on the whole *Ruslan* meant more to them than the earlier opera). Not that Tchaïkovsky's own musical personality fails to manifest itself, of course. Sometimes it makes itself felt through academic *gaucheries*, as when later in that same choral scene, at the words ' Tikhaya nochen'ka,' he cannot resist the temptation to sharpen the leading note in the accompaniment to a melody in the Æolian mode; sometimes through that unmistakable kind of cantilena, that species of Bellini-with-a-Russian-accent, to which Tchaïkovsky alone has ever had the real secret, though Rakhmaninov and Glazunov and many others have produced clever imitations (cf. Vakula's arioso at the end of the first scene of Act II, or the melody in G flat which dominates the finale of that act). The polonaise of the Court scene is one of those conventional Russian polonaises that crop up wherever festive, ceremonial music is required; it is less brilliant than the corresponding one in Korsakov's *Christmas Eve*, less tuneful than that in *Onegin*. But the minuet is graceful and pretty, and also noteworthy as the first of a whole series of rococo insets in Tchaïkovsky's stage-works. Again, in the course of Chub's hospitable invitation in the finale of the last act, the grazioso ' ballet ' element in Tchaïkovsky's musical make-up peeps out rather incongruously.

Broadly speaking, the operatic convention adopted in *Vakula* is the same as that of *The Oprichnik*—or the average Western opera of the same period : the convention of set numbers embedded in a more or less continuous texture. Thematic reminiscence is used even more sparingly than in *The Oprichnik*; indeed, the only theme with any claim to be considered a leitmotive in even the loosest sense of the word is Ex. 97a, which is referred to three or four times later : in the finale of Act I, when Vakula enters his mother's hut in the next scene, and in the final scene of the opera. (Oddly enough Ex. 97b is a form of the ' Vakula ' theme of *Christmas Eve*.) The overture to the opera is sectional, like that to *The Oprichnik*, but considerably longer, and as there are no dramatic elements to be opposed to each other the piece is a purely musical composition on themes from the opera :

> Introduction (andante con moto).
> Song of the *kobza*-players from the final scene (andante).
> Allegro giusto in sonata form, based on a new version of the devil-and-Solokha hopak for first subject and a new version of the Vakula theme for second.
> Song of the *kobza*-players.
> Coda (più mosso and allegro vivace), based on the final chorus.

After *Vakula* Tchaïkovsky was attracted in turn by *Ephraim*, a libretto by his friend K. S. Shilovsky about happenings at the court of Pharaoh at the time of Moses (obviously inspired by *Aïda*, which had been produced in Petersburg two or three months earlier), by a *Francesca da Rimini* by K. I. Zvantsev (of which the only result was the well-known symphonic fantasia), and the already-mentioned *Othello* libretto by Stassov. In May 1877 his brother Modest sent him the scenario of an opera based on Charles Nodier's *Ines de Las-Sierras*, but in the very letter in which the composer rejects *Ines* as 'too episodic and too little poetic' he tells the story of Elizaveta Lavrovskaya's suggestion that he should compose a *Eugene Onegin*. On the face of it, it seems rather a crazy idea; Pushkin's poem is a 'novel in verse,' not a drama, and it lacks most of the elements of drama; most of its charm lies in the tone and the poetry of the narrative.[1] 'It struck me as wild, and I made no reply,' says Tchaïkovsky himself. But after a time he thought it 'possible'; bought a Pushkin with some difficulty—it was Vol. 1 of the 1838 edition, for the copy has been preserved—spent a sleepless night and produced a scenario corresponding very closely to the action of the opera as we know it and which I quote in place of a synopsis :

> *First Act.* Scene 1 : Mme. Larina and the nurse are sitting in the garden, making preserves. Duet. A song is heard from the house : Tatyana and Olga sing a duet with harp-accompaniment. Enter reapers (with the last sheaf); they sing and dance. Suddenly the servant announces guests. Enter Eugene and Lensky. Ceremony of introduction and entertainment (bilberry wine). Eugene exchanges impressions with Lensky and Tatyana with Olga : quintet *à la Mozart.* The older women go away to prepare dinner. The young people stay and walk in the garden in pairs (as in Faust). Tatyana is reserved at first, then falls in love.
> Scene II : Tatyana's letter.
> Scene III : Scene between Onegin and Tatyana.

[1] The English or American reader is referred to Professor Oliver Elton's translation (Pushkin Press, 1943), or that by Babette Deutsch in a volume of Pushkin translations edited by A. Yarmolinsky (Nonesuch Press, 1940).

Second Act. Scene I : Tatyana's name-day. Ball. Lensky's jealousy. He insults Onegin and challenges him. General confusion. Scene II : Lensky's aria and the duel.

Third Act. Scene I : Moscow. Ball in the Nobles' Hall. Tatyana meets a whole string of aunts and cousins. They sing a chorus. Appearance of the general. He falls in love with Tatyana. She tells him her story and agrees to marry him.

Scene II : Petersburg. Tatyana awaits Onegin. He appears. Big duet. Tatyana still loves him and fights a hard inner battle with herself. Her husband comes. Duty triumphs. Onegin rushes off in despair.[1]

In the definitive form of the opera the principal changes were these :

In Act I, scene 1, there is no ' ceremony of entertainment ' and no ' quintet *à la Mozart* '; the nurse Filipyevna disappears before the young men enter and Mme. Larina leaves her daughters alone with the visitors almost immediately. Then follows a *quartet* which might be charitably regarded as *à la Mozart*.

Act III, scene 1, was entirely abandoned in favour of a different ball scene, in Petersburg. Instead of a shy debutante, Tatyana is already a polished woman of the world and already married to ' the general,' now christened ' Prince Gremin.' Onegin sees her at this ball.

The very end of the opera gave Tchaïkovsky considerable trouble. Tatyana repulses the man who had once repulsed her (' But now, to-day, my turn has come.') And in Pushkin the scene ends with her quiet, firm avowal (I quote from Professor Elton's admirable version) :

> . . . I love you (why sophisticate it?),
> But am another's, pledged; and I
> To him stay constant, till I die.'
> ....
> So she departed : and Evgeny
> Like a man thunderstricken stood

till the sound of the husband's approach breaks the spell. In his own copy of the poem Tchaïkovsky first of all underlined the words ' So she departed,' as if he had intended to follow the poet closely, then crossed out the underlining, allowed Tatyana ' overcome with emotion ' to ' sink on Onegin's breast ' and added six pages (in vocal score) of passionate love-duet before she finally nerves herself to dismiss her lover. (There is no final appearance of the husband, as

---

[1] Unlike the earlier operas I have discussed, the story of *Onegin* must be well enough known to every reader to make further elucidation of this scenario unnecessary.

in the poem and the first draft of the scenario.) Even so, the definitive version of the end (made before the first professional performance of the opera at the Bolshoy Theatre, Moscow, on January 11/23, 1881) is said to be closer to Pushkin than the version given at the actual first performance (by students of the Moscow Conservatoire in the Maly Theatre on March 17/29, 1879). One curious point: in the original libretto Onegin's final words were ' O death, O death, I go to seek thee!'; according to N. Rukavishnikov[1] ' the composer apparently did not care much for this phrase and made no protest when it was changed.' But no one knows who was responsible for the substituted line, ' Anguish! Dishonour! How pitiful my fate!'

But, broadly speaking, the libretto is Tchaïkovsky's own.[2] He preserved Pushkin's own verses wherever possible and imitated his style to the best of his ability in the necessarily numerous interpolations, though these changes and interpolations in a passionately loved classic—almost as much as the lack of conventional drama and the not so very long out-of-date costume of the 1830's—were probably a principal cause of *Onegin's* slow success in its early days.[3] Thanks to the preservation of Tchaïkovsky's own copy of the poem, we can even trace in his underlinings and crossings-out, not only his shaping of the libretto from most unpromising material, but (as Rukavishnikov says) his ' deep sympathy for Tatyana and Lensky and a certain coldness towards Onegin.' For instance, in the margin of stanza xxiii of Chapter I, describing Onegin's fashionable room, the composer has scribbled: ' unpleasant.' But Chapter IV, stanza xi, where Onegin is touched by Tatyana's letter, is marked and there are signs that Tchaïkovsky at first had some thought of setting the five following stanzas—Onegin's ' sermonising'—more or less as they stand; he has scribbled a more singable alternative for one line; but the final text of Onegin's aria in Act I, scene 3, though it still embodies a number of Pushkin's lines, was practically written afresh. The poem written by Lensky during the night before the duel (VI, xxi and xxii) was used in its entirety, though with some

---

[1] In a fascinating study of ' Pushkin in Tchaïkovsky's Library ' (*Sovetskaya Muzika*, January 1937) to which I am indebted for a number of particulars concerning Tchaïkovsky's work on his three Pushkin libretti.

[2] The French and Russian texts of the couplets sung by the French guest, Triquet, in Act II, scene 1, were written by K. S. Shilovsky, who also had some hand in the expansion of the original draft scenario. Judging from Tchaïkovsky's letter to his brother-in-law of May 19/31, 1877, and other statements, Shilovsky embarked on the whole libretto, but nothing came of this.

[3] Having seen a vocal score of the opera, Turgenev wrote to Leo Tolstoy (November 15/27, 1878): ' Undoubtedly notable music. The lyrical, melodic passages are particularly good. But what a libretto! '

expansion at the end, as the text of his famous aria in Act II, scene 2; before the line ' Will come, fair maiden,' Tchaïkovsky has noted in the margin: ' ret. of I theme ' (the first theme does actually return here), and he ringed round the last two lines of the twenty-second stanza, marking them ' conclusion ' (they provide the basis of the andante mosso coda), showing that the musical form of the aria had begun to take shape in his mind at a very early stage—possibly even at the first reading. Similarly stanzas xx and xxi of Chapter II were adapted—the third person being changed to first—for Lensky's arioso in the first scene.

But the majority of Tchaïkovsky's marginal markings, and the majority of his more wholesale borrowings from the original text, relate to Tatyana, with whom he was from the first ' absolutely in love.' It was Tatyana who aroused that ' love and pity, as for a real person ' which he needed if he was to be genuinely inspired. He told Kashkin many years afterwards : ' I had so familiarised myself with the figure of Tatyana that she had become for me a living person in living surroundings. I loved Tatyana and was terribly indignant with Onegin, who seemed to me a cold, heartless cox-comb.[1] He began to set Tatyana's famous letter even before he prepared his libretto.[2] Indeed, two-thirds of the whole opera was written or at least roughed out in short score, by June 23/July 5, 1877 —that is, in little more than five weeks after Mme. Lavrovskaya's suggestion; the non-completion of the score till January of the following year was due partly to work on the Fourth Symphony, another favourite work which was composed side by side with *Onegin*, but mainly to the composer's catastrophic marriage and the illness that followed it.

The best way to approach the music of *Onegin* is by beginning where Tchaïkovsky began: with Tatyana's letter. Though as it was composed before the libretto existed, we should remember that this could not have been the whole letter scene as we now know it, but only the letter itself, beginning with the words ' I write to you without reflection ' (in H. G. Chapman's English version of the libretto) or rather with the orchestral passage, moderato assai, quasi andante, leading up to them and continuing under them with the

[1] For his account to Kashkin of the manner in which this illusion of Tatyana's reality, and the parallel between her behaviour and Antonina Milyukova's, became a factor—or so he alleged—in his decision to marry the latter, I must refer the reader to the chapter on ' *Eugene Onegin* and Tchaïkovsky's Marriage ' in my book *On Russian Music* (William Reeves, 1939).

[2] According to Kashkin, he had thought long before of setting the letter as a solo song.

voice part as purely incidental as in any of the Wagner passages to which Tchaïkovsky objected. (One notices the same thing at Tatyana's entrance in the ball scene in Act III, where all the essential music lies in the orchestra—the charming and characteristic clarinet melody—and the vocal parts are simply patched on; Tchaïkovsky had been at Bayreuth the year before he wrote *Onegin* and, however un-Wagnerian the stuff of his music, he was not altogether un-affected by Wagner's methods.) But the orchestral conception is masterly; the simple oboe line crossed by the dropping fourths and fifths of flute, clarinet and horn and the light splash of the harp magically not only conveys the naïve character and romantic mood of the writer but suggests, almost pantomimically, the act of writing in a way comparable with, though not like, the 'writing' passages in *Boris Godunov* and *Khovanschina* (the scene in Pimen's cell and the scene of the public scribe). This fusion of emotional expression with graphic tone-painting is sustained throughout the letter, even through the less successful 'No, never any other' passage, and towards the end, as Tatyana's passion approaches its climax, the dual quality of the music also touches a new level in a horn phrase of melting warmth (Ex. 99) which contains the purest essence of Tchaïkovskian melody while the harmony of the second bar touches the very nerve centre of Russian romantic harmony (the flattened sixth). As I pointed out elsewhere,[1] that horn phrase, or rather its first few notes, became a sort of motto-theme for the whole opera, though doubtless an unconscious one. (To have used it deliberately as it is used would have been pointless.)

We hear it first in the duet behind the scenes which opens the first act. It occurs in a little phrase piped out by flute and oboe at the end of the quartet when Onegin first looks at the shy girl 'rather familiarly' and then goes up to her. We hear it again in the viola phrases which close the love scene between Olga and Lensky, and once more (in the orchestra) near the beginning of the second scene, when Tatyana says to her old nurse: 'Amuse me; and tell me some tale of long ago.' In the letter scene itself it occurs quite early in a different musical context. It assumes two different forms in Gremin's aria in Act III, and it occurs again in Tatyana's sweeping phrase which dominates the last passionate scene of the opera.

Indeed, the whole score—from the short monothematic introduction to the final avowal—is saturated with the spirit, if not the letter, of that warm, lyrical motto-theme. Although he gives his name to the work, Onegin himself is not the principal figure as he

[1] *On Russian Music*, p. 233.

is in Pushkin's poem. It is Tatyana who takes the centre of the stage, as indeed she nearly does in Pushkin; Tchaïkovsky could identify himself with her shy, affectionate, quintessentially feminine character more completely than with any male character in his operas, more even than with Hermann in *The Queen of Spades*; and to paint her musical portrait he only had to pour out freely the peculiar kind of lyrical melody which constitutes the most individual element in his musical make-up. So, like Mozart's heroines, she is not merely a character set to appropriate music; she exists *as* music. To a less extent, that is true of Lensky also. He, too, is a piece of musical self-projection on Tchaïkovsky's part; though, being a less definite and less intensely sympathetic figure than Tatyana, even the best of his music—his arioso in Act I and the famous aria before the duel—has less warmth and less character than hers. But the titular hero comes to life musically only when he echoes Tatyana's music—as he does with superbly ironic effect in the penultimate scene: discovering his passion for the transformed Tatyana in the very music of the opening of the letter scene, here beautifully led up to. Or in his ' sermonising ' aria (Act I, scene 3) where once again the ' motto ' from Ex. 99 steals into the vocal line (' You *are what I do most admire* ').

The rest of the music is ' background.' Not ' background music ' in the common sense of the phrase, but music painting the background of the novel; for, just as Pushkin called his poem a ' novel in verse,' it remains a musico-poetic novel—rather than a drama— when transferred to the stage.[1] In the first act it paints the country setting with liberal quantities of attractive folk-music (or folkish music) : the chorus and dance of the reapers, the scene of Tatyana and the nurse, the oboe-pipe of the shepherd sounding so magically cool and fresh after the passion of the letter scene, the Glinka- like chorus of girls gathering berries (taken direct from Pushkin) which so effectively and ironically frames the Tatyana-Onegin scene in the garden. Throughout a great deal of the second and third acts it has to paint ball settings, the country ' hop ' at the Larins and the fashionable assembly in St. Petersburg, and there too Tchaïkovsky was in his element with valse and mazurka and polo- naise.[2] Everything in *Onegin* seems specially made for Tchaï-

---

[1] There is a more modern parallel in Delius's *Fennimore and Gerda*, based on Jens Peter Jacobsen's novel, *Niels Lyhne*.

[2] The écossaise in the last act was added in August 1885 at the request of Vsevolozhsky, Director of the Imperial Theatres, and there is extant an amusing letter of Tchaïkovsky's to his publisher in which he admits that, after a long discussion with

kovsky; even Triquet's pseudo-rococo couplets ,were not arbitrarily inserted by him like the couplets in *Cherevichki*; they are justified by the poem (V, xxvii).[1] That is why *Onegin* is his operatic master-piece. From a purely musical point of view, *Vakula* is perhaps more beautiful. It is, as Tchaïkovsky recognised, more finely wrought, *too* finely wrought; *Onegin*, besides possessing a heroine equally attractive musically as Oksana and twenty times more attractive dramatically, has more of that broad simplicity, that human warmth, without which no opera—however fine musically—can hope to keep the stage.

Yet Tchaïkovsky himself feared that even *Onegin* would be ineffective. On August 30/September 11, 1877, 'when the first fire had passed off' and he could 'consider the composition objectively,' he confided to Nadezhda von Meck his fear that it was 'condemned to fail and to be ignored by the mass of the public. Its content is very unsophisticated, there are no scenic effects, the music lacks brilliance and rhetorical effectiveness.' It is true there may be some chosen spirits who 'hearing this music, will be touched by those emotions which agitated me when I wrote it.' But 'on the stage *Onegin* won't be *interesting*. For it won't satisfy the first require-ment of opera—*scenic movement*.' His only hope is that it will please those who are capable of appreciating in opera 'the simple, everyday feelings common to all mankind.' Later, writing to Taneev in more pugnacious mood, he could 'spit on all stage effect.' But he was always sure that *Onegin* could have no future in the theatre. And he almost rejoiced in the fact, for he dreaded to see these ideal characters reduced to the painful realities of the opera stage.

In a letter to Nadezhda von Meck of December 16/28, 1877, he writes:

> Where shall I find the *Tatyana* whom Pushkin imagined and whom I've tried to illustrate musically? Where is the artist who can even approach the ideal Onegin, that cold dandy penetrated to the marrow with worldly *bon ton*? Where is there a Lensky, an eighteen-year-old youth with the thick curls and the impetuous and original ways of a

---

Vsevolozhsky of the kind of dance to be inserted, he agreed on an écossaise without in the least knowing what an écossaise was like: 'I believe Schubert wrote écossaises. If not, perhaps you can tell me where I can find one for a model. . . . I *must* have an écossaise.' The one he actually wrote, Modest tells us, was composed, orchestrated and sent to Petersburg in one day; it sounds like it.

[1] A few months before taking up *Onegin* Tchaïkovsky had set Almaviva's couplets 'Vous l'ordonnez' in *Le Barbier de Séville* for a student performance in the Maly Theatre, Moscow.

young poet *à la* Schiller? How Pushkin's charming picture will be vulgarised when it's transferred to the stage with its routine, its senseless traditions, its veterans of both sexes who—like Alexandrova and Kommisarzhevsky *i tutti quanti*—shamelessly take on the rôles of sixteen-year-old girls and beardless youths!

The whole thing was not so much an opera as ' lyrical scenes ' conceived for ' limited resources and a small stage.' It is very odd that, having found the subject which perfectly satisfied his demands for real and sympathetic characters, for strong, simple human emotions, Tchaïkovsky should ever have felt so doubtful about it— after the first overpowering burst of enthusiasm—and that he should never have returnel to anything like it, except partially in *The Queen of Spades.*

In one respect the music of *Eugene Onegin* accidentally, though strikingly, symbolises the change that came over Tchaïkovsky's music at about this period: the folk-music is all in Act I, there is none in the rest of the work. In most of the works we have discussed up to this point—*The Voevoda, The Oprichnik, Snow Maiden, Vakula the Smith,* in fact all except *Undine*—there has been a strong national flavour in much of the music, a flavour that has never failed to heighten its charm. After *Onegin*—or rather, after the first act of *Onegin*—that flavour suddenly becomes much fainter and except in the first act of *The Sorceress,* almost disappears.[1] For a time Tchaïkovsky turns abruptly away from Russian subjects. He even returns to the old *Undine* theme, having come across Zhukovsky's translation of the tale again in his sister's library at Kamenka, and commissions his brother Modest to prepare a scenario; only to discover, as a result of re-reading *Romeo and Juliet,* that ' Undine, Berthalda, Huldbrand and the rest are childish nonsense.' He will ' of course write a *Romeo and Juliet* '; it will be ' my supreme masterpiece '; and one can only regret that he allowed himself to be frightened away from the subject by its ' awful difficulty ' and the fact that Gounod had already used it. The fact that Verdi had written a *Giovanna d'Arco* did *not,* however, deter him from essaying a *Maid of Orleans.*

This idea first came to Tchaïkovsky in April 1878, at the same time as the revival of interest in *Undine* and in the same way: among Zhukovsky's works he came across his translation of

---

[1] On the other hand, even in *The Maid of Orleans,* where Tchaïkovsky was deliberately trying to be non-Russian, the French king lapses into an unmistakably Russian accent (his first recitative in the finale of Act III), and the opening chorus of girls is Glinka-like in texture.

Schiller's *Jungfrau von Orleans*. But nothing came of it till seven months later. Then at the end of November he tells Madame von Meck that he is ' seriously attracted ' to this subject for his next opera. He wants to get hold of the libretto of Auguste Mermet's *Jeanne d'Arc* produced in Paris a couple of years before; he has already bought Verdi's ' extremely bad ' work and thinks it will be useful to compare the libretto with Mermet's, which he has heard highly praised[1]; in Paris he must also buy some books on Joan of Arc. And Nadezhda von Meck promptly makes him a present of a very expensive one, Henri-Alexandre Wallon's *Jeanne d'Arc*, reading which he ' wept a great deal over the passage describing her execution (when she was led to the stake she screamed and begged to be beheaded instead of burned). I felt infinite sorrow for all mankind . . . ' (letter to Modest, December 10/22, 1878). But he was still puzzling over the libretto and had not yet settled on a definite plan. ' A great deal in Schiller pleases me, but I must confess his contempt for historical truth somewhat discourages me.

He wished to keep to Schiller's—or, rather, Zhukovsky's—text as closely as possible, but there were, of course ' too many characters and too many secondary episodes.' And there were other points:

> For example, Schiller has a scene where Joan fights with Lionel. For various considerations, I should like to substitute Montgomery for Lionel. Is this possible? Are these historical characters? To know all this, I shall have to read a few books. Meanwhile I've taken direct from Zhukovsky one scene which, in any case, I shall have to have, even if I don't find it in Mermet: the scene where the King, archbishop and knights recognise Joan as an ambassador from on high.

Finally he came to the conclusion that ' although Schiller's tragedy doesn't conform to historical truth, it surpasses all other artistic portrayals of Joan in deep psychological truth.' Even before this, without a libretto, without even a scenario, he had begun the music of that essential scene of Joan's recognition on December 5/17 and had finished it (i.e., all the second part of Act II) in five days. Then, at Clarens, on the last day of the old year (January 12, 1879, new style) Tchaïkovsky wrote the chorus of girls that opens the first act—and completed the whole work, words and music, on February 21/March 5, though the scoring was not finished till the following August. The music came easily enough, but the libretto cost him endless trouble and he gave Nadezhda von Meck

---

[1] When he did get Mermet's libretto, he found ' his scenario very bad, though with two or three effective scenes which I may be able to use.'

an amusing account of the number of penholders gnawed away in the effort to compose a few lines. He had particular difficulty with the rhymes and lamented the non-existence of a Russian rhyming dictionary. The final scenario was based mainly on Schiller-Zhukovsky (the text 'preserving many of Zhukovsky's verses' as the title-page of the opera reassures us) but with one or two additions or modifications from Wallon's book, Jules Barbier's tragedy *Jeanne d'Arc* (final scene) and the Mermet libretto (beginning of Act I):

> *Act* I. Joan (soprano)[1] and village-girls are decorating the Druids' oak. Enter her father Thibaut (bass) and her lover Raimond (tenor); Thibaut presses Joan to marry. She says she is destined for 'another fate'; Thibaut reproaches her for commerce with evil spirits. Distant fires are seen. Enter fugitive villagers, one of whom, the aged Bertrand (bass), describes the wretched state of France. Joan prophesies the expulsion of the English and says Salisbury[2] is already killed; she is disbelieved but her second-sight is immediately confirmed by a soldier (bass) who has just come from Orleans. The people are convinced. Left alone, Joan realises that ' her hour is come ' and takes a passionate farewell of her home —strengthened and comforted by a chorus of angels.

> *Act* II. The castle at Chinon. The King (tenor), with Agnes Sorel (soprano) and Dunois (baritone), is being entertained by the songs of minstrels and the dances of gypsies and buffoons. Dunois tries to nerve the King to action, but he cannot bring himself to leave Agnes. A wounded warrior, Lauret (bass), is brought in with news of another defeat and dies at the King's feet. Agnes consoles the King. Short love-duet. Enter a chorus of people hailing ' the Saviour Maid '; Dunois announces the victory; the Archbishop (bass) tells how an unknown girl has turned the tide of battle. Enter Joan, who picks out the King from among the courtiers, tells him his secret prayers, and relates the story of her life; all present recognise her as an emissary of Heaven.

> *Act* III. Scene 1 : Near a battlefield and the burning English camp. Enter Lionel, a Burgundian knight (baritone), pursued by Joan. They fight, but when she has him at her mercy, she sees his face— and spares him. Unwillingly they fall in love. Dunois appears with a detachment. Instead of fleeing Lionel surrenders to him and offers to join the King's party; Dunois joyfully accepts him.

---

[1] In Russian she becomes ' Ioanna ' after Schiller's ' Johanna.' Though written for a soprano the rôle was taken at the first performance (Maryinsky Theatre, Petersburg, February 13/25, 1881) by a mezzo, Mme Kamenskaya, and various transpositions and adjustments had to be made. For the sake of the same fine exponent of the part, further temporary changes were made in 1882, but the definitive form of the opera remains the same as the original form.

[2] Which Tchaikovsky sets as a four-syllable word: ' Sa-lis-bou-ry.'

Scene 2: The Square before Rheims Cathedral. As the Coronation procession leaves the Cathedral, Thibaut denounces Joan as an agent of Hell, and when he and the Archbishop ask Joan if she 'considers herself pure and holy' she remains silent because of her guilty love for Lionel. Lionel comes forward as the champion of her innocence but his challenge is answered by thunder. 'It is the voice of Heaven!' say the people. 'She is guilty!' The King banishes her from Rheims. When Lionel tries to accompany her, she repulses him as ' her foe and the ruin of her soul.'

Act IV. Scene 1: Joan is sitting in a wood, deep in thought. She admits the reality of her love for Lionel—who promptly appears. They embrace. Their love-duet is interrupted first by the angelic voices who tell Joan she will atone for her sin by suffering and death, then by the advent of ' British ' soldiers who kill Lionel and take Joan prisoner.

Scene 2: Rouen. Joan is led to the stake and the fire is lit.

Absurd and distasteful as this romantic manipulation of historic facts undeniably is, Tchaïkovsky could at least plead that he had kept nearer the truth than Schiller, who allowed Joan to escape from her captors, rescue the wretched Charles VII (who had got captured too) and die on the battlefield, standard in hand, surrounded by her friends. Just before his death, however, Tchaïkovsky—plagued by his brother Modest—was contemplating the substitution of Schiller's ' rose-coloured death scene,' as Schlegel called it, for his own gloomily veracious one. He might also have contended that the ridiculous Joan-Lionel fight and love-affair had the respectable operatic precedent of Tancred and Clorinda, and pointed out that his transformation of Schiller's Lionel from an English general into a Burgundian knight has the very faintest justification in the fact that the historic Joan surrendered at Compiègne to a Burgundian named Lionel. But Tchaïkovsky's Lionel has very little in common with Schiller's. Schiller's Lionel does not surrender to Dunois or change sides; indeed, he sees Joan only once more, when she is a prisoner; their love remains on a purely ideal and abstract plane. The Lionel at the end of Act III, scene 2, is essentially Schiller's Dunois; the Lionel of Act IV, scene 1, is purely a creation of Tchaïkovsky's own. But there is little point in discussing the origin or behaviour of a baritone in fancy dress. And in saying that, we put our finger on the crippling weakness of the whole opera.

As we have seen from his remarks to Karl Waltz, ' medieval dukes and knights and ladies captivate my imagination but not my *heart*, and where the heart is not touched there can't be any music.'

Not only Lionel but Charles VII and Dunois and Agnes and even the grim old peasant father are merely characters in fancy dress; they never touched Tchaïkovsky's heart and never evoked from him any real music. But Joan herself? We know at least that he was deeply moved by her martyrdom, though even this was ultimately portrayed simply by a gloomily effective funeral march which emphasises only the pitiless cruelty of her captors and expresses neither Joan's courage and nobility nor her human weakness, reflects none of that ' infinite sorrow for all mankind ' aroused by the reading of Wallon's description. On the whole, Joan too remains only a lay figure—except in one passage: her ' narrative ' in the second act and her recognition as the emissary of Heaven. That passage, as we have seen, was written first as Tatyana's letter scene was written first and it rises even higher above the rest of the opera than the letter scene does in *Onegin*. Even the 'cello melody to which she enters—it recurs again at the end of the act, and in the Coronation scene when the King points to Joan as ' the ambassadress of Heaven '—though simple ' processional ' music, has a quiet dignity that saves it from the banal; Joan's snatch of recitative, ' I saw thee, but only where none but God saw thee,' has the exquisite sweetness of nineteenth-century French opera at its best; and the King's outburst, ' I believe, I believe : this cannot be by man alone,' oddly reminds one of the opening of Elgar's A flat Symphony (perhaps because both were evidently written under the influence of the A flat passage of Chopin's F minor Fantaisie). But all this is only the prelude to Joan's narration proper, which is so beautiful that its neglect in favour of the far inferior ' farewell ' aria in Act I is quite incomprehensible. I quote the opening (Ex. 100) : ' Holy father, they call me Joan; I am the daughter of a simple shepherd,' or as Schiller has it :

> Ehrwürd'ger Herr, Johanna nennt man mich.
> Ich bin nur eines Hirten niedre Tochter

for Tchaïkovsky has set Zhukovsky's version quite straightforwardly. And the phrase a little later to which Joan sings the words of the heavenly apparition, ' Rise up and leave your flock ' (' Ich bin's. Steh auf, Johanna. Lass die Herde '), was used throughtout the opera—though generally sung elsewhere by an invisible choir of angels—as the motive of the ' heavenly voices.' (There are one or two other cases of thematic reminiscence in the score—notably the ironic use of the melody to which the Archbishop has acclaimed Joan in the finale of Act II, when he is challenging her innocence in the

finale of Act III—but nothing approaching a Wagnerian leitmotive.)[1]
Here in this narration, and here alone, is Joan herself adequately
characterised in the music; having written it Tchaïkovsky seems to
have been deserted by his inspiration.

There is very little in the rest of the score that even bears the stamp
of Tchaïkovsky's musical personality. Perhaps the most Tchaïkovskian things, both melodically and orchestrally, are Joan's familiar
' farewell ' aria and her two duets with Lionel, but all three are
weak Tchaïkovsky. And the G flat coda of the duettino for Agnes
and the King, though recognisably from the same hand, also helps
one to recognise the general influence on Tchaïkovsky's style of the
famous duet in the same key in the fourth act of *Les Huguenots*.
But if Tchaïkovsky had always been conscious of Meyerbeer, he
had never been so much so in *The Maid of Orleans*. The whole
work is so deliberately French, so completely conceived in terms of
the Paris Grand Opera and its great crowd effects, that it is not
unkind to assume that the secret motive controlling its inception
and execution was the hope of a great operatic triumph in Western
Europe. And one must admit the success, the stagey effectiveness,
of some of the music conceived in these terms: for instance, the
finale of Act II, the Coronation music, the final scene. Nor do we
need the testimony of Tchaïkovsky's letters to gather that at this
period he was particularly interested in contemporary French opera,
the post-Meyerbeerian and more lyrical stage-works of Massenet
and the rest; many pages of *The Maid* reflect their palest and most
sugary melodiousness, while Agnes' arioso in Act II might have
been written by Gounod[2] in one of his happier moments. Yet
another French symptom is the long ballet—twenty-one pages of
piano score—forcibly inserted in the second act. A couple of lines
in Schiller do offer a slight pretext for the chorus of minstrels,
but this ballet, lacking even the slight dramatic justification for the
dances in *The Oprichnik* and *Vakula* (to say nothing of *Onegin*,
where the ballet is essential), simply holds up the action. However,
as music the ballet is by no means the worst part of the score, and

[1] A reminiscence of a different kind is prominent in the King's music in Act II,
where Tchaïkovsky did not realise that he was remembering the opening of the
Jupiter Symphony.

[2] ' Gounod is a first-rate master, if not a first-rate creative genius,' Tchaïkovsky
had written a year or two before (April 8/20, 1877). ' In the sphere of opera, I
consider that, with the exception of Wagner, there is no living composer to whom it
would not be an honour to enter into rivalry with Gounod. So far as I am concerned
I should consider myself a happy man if I could write an opera half as beautiful as
Faust.' Tchaïkovsky's admiration for Gounod was really limited to that one work.

the final buffoons' dance with its angular syncopations (Ex. 101) to which piquantly scored counterpoints are added later, might well be included in the orchestral repertoire. That can hardly he said of the introduction to the opera, much longer that the brief mono-thematic prelude to *Onegin* but less well organised than the over-ture to *Vakula*; it begins promisingly with a beautiful little flute theme treated somewhat like the descent of the Grail, with increas-ingly full scoring, breaks off into the alarm music of the first scene, builds up to Joan's song in the finale of Act I, returns to the open-ing music—and then peters out in a long and quite incredibly empty and showy flute cadenza.

In less than four months after the production of *The Maid of Orleans* Tchaïkovsky informed his publisher that he was contem-plating yet another opera : ' This is now the only form of composi-tion capable of arousing my enthusiasm. I've got hold of a very decent libretto, given me by K. Y. Davidov, who had himself begun to write an opera on it but gave it up for want of time. The libretto is based on Pushkin's *Poltava* and has been put together by Burenin.[1] So you can take it that if I write anything big it will be an opera ' (letter of June 4/16, 1881). During the next two or three months he wrote four numbers—though which four I do not know—for this new opera, afterwards named *Mazeppa* after its villain-hero, but he wrote with no enthusiasm; he had at this period lost all taste for composition, everything seemed ' *remplissage*, routine and hackneyed technical devices.' (A decade or so later Rimsky-Korsakov was to pass through a precisely similar phase.) By October *Mazeppa* was abandoned; Tchaïkovsky had returned to ' the old yet ever new subject of *Romeo and Juliet* ' and it was probably at this time that he began to sketch out the love-duet, partly based on material from his overture-fantasia, which was posthumously completed and scored by Taneev. But before the month was out, he was clamouring for a copy of Luka Antropov's play *Vanka the Steward*, based on a story by D. V. Averkiev. The subject was ' very sympa-thetic '—mainly, it appears, because it centred on a love scene in a garden at night, ' more or less on the lines of *Romeo and Juliet*.' And sure enough, at the end of November he began to compose a love scene in a room with doors open on a garden at night; but it was the scene between Mariya and Mazeppa. ' One fine day,' he told Nadezhda von Meck (May 29/June 10, 1882):

---

[1] Viktor Petrovich Burenin, a poet and critic who died as recently as 1926 at the age of eighty-five.

I re-read the libretto and skimmed over Pushkin's poem, was touched by several scenes and verses—and began with the scene between Mariya and Mazeppa, which had been transferred unchanged from the poem to the libretto. Although up to now I have not experienced the profound joy that I felt in composing *Eugene Onegin*, for example; although on the whole the composition progresses quietly and I don't feel particularly attracted by the characters—still I'm writing and I've already achieved something.

Actually the bulk of the composition was done between the date of that letter and September 15/27, and the orchestration was finished by April 28/May 10, 1883. The first performance was given in the Bolshoy Theatre, Moscow, on February 3/15 of the following year.

Although Tchaïkovsky preserved Burenin's scenario, he made considerable cuts and changes in the actual libretto, inserting or adapting Pushkin's own verses where possible. This was not often, for *Poltava* is a narrative poem of which only the first two cantos are concerned with Mazeppa's love and treason (the subject of the opera) while the third and most important, the crown of the whole, is devoted to a marvellous description of the Battle of Poltava and to the glorification of Peter the Great and the triumph of the new Russian state over both foreign invaders and Ukrainian separatists. But it is interesting to the Russian if not to the English reader to trace how the composer takes, for instance, the words in which Pushkin addresses Mariya and adapts them to be sung by Mariya herself; the two copies of *Poltava* in which he made his marginal notes and scribbled new bits of libretto are still preserved (or were until the present war), and in one instance he has begun to sketch a musical idea (Ex. 102) beside the passage that suggested it: which is interesting as evidence of the way in which musical germs occurred to him, though the equivalent passage in the finished opera bears no relation to it; even the word ' Poslusha ' (' Listen! '), is changed to ' Skazhi ' (Tell me!).

The action of Mazeppa in its definitive form is as follows:

Act I. Scene 1 : Garden of the rich Cossack Kochubey; girls are fortune-telling by throwing wreaths into the river. Enter Kochubey's daughter, Mariya (soprano), who after the departure of the girls confesses her love for their guest, the elderly hetman Mazeppa.[1] Enter the young Cossack Andrey (tenor), who tells her of his hopeless love for her. Exeunt both. Enter Mazeppa (baritone), Kochubey (bass), the latter's wife Lyubov (mezzo-soprano),

[1] His little adventure on the horse had happened some forty years earlier.

Mariya, guests, musicians, servants, etc. Entertainment with songs and dances. Left alone after the entertainment, Mazeppa asks Kochubey for his daughter's hand; Kochubey refuses on account of the hetman's age and the fact that he is Mariya's godfather. They quarrel violently and the noise brings back the others. Mazeppa fires his pistol, summoning his men, calls on Mariya to chose between him and her parents—and carries her off.

Scene 2[1] : Room in Kochubey's house. With him are his wife and friends, including Andrey and Iskra, governor of Poltava (tenor). Women lamenting for Mariya. Urged to revenge by his wife, Kochubey resolves to reveal to the Tsar Mazeppa's secret intrigues with the Swedes. Andrey volunteers to go to the Tsar.

Act II. Scene 1 : Dungeon in Belotserkovsky Castle; Kochubey chained to a pillar. The Tsar, trusting Mazeppa implicitly, has given his accusers into his power. Enter Orlik (bass), who demands to know where Kochubey's treasure is concealed; at the end he summons a torturer.

Scene 2 : Room in Mazeppa's castle; he is looking out into the starlit garden. Orlik comes to tell him that the torture has failed to make Kochubey reveal his secret. Enter Mariya, who knows nothing of her father's fate; she reproaches Mazeppa with his recent coldness and he reveals to her his plan to set up an independent Ukrainian state with himself as its head. Exit Mazeppa. Enter Lyubov, who tells Mariya the whole story and persuades her to plead with Mazeppa for her father's life.

Scene 3 : A field by the scaffold. A crowd of people, including a drunken Cossack (tenor). Enter executioners, Mazeppa on horseback, Orlik, and Cossacks; later Kochubey and Iskra guarded. Kochubey prays. At the moment the axes fall, Mariya and her mother rush in. Curtain.

Act III. Symphonic picture : 'The Battle of Poltava.' The curtain goes up, revealing the same scene as Act I, scene 1, but everything is now neglected and half-ruined. Fugitive Swedish soldiers cross the stage, pursued by Russians, including Andrey. He sings a long aria, then hides as he hears horsemen approaching. Mazeppa and Orlik pause in their flight. Andrey emerges from concealment and attacks Mazeppa, who shoots him. Enter Mariya, out of her mind. Orlik drags Mazeppa away. Mariya takes Andrey's head in her lap and, thinking herself back in the days of their childhood, sings a lullaby as he dies.

That, as I have said, is the definitive form of the action; as the opera was originally produced, the end was more protracted, the chorus entered after Andrey's death and Mariya, remembering the floating wreaths in the first scene, threw herself into the river. But

---

[1] The division of the first act was an afterthought. Apparently the action was originally conceived as continuous, without change of scene.

within a month after the first production Tchaïkovsky made up his mind to end with the lullaby, which he extended considerably. At the same time he cut some of the music at the end of the first scene, which tended to hold up the action, and made a number of drastic changes (mostly cuts but also some additions) in the big scene between Mariya and Mazeppa. At some later date he wrote an additional arioso in G flat for Mazeppa, to words by V. A. Kondourov, to be inserted *ad lib.* just before this scene.

We have seen that Tchaïkovsky began *Mazeppa*, as he had begun *Onegin* and *The Maid of Orleans*, with a scene in the middle of the opera, a scene that specially appealed to him. The scene between Mariya and Mazeppa has not left its musical mark on the rest of the opera as the horn-theme in Ex. 99 did on so much of *Onegin* —though oddly enough, Mariya's first words in the scene are sung to a motive very nearly identical with the opening of the horn-theme in the earlier opera, and the motive recurs elsewhere: in Act I when Mariya is left alone by the other girls, in the first scene between Mazeppa and Kochubey, in Kochubey's monologue in the dungeon scene, and in the accompaniment to Andrey's aria in Act III. But dramatically the scene is as important as Tatyana's letter scene or Joan of Arc's narrative, for it reveals at full length the character of the central figure—or in this case of the two principal characters. (The others are negligible; Kochubey comes to life only when he is half-dead from the torture, in the dungeon scene, a powerful, gloomy piece of work though over-praised by some Russian critics; and Andrey is simply a tenor ' stooge ' with some attractive but not quite first-rate lyrical music to sing. Both Mazeppa and Mariya are favourite types of Russian opera—and Russian fiction—but they are not quite stock figures from the Western point of view. Mariya is the less interesting, being one of those negative, all-suffering heroines in whom the Russian soul delights—or used to delight—and who inhabit the pages of every classical Russian novel and every classical Russian opera; like so many of her sisters, she lacks the positive traits which distinguish Sonya in *War and Peace* or Tatyana Larina in *Onegin*, both of whom really belong to this class. But Mazeppa is by no means the mere villain my bald summary of the action makes him appear to be; he is a romanticised, Byronised figure,[1] a ' divided ' character like a Dostoevsky

---

[1] Pushkin's Mazeppa ' is treated romantically and, though he is painted as a villain, his dark cunning character is calculated to exercise a powerful charm over the reader,' says D. S. Mirsky, in his *Pushkin* (Routledge, 1926).

hero, or Pushkin's and Mussorgsky's Boris Godunov, or Ivan the Terrible in *The Maid of Pskov*. He is potentially first-rate material, and Tchaïkovsky's limitations as a musical dramatist are precisely defined by the nature of his failure with him. For Tchaïkovsky to paint a character successfully in music, it was necessary for him to feel strong sympathy, to experience at least partial self-identifica tion, with it; and as we have seen he ' did not feel particularly attracted ' by any of the characters in *Mazeppa*. Though himself a divided character, he was incapable either of entering into Maz-eppa's or of drawing it objectively as a real, living whole. So, instead of a character living in terms of music like Mussorgsky's Boris or even Rimsky-Korsakov's Ivan the Terrible, we get only a character who behaves like an unmitigated villain and who has throughout the opera a sort of leitmotive (Ex. 103) suggesting his cruelty (I quote the form in which it is first heard, at the opening of the orchestral introduction to the opera), but who also breaks into beautiful and expressive music (e.g., the arioso in which he tells Kochubey of his love for Mariya) or poetises about the beauty of night in the Ukraine (beginning of Act II, scene 2) or sentiment-alises over Mariya and her youthful love for him (the inserted arioso in G flat). But the only place in the whole score where his character even begins to become integrated is the big scene with Mariya, and even here his portrait is musically inadequate.

When Mazeppa is telling Mariya of his ideal of a free and inde-pendent Ukraine, neither ' under the protection of Warsaw ' nor ' under the the despotism of Moscow,' Tchaïkovsky introduces a modified quotation, or rather allusion, of a kind common enough in literature but exceedingly rare in music : the orchestra underlines Mazeppa's words with a passage (see Ex. 104a) marked in the score by square brackets and the letters ' Zh.z.Ts.G.' (i.e., *Zhizn' za Tsarya Glinki*)—compounded of the mazurka from *Life for the Tsar* (Ex. 104b) and the ' Slavsya ' from the same opera (Ex. 104c), symbols of Warsaw and Moscow respectively. The point is, of course, far too subtle for an opera audience, perhaps too subtle for any audience. More obvious and more effective, if much less inter-esting, are the musical symbols of Russian victory in the ' Battle of Poltava ' intermezzo : the famous ' song of glorification ' ' Slava ' (introduced by Beethoven in the second Razumovsky quartet, by Mussorgsky in the Coronation scene of *Boris*, and by Rimsky-Korsakov in *The Tsar's Bride* and his *Overture on Russian Themes*), the liturgical chant which Tchaïkovsky himself had used

for the opening and climax of his *1812* Overture only a year or two
before, and a military march of the Petrine period.[1]

To what extent actual Russian, or rather Ukrainian, folk-tunes
are introduced in the rest of the score I cannot say. But the folkish
element plays an important part in the first act. The beautiful
opening chorus of girls in 5/4 time, for instance, might well have
been written by Glinka. And the whole of the following scene—
the entrance of Mazeppa, Kochubey and the rest, the choral song,
and the ensuing hopak (generally known as 'the Cossack Dance ')—
is attractively dyed in national colours, though even in the hopak
Tchaïkovsky rather unhappily uses a secondary cantabile melody of
his own as a foil to the folk or folkish, main theme (cf. the finale
of the Second Symphony and the finale of the Serenade for strings).
Otherwise the national element in the music is more or less limited
to the 'folk scene,' actually so called by the composer, with the song
of the drunken Cossack which Tchaïkovsky hotly defended to
Jurgenson, which precedes the grim and theatrical scene of the
execution. (Incidentally, in Pushkin Mariya arrives not in time to
see the execution but to see the scaffold being taken to pieces and
' two Cossacks lifting a coffin on to a cart.') But here again Tchaïkovsky, challenging comparison with Mussorgsky in the field of
choral realism, only demonstrates his inferiority, precisely as in the
similiar scene in *The Oprichnik*. Only in the irony of the contrast
between the song of the drunken Cossack and the scene of death
is there a dramatic value comparable with similar things in Mussorgsky, e.g., the lovely snatch of folk-song sung by Shaklovity over
the body of the murdered prince in *Khovanshchina*. There are
several touches of such irony in *Mazeppa* : for instance, the quotation of the melody to which Mariya has hailed Mazeppa as future
Tsar of the Ukraine again when, mad, she faces him in the last scene
(cf. the two appearances of the Archbishop's music in *The Maid of
Orleans*), and—still more effective, indeed a real master-stroke—the
lullaby which she sings over the body of Andrey.

This simple and beautiful song might well be given occasional
hearings in our concert-halls, but there are few musically outstanding numbers in *Mazeppa*. The melodic inspiration neither rises to
the level of Tchaïkovsky at his best nor falls to that of Tchaïkovsky
at his worst. It keeps—particularly in such numbers as Mariya's
arioso and duet with Andrey, Mazeppa's arioso in the first act, the

---

[1] In a letter to A. F. Fedotov, Tchaïkovsky some years later expressed his distaste
for the depicting in sounds of ' every sort of fight, assault, attack, etc.'

lament of Lyubov and the women, with its characteristic wood-wind embroideries, and Andrey's aria in the last scene—to a respectable level of warm and always unmistakably Tchaïkovskian lyricism, but never leaves one with anything to remember. One favourite device of Tchaïkovsky's—the orchestral echoing of the voice part, usually by a solo wood-wind instrument, to bridge the cæsuras (cf. the middle section of Lensky's aria in *Onegin* or the end of Ex. 100)—is used in *Mazeppa* more perhaps than in any other opera of Tchaïkovsky's; it becomes particularly wearisome when the voice part consists merely of short-winded arioso phrases.

Tchaïkovsky's choice of subject for his next opera[1] was once again decided by a single scene. His brother Modest tells the story:

> Peter Ilyich was at that time [i.e., January 1885] in search of an opera subject. I happened to be in Moscow and one day mentioned quite in passing that the scene of the meeting between ' Kuma ' and the young Prince in Shpazhinsky's drama *The Sorceress* would be very effective in an opera, though without recommending the drama itself for a libretto. Peter Ilyich immediately bought a lithographed copy of this play and went into raptures over the scene in question. That was decisive. The next day a letter was written to the author of *The Sorceress* with a request for the drama to be turned into an opera libretto.

Shpazhinsky agreed (January 21/February 2, 1885) and set to work forthwith, while Tchaïkovsky passed the time with the transformation of *Vakula the Smith* into *Cherevichki*.

The action of *The Sorceress* in its operatic form is as follows:

Act I. A low inn on the banks of the Oka, near Nizhny-Novgorod. Foka (bass) and Paisy (tenor), a vagabond monk, mingle with the drinkers who are gaming and quarrelling. Enter Foka's niece, the innkeeper Nastasya (nicknamed ' Kuma ' = ' gossip ') (soprano) with her friend Polya (mezzo-soprano). Boats pass on the river; the young Prince Yury (tenor), his huntsman Zhuran (bass) and their men are returning from a bear-hunt; when Yury has passed, '.Kuma' 's quietness suggests that she has fallen in love with him. Lukash (tenor), one of the drinkers, brings the alarming intelligence that Yury's father, Prince Nikita Kurlyatev (baritone), the Grand Ducal vice-regent of Nizhny-Novgorod, is approaching with the puritanical old clerk Mamïrov (bass), who has brought his master to see for himself the scandals of this inn of ill-repute. The drinkers are all frightened, but ' Kuma ' keeps her presence

---

[1] Among the other opera subjects that temporarily attracted Tchaïkovsky's attention in the early eighteen-eighties was the legend of Sadko, afterwards used by Rimsky-Korsakov.

of mind and at once bewitches the Prince by her beauty and simplicity. She brings him wine and calls the inevitable *skomorokhi* (tumblers) to amuse him. Mamïrov is furious and 'Kuma' mischievously induces the Prince to order him to dance too. General mockery of the old puritan.

Act II. The garden of the Prince's house. His wife, Princess Evprak-siya (mezzo-soprano), is pale and ill with jealousy, for he visits 'Kuma' every day. Her waiting-woman Nenila (contralto), who is Maimïrov's sister, vainly tries to console her, and Mamïrov himself inflames her jealousy still further. Enter Yury, who tries in vain to worm from his mother the secret of her trouble. Scene between Mamïrov and Paisy, who is ordered to act as a spy on 'Kuma.' Angry scene between the Princess and her husband, who makes no secret of his passion for 'Kuma.' Scene in which an angry crowd of townspeople break into the garden in pursuit of one of the Prince's men who—taking advantage of their master's preoccupation—have been committing all sorts of crimes; Yury pacifies them. Re-enter the Princess with Nenila; Paisy reports that the Prince has gone to 'Kuma' as usual and Yury thus learns the reason for his mother's grief. He swears that he will kill 'Kuma,' the 'sorceress' who has bewitched his father.

Act III. 'Kuma' 's hut. The Prince is making love to her; she is cool, and when he becomes over-pressing she threatens to commit suicide rather than yield. Exit the Prince; enter Polya and Foka, who warn her of Yury's determination to kill her. 'Kuma' insists on being left alone, and presently Yury and Zhuran enter the moonlit hut. 'Kuma' reveals herself, and Yury is at once captivated by her beauty. She has little difficulty in convincing him of her innocence; Zhuran is sent away; love scene.

Act IV. A gloomy forest near the bank of the Oka. Hunting horns are heard, and the wizard Kudma (bass) emerges from his cave, only to retire on the approach of the hunters. They pass on but Zhuran waits to meet Yury. From their conversation it appears that he has arranged to meet 'Kuma' here and fly with her; exeunt both to join the bear-hunt. Enter Paisy with the Princess, who persuades the wizard to give her a poison for 'Kuma'; they go into the cave. On the Oka a boat appears with 'Kuma,' who is set ashore with her belongings. The Princess, who is unknown to 'Kuma,' comes out of the cave, gains her confidence and, pretending to give her a drink from the spring, administers the poison to the accompaniment of the wizard's mocking laughter. Hunting horns; the Princess bids 'Kuma' farewell; Yury rushes in joyously —but the poison is already beginning to work and 'Kuma' dies in his arms while his mother returns to rejoice in her revenge. 'Kuma' 's body is borne away by the hunters; exit the Princess, cursed by her son. Yury is left alone lamenting, when a number of boats appear on the river. It is the Prince with his men, in pursuit of 'Kuma' and Yury. The Prince thinks Yury is concealing her, will not believe the truth and—just as the Princess reappears—kills his son in an outburst of jealous fury. The young Prince's body is borne away and his father, left alone in the dark forest, goes mad to the accompaniment of thunder, lightning and the wizard's laughter.

It is difficult to understand why Tchaïkovsky was ever attracted by this extraordinary melodrama. Apart from its absurdities and unrealities, it contains far too much action, too many secondary characters and too many superfluous episodes. As the composer told his librettist's wife, 'He [Shphazinsky] knows the stage admirably but he can't adapt himself to the demands of opera. He uses too many words; dialogue predominates too much over lyricism' (letter of October 27/November 8, 1887). Tchaïkovsky himself had to make drastic cuts in the libretto—even, when the composition was finished, in his music—and the letter to Shpazhinsky in which he points out that after 'Kuma' has bewitched the son as well as the father 'it's impossible to drag out two more whole vast acts,' has already been quoted.[1] But the attempt to cram the content of those two long acts into a single one only resulted in Act IV of the opera becoming ridiculously crowded.

Even more than in *Mazeppa* one feels the lack of sympathetic or even interesting characters. All the protagonists are lay figures except 'Kuma,' and she is not quite credible. Her beauty, her charm—which have the effect of witchcraft on every man who sees her—constitute the mainspring of the action; yet in musical fact she has not even the charm of Oksana in *Vakula*. But Tchaïkovsky *conceived* her as a more remarkable character, and it is worth quoting at length from a letter to Emilya Pavlovskaya, his favourite Tatyana and Oksana, for whom the rôle of 'Kuma' was conceived and who actually created it (at the Maryinsky Theatre, St. Petersburg, October 20/November 1, 1887). When Pavlovskaya first heard of his intention to compose *The Sorceress*, she had taken an opportunity of seeing Shpazhinsky's play and conceived a violent dislike to it, particularly to the leading rôle, which seems to have been originally conceived on coarser, more realistic lines—as Mérimée's Carmen is more realistic than Bizet's. 'My conception of Nastasya's type is quite different from yours,' the composer wrote to his prima donna (April 12/24, 1885).

Of course she is a *loose woman,* but her charm does not lie merely in her ability to talk well. That would be enough to attract the people to her inn. But it wouldn't be enough to turn the young Prince from a

[1] See p. 129.

bitter enemy, who has come to kill her, into a lover. In the depths of this loose woman's soul lie a certain *moral power and beauty* which up to now have had no opportunity to unfold themselves. *This power is love.* She is a strong womanly nature who can love only once and can sacrifice *everything* for her love. While her love is still unborn Nastasya squanders her power so to speak in small change, i.e., she makes a joke of compelling everyone who comes in her way to fall in love with her. She remains a sympathetic, charming, though spoiled woman; she knows she is charming, is content to be, and—since she is neither guided by religious faith nor, being an orphan, has received a proper upbringing—pursues the single aim of having a good time. Then appears the man who has power to touch the slumbering better chords of her inward being and—she is transformed. Life loses for her its value so long as her goal is not reached; her charms, which hitherto have possessed an elementary, instinctive power of attraction, now become a powerful weapon which in a moment overcomes the hostile power, i.e., the hatred of the young Prince. Then both surrender themselves to the mad torrent of love which leads to the inevitable catastrophe —her death—and this death leaves the spectator with a sense of peace and reconciliation. At any rate it will be so in my libretto, though it's different in the drama. Shpazhinsky understands perfectly well what I want and will work out the characterisation in accordance with my intentions. He will soften some of the rough edges of Nastasya's *manières d'être* and bring the hidden power of her *moral* beauty more into the foreground. *He and I,* later *you* too (if you will come to terms with this rôle), will so arrange it that in the last act everyone will have to weep. As regards costume and make-up, there's no need for headaches about that. We'll arrange it so that there's nothing repellent. If Savina [the actress whom Pavlovskaya had seen play the part in its original, non-prettified form] was badly dressed there's no need for you to be.... My enthusiasm for *The Sorceress* has not made me untrue to the fundamental requirement of my soul: to illustrate in music Goethe's words, *Das Ewig-Weibliche zieht uns hinan.* The circumstance that the power and beauty of Nastasya's womanliness long remain covered under a cloak of sin only heightens the theatrical interest. Why do you love the rôle of la Traviata? Why are you so fond of Carmen? Because power and beauty peep out from these characters, though in coarse form. I assure you that you will also grow fond of the *Sorceress.* I won't say much about the other characters. I will only tell you that in my version the Princess will also be a strong personality. If this character has struck you only as the type of a *jealous and amorous old woman,* it is probably because you have seen it badly played. She is not jealous of the elder Prince's person but on account of her noble rank; she is a rabid aristocrat to whom the preservation of the honour of her sex is everything and who is capable of giving her life or committing a crime for honour's sake.

There is no need to look any further for the reasons why *The Sorceress* is a failure. A dramatic composer may sometimes ' soften some of the rough edges ' of a character with impunity—Verdi and Bizet and their librettists did so in the cases Tchaïkovsky mentions— but anxiety to conciliate a prima donna who disliked realistic rôles could only be unfortunate. *The Sorceress* is, or ought to be, a dramatic, realistic opera; as it is, it is only a convincing demonstration that Tchaïkovsky was not a truly dramatic composer. He was not objective enough; his power of dramatic expression was paralysed directly it was dissociated from more or less Tchaïkovskian types of character. Brutal Princes and haughty Princesses and enchanting hussies were quite outside his range, and the attempt to convert the enchanting hussy into something like a rustic Tatyana completely failed.

The Sorceress is particularly disappointing in that it begins so well. The first act, where there is practically no drama but only lively tableaux, is delightfully colourful. These drunken roistering scenes may not be very realistic judged by Mussorgskian standards (as we can, unfortunately, hardly help judging them now), but by the conventional operatic standards still generally valid in the 1880's —Tchaïkovsky's own standards—they are first-rate. The instrumental introduction, mainly based on Nastasya's song later in the act, sets the note: a folkish melody with Glinka-like treatment. And the opening chorus, the approaching chorus of girls, the 5/4 opening of the scene of the arrival in boats of more convivial citizens from Nizhny-Novgorod, the little scene between Nastasya and Lukash (the bell passage just before would pass unnoticed if transferred to Borodin's *Igor*), the sonorous E flat theme which permeates the scene of the passing of Yury and his men, Lukash's ' Come along, you pretty girls ' and the girls' reply, the thoroughly Russian character of the recitative in which the old Prince first addresses ' Kuma ' and in which she replies, the song in which she defends herself and at the same time attacks Mamïrov, the recommencement of the jollification (with the Prince joining in)— all these are beautiful or racily characteristic music. Only the tumblers' dance at the end of the act is a little less colourful than might have been expected, and the unaccompanied decimet with chorus, which opens the finale, though notable as a technical feat, is disappointingly operatic.

But when the drama begins, the music (one might almost say) finishes. There are a few good moments here and there in the three remaining acts, generally when the music recaptures the Russian flavour of Act I: the chorus of girls at the beginning of Act II, the music that accompanies Yury's first entry, the really lovely eight bars in which in Act III Nastasya addresses Yury as her ' falcon,' the male chorus dying away in the distance as the old Prince is left alone on the stage towards the end of the last act. But for the rest this Russianness is either strongly diluted—as in the prelude to Act IV, where a melody with a folk-song cadence, taken from the passage where the boat bearing Nastasya and her belongings comes into sight, is incongruously mixed with the conventional blood-and-thunder music of the theatrical hack. Nor is this weakening of the national flavour compensated for, as in *Onegin*, by the power of Tchaïkovsky's own peculiar lyricism. The duet for the Princess and her son in Act II, though pretty, is weak and utterly inexpressive of either the singers' characters or the words they sing. The elder Prince's love-song in Act III is again pretty in the Gounod vein. ' Kuma ' 's arioso in the last act is pitifully weak by comparison with Natalya's arioso in the *Oprichnik* of twenty years earlier, while the ' poison ' duet that has come just before is to English ears absurdly suggestive of Gilbert and Sullivan. Indeed, the high-water mark, such as it is, of Tchaïkovsky's more personally lyrical invention in *The Sorceress* is the melody that crowns the love-duet at the end of Act III, (' When thou, by telling all, calmest the anger in my soul ': Ex. 105). That was the best he could do for the emotional culmination of the whole drama.

Nor does he rise to the wonderful opportunities offered by some of the dramatic moments. Consider the scene in which Nastasya, alone in the moonlit hut, awaits the coming of the man she loves—coming to kill her. (Incidently this scene is an excellent example of Tchaïkovsky's favourite device of using some attractive, unpretentious little orchestral theme, not a leitmotive or anything like one, to punctuate a scene and give it unity). However adequate the declamation, the orchestral figuration—and they are no more than adequate—the stale diminished-seventh harmony deprives them of all force. Yury's actual entry and his immediate enslavement by Nastasya's beauty are even more completely thrown away. And the final scene of the elder Prince going mad in the forest is inferior to the scene of the Miller's madness in Dargomïzhsky's *Rusalka*, to say nothing of the hallucination scene in *Boris Godunov*.

Tchaïkovsky was, in his own words, eager ' to get his revenge. after the unlucky *Sorceress*,' and during this period, when he was ' ready to rush at any subject you like,' he expressed regret that his brother Modest was preparing a libretto on Pushkin's story *The*

Queen of Spades for another composer, N. S. Klenovsky. But when, in March 1888, Klenovsky after all turned down Modest's 'book' Peter had lost interest in the subject; he wanted to write a symphony, he told Modest; he would return to opera only if he came across a subject that would really *warm* him. 'A subject like *The Queen of Spades* doesn't move me at all and I could never make anything worth while of it.' And there for nearly two years the matter rested. Then, in December 1889,[1] Vsevolozhsky, the Director of the Imperial Theatres, who seems to have had a special affection for this subject—it was he who had suggested it to Klenovsky and Modest Tchaïkovsky in the first place—approached Peter with the suggestion that he should set Modest's libretto, and set it in time for the next season. Tchaïkovsky agreed; his brother had to read his libretto to an 'improvised commission' which discussed it and the staging and even the casting before even a note of the score was written. Accordingly Tchaïkovsky rushed off to Florence for peace and quiet, and set to work on January 19/31, 1890, finishing the sketches on March 3/15, the vocal score on March 26/April 7 and the full score on June 8/20. Vsevolozhsky got his opera in time for 'the next season,' and it was duly produced at the Maryinsky Theatre on December 7/19 of the same year.

Pushkin's Hoffmannesque short story, told with purely Pushkinian irony, may be summarised as follows[2] : A young Engineer officer named Hermann is fascinated by gambling, but being of German origin (hence, in Russian eyes, ridiculously prudent and methodical), never gambles himself. In his presence one of the gamblers, Tomsky, tells the story of how his aged grandmother acquired in her youth the secret of an infallible winning sequence of three cards. Hermann is fascinated by the idea of wheedling the secret out of the old Countess, begins hanging about outside her house, and is soon struck by the beauty of her orphan *protégée* and companion Lizaveta. The wretched, repressed Liza is captivated by this unknown admirer and when he sends her a love letter she gives him a rendezvous in her room. But Hermann takes the opportunity to conceal himself first in the Countess's room and, when the old lady is left alone, frightens her literally to death in trying to make her reveal her secret. He then visits Liza and cruelly tells her the whole story. Three days later he attends the Countess's funeral and

---

[1] A month or two earlier there had been some question of a libretto by no less a writer than Chekhov on Lermontov's *Bela*, which Tchaïkovsky wished to compose.

[2] There is a good translation in the Everyman's Library volume, *The Captain's Daughter, and Other Tales* by Pushkin, translated by Natalie Duddington.

approaches her coffin with the other mourners to give her a last kiss —and he has an illusion that she winks at him sarcastically. That night he is visited by her ghost, who reveals that the secret sequence is three, seven, ace. Hermann goes to a gambling club, where the wealthy Chekalinsky is banker, backs the three and wins an enormous sum; backs the seven and wins again—what the game was I am unable to discover—and then by some blunder, instead of the ace, plays the Queen of Spades and loses everything. At that moment he has the illusion that the Queen is winking at him: ' he was struck by an extraordinary likeness.' . . . And in a brief epilogue Pushkin tells us that Hermann is now in an asylum where he keeps muttering with incredible rapidity, ' Three, seven, ace! Three, seven, Queen,' and that Lizaveta married ' a very nice young man in the Civil Service, son of the old Countess's former steward.'

Modest Tchaikovsky took this dry and fantastically humorous tale and saturated it with the sham romanticism of the novelette, providing Liza with a wealthy fiancé, tagging on a gloomily tragic ending and making every opportunity for interpolating songs and even a whole ' pastoral interlude ' that have nothing to do with the action. Among other changes, the Countess becomes Liza's grandmother instead of Tomsky's. The general result is as follows:

Act I. Scene 1 : A public garden in St. Petersburg; children, nurses, etc. Meeting between Chekalinsky (tenor), Surin (bass), Hermann (tenor) and Tomsky (baritone). Hermann confides to Tomsky that he is madly in love with an unknown beauty. Enter Prince Eletsky (baritone), whom they congratulate on his engagement. Enter the Countess (mezzo-soprano) with Liza (soprano), who turns out to be Eletsky's betrothed and Hermann's unknown. While the Countess is talking, Tomsky tells the other men the ' three-card ' story. A thunderstorm disperses the promenaders; Hermann is left brooding over the story.

Scene 2. Liza's room. She, her friend Polina (contralto) and other girls are singing and dancing till the French governess (mezzo-soprano) comes in and stops them. Liza, left alone, reveals that instead of her betrothed she is fascinated by the unknown officer who looks like ' a fallen angel.' At that moment he enters from the balcony. Liza is with difficulty persuaded not to alarm the household, but she is about to dismiss him when the Countess enters, while Hermann hides—and the ' three-card ' story comes back to his mind. When the Countess leaves the room, Hermann again protests his love and this time Liza yields.

Act II. Scene 3 : A masked ball. Eletsky is disturbed by Liza's troubled mood. Surin and Chekalinsky, who have discovered the secret of Hermann's preoccupation with the ' three-card ' story,

play tricks on him; he takes their whisperings for spirit-voices. A
'pastoral interlude,' Karabanov's *Faithful Shepherdess* is performed for the amusement of the guests, the principals being
Prilepa (soprano),[1] Milovzor (played by Polina) and Prilepa's
wealthy admirer, Zlatogor (played by Tomsky). Liza gives Hermann the key to the garden so that he may get to her at night more
easily. It is announced that the Empress is coming—the period is
that of Catherine the Great—and great excitement is built up. As
Her Majesty is about to enter, the curtain falls.

Scene 4: The Countess's bedroom. Hermann conceals himself.
The Countess is put to bed by Liza and her attendants. Hermann
emerges and frightens the old lady to death. Liza appears and
finds that Hermann's card mania is stronger than his love.

Act III. Scene 5: Hermann's quarters in the barracks. Hermann
alone. Liza has not lost all faith in him and has written asking
him to meet her by the canal, opposite the Winter Palace. He
fancies he still hears the singing at the Countess's funeral. The
ghost enters and tells him the secret.

Scene 6[2]: Liza alone at the rendezvous by the canal. Hermann
comes but can talk of nothing but the secret of the cards. He
finally repulses Liza brutally and she throws herself into the canal.

Scene 7: The gambling club. Enter Hermann, who wins twice,
then plays against Eletsky, stakes everything, and loses on the
Queen of Spades. The Countess's ghost appears to him; in a frenzy
he stabs himself and dies. The assembled gamblers sing a brief
prayer for his 'suffering spirit.'

Although Modest Tchaïkovsky was mainly responsible for the
libretto of *The Queen of Spades*, the composer took an active part
in shaping it. Indeed, the manuscript reveals that Modest wrote
only on the right hand half of each sheet of paper, while the left
half is often covered by his brother's comments, substituted verses
of his own and musical sketches. The text of Eletsky's aria in
Scene 3 is wholly the composer's. As with Shpazhinsky, Tchaïkovsky
had to press for cuts. 'You've done the libretto very well,' he wrote
on January 23/February 4, 1890, 'but there's one thing wrong—
too many words. Please be as short and laconic as possible. I shall
leave out a few things.' These 'few things left out' include three
couplets of Hermann's arioso in the first scene, much of his original
monologue at the end of that scene, a second interlude—Derzhavin's

[1] There was originally some idea, rejected by the composer, that Prilepa might be
played by Liza. In Rosa Newmarch's English version Prilepa becomes Chloë and
Milovzor, Daphnis.

[1] This scene was inserted by the composer, against the advice of Modest and
Laroche, partly because otherwise the last act would have been practically womanless,
partly because 'the spectator must know what becomes of Liza. Her rôle can't end
with Scene 4' (as it practically did in Pushkin's story).

'Ode in Honour of Prince Vyazemsky'—in Scene 3, and much of the original scene between Liza and the Prince. On the other hand he actually added a few words to the Prince's part 'so as to bring it forward'; he always liked to strengthen subordinate rôles.

Tchaïkovsky liked the text for recitatives to be in rhythmic prose. 'I'm awfully pleased with the way you've re-done Hermann's words in the chief scene—the scene of the old lady's death: Pushkin's text has remained almost unchanged, but there's rhythm,' he wrote (February 25/March 9). And in song passages he disliked short lines, which would hamstring long-breathed melodic phrases : 'I've decided to leave out everything that Hermann says in short lines.'

But as Tchaïkovsky himself remarked, he stands 'not by the word but by the scene,' and Yarustovsky makes some interesting comments on his skill in building, and inducing his librettist to build, effective scenes :

The soundest dynamic development of a dramatic line in opera is usually constructed according to the so-called law of 'repeated complexes,' one of the principal laws of dramaturgy which opera has acquired from drama. Let us examine, for instance, the composition of the second scene of The Queen of Spades. We clearly observe the threefold repetition of a scenic-emotional situation, each time interrupted by a counter-action : after a 'neutral' episode (romance, duet, dances) Liza is left alone; her emotional state gradually changes and develops; appearance of Hermann. Again a gradual development in the emotional condition of both, a culmination—and again an interruption —the appearance of the Countess; finally—the third 'wave,' forming the climax of the whole scene. . . . We may observe a similar development in the letter scene in Onegin, in the scene of 'Kuma' and the young Prince in The Sorceress, and in a whole series of other scenes.

It may be added that the emotional parallel between the second and third 'waves' in Scene 2 is reflected in the musical substance of each wave and thus helps to condition the musical form on an almost symphonic scale.

The Queen of Spades seems to offer little that could arouse a composer's sympathy as Tchaïkovsky needed to have his sympathies aroused if he was to do good work. Hermann is a contemptible figure (in Pushkin actually ridiculous), the old Countess a repellent one, and even the unfortunate Liza is not particularly attractive. But a letter which Tchaïkovsky wrote to his brother a few hours after the completion of the composition-sketch throws a valuable light on his emotional state and also perhaps explains why The Queen of Spades, by no means Tchaïkovsky's second best opera, is his second most popular :

I composed the actual end of the opera yesterday morning. When I got to Hermann's death and the final chorus I was suddenly overcome by such compassion for Hermann-that I began to weep. This weeping gradually changed into a very pleasant hysteria, i.e., it was so sweet to weep. Afterwards I discovered the reason (I had never wept in that way for a hero before and was anxious to explain my pleasure in weeping). I found that Hermann had been not only a pretext for writing this or that music, but a genuine, living and even sympathetic man. Because Figner [a famous tenor of the Maryinsky stage] is sympathetic to me and because I had always visualised Hermann as played by Figner, I had felt such warm sympathy with his fate. Now I believe that my warm, living feeling for the hero of the opera is also favourably reflected in the music.

The score of *The Queen of Spades* is saturated with hysterical emotion and, lying chronologically between the Fifth and Sixth Symphonies, belongs almost entirely to their emotional world.

The orchestral introduction, an odd piece of patchwork, might easily belong to either of the last two symphonies, particularly in its harmonic intensification and the almost *Tristan*-esque working up of the not very distinguished love-theme from Scene 2 (which returns in the closing scene of the opera). So might the passage where Hermann realises that the Countess is dead, practically the whole of the scene by the canal, the mournful descending melody that accompanies Hermann's first entrance and his arioso in the first scene—indeed, most of the music associated with the 'hero' himself. That 'mournful descending melody' (cf. also the melody accompanying the appearance of Liza and the Prince in Scene 3) has a close family likeness to the phrase which recurs throughout the opera when the 'three cards' are mentioned, itself an echo of Lensky's aria in *Onegin* and a foreboding of the opening of the finale of the Sixth Symphony (Ex. 106). In each case this rather weak and sentimental melodic shape is associated with nothing less than the idea of death. The 'coming day' brings death to Lensky —and he feels forebodings. The complete words of this particular passage from *The Queen of Spades* are as follows in Rosa Newmarch's translation:

> Thou shalt die when a third man, impell'd by despair,
> Shall strive from thy bosom the secret to tear
> Of three cards!

And recent research has shown beyond much doubt that 'death' was the secret programmatic idea at the back of the finale of the *Pathétique Symphony*.[1] A particularly interesting point is

[1] Cf. footnote to p. 75.

Tchaïkovsky's transformation of the end of Ex. 106a into a 'fatal' motto-theme (Ex. 107), first heard in the introduction, which recurs dozens of times throughout the score as no other single theme recurs in any other of Tchaïkovsky's operas.

The other main element in the music of *The Queen of Spades* is that of eighteenth-century pastiche. As we have seen, Tchaïkovsky always delighted in opportunities for this—the minuet in *Vakula*, Triquet's couplets in *Onegin* and many examples outside the operas—but he had never allowed himself so many as in *The Queen of Spades*: the duet for Liza and Polina, the whole long interlude of *The Faithful Shepherdess* (a miniature dramatic cantata taking up twenty-eight pages of the vocal score), and Tomsky's song in the last scene (a setting of a poem by the eighteenth-century writer Derzhavin). And the Countess, recalling the days of her youth, actually sings the air 'Je crains de lui parler la nuit,' from Grétry's *Richard Cœur de Lion*—anachronistically, for the Countess's youth must have begun to fade half a century before the composition of Grétry's opera. As pastiche, the duet for Prilepa and Milovzor and the finale[1] of *The Faithful Shepherdess* are perhaps the best of all Tchaïkovsky's essays in sham rococo.

But these rococo insets are not the only parenthetic episodes, padding out the length but holding up the action. There are, for instance, Polina's romance in the second scene (the best example of truly Tchaïkovskian melody in the whole score), the girls' chorus which follows it (which, with the nursemaids' song in the opening scene, provides the sole whiff of folk-music), the choral polonaise heralding the spoof entry of the Tsaritsa (an effect devised by the composer himself, *vide* his letter to Modest of February 20/March 4, 1890, in order to get an effective ending to the scene). Hermann's song 'What is our life? A game!' in the last scene, though it has more point, more dramatic justification than these, is also a parenthesis; it must be reckoned among the 'French' elements in the score, with the episode of the boys playing at soldiers in the opening scene (standing midway between the scene that obviously suggested it in *Carmen* and the toy soldiers of *Nutcracker*), the governess's arioso (where the Frenchness is of course deliberate), and the opening of Scene 4 (which stands in a direct line between the first movement of the Fourth Symphony and the Flower Valse in *Nutcracker*).

One other page of *The Queen of Spades* is worth looking at and

---

[1] Of which the principal theme seems to have been adapted without acknowledgment from a chorus in Bortnyansky's opera *Le Fils Rival* (produced 1787).

performing: Liza's ' Ah, I am worn with my sorrow,' sung as she waits for her lover by the canal. It is not first-rate Tchaïkovsky but it stands out in a score which, despite its popularity in Russia, Tsarist and Soviet alike, is decidedly weak from the lyrical point of view. Such things as the square-cut and painfully conventional ' Chorus of promenaders ' in Scene 1, Liza's monologue in Scene 2 almost till the moment of Hermann's appearance, Hermann's ' Forgive me, bright celestial vision,' Eletsky's aria in the fête scene, Hermann's pleading with the old Countess and the duet in Scene 6 compare rather dismally with the lyrical beauties of Tchaïkovsky's early operas. They lack even the stamp of his personality.

Tchaïkovsky's last two stage works are of slight importance. They are the incidental music to *Hamlet*, written hurriedly and very much against the grain in January 1891, for Lucien Guitry's benefit on February 9/21, and the one-act opera *Iolanta*, a setting of a libretto by his brother Modest based on Zvantsev's translation of Henrik Hertz's *Kong Renés Datter*, which in turn originated in a story by Hans Andersen. The *Hamlet* music cannot compare in interest or importance with the *Snow Maiden* music. The overture is a shortened version of the big overture-fantasia *Hamlet*, rescored for the small orchestra of the Mikhaylovsky Theatre, which also provides the material for two of the melodramas and the brief final march (presumably for the entry of Fortinbras.) The entr'acte before Act II is a cut-down version of the ' alla tedesca ' movement from the Third Symphony, the trio being omitted; that before Act III is note for note the same as the melodrama that accompanies Kupava's complaint in Act II of *Snow Maiden*; that before Act IV is the elegy composed seven years earlier for the jubilee of the actor I. V. Samarin. Only the entr'acte before Act V, used again later as a funeral march, was specially written. But comparison of the two versions of the overture is not uninteresting:

Overture Fantasia (1888)	Theatre Overture (1891)
Lento lugubre (Ex.45)	Lento lugubre (with a single new bar in place of bars 20–54 of the original)
Andante non troppo	Andante non troppo
Allegro vivace :	Allegro vivacissimo (throughout, with only minor changes of tempo)
Ex.42 (F minor)	Ex.42 (F minor) (identical for 21 bars)

OVERTURE FANTASIA (1888)	THEATRE OVERTURE (1891)
40 bars working round to	12 bars working round to
Andante: Ex.43 (B minor)	Ex.43 in double note-values (C minor)
Moderato con moto: 33 bars on Ex.44 (D major, etc.)	(Ex.44 omitted altogether)
Allegro vivace: 8 bars on Ex.46 (E flat) 12 bars leading to recapitulation of Ex.42	8 bars on Ex.46 (E flat) 4 bars leading to recapitulation of Ex.42 (identical for 15 bars)
29 bars working round to Ex.43, now in double note-values (B flat minor)	19 bars working round to Ex.43, still in double note-values (B flat minor)
Moderato con moto: 28 bars on Ex.44 (D flat, etc.)	
Allegro: 28 bars, return of Ex.45	(Ex.44 and return of Ex.45 omitted)
Allegro vivace: Ex.46 worked to a climax	Ex.46 worked to a climax
Poco più animato: 16 bars on Ex.42. . . . 21 transitional bars	16 bars on Ex.42 11 bars on Ex.46
Grave: 12 bars on Ex.45	

Iolanta was a commissioned work, a one-act opera intended to be produced (as it actually was on December 6/18, 1892) with the two-act ballet *Nutcracker*. The subject was chosen by Tchaikovsky himself, though having chosen it he temporarily took a violent dislike to it, and the composition, begun in July 1891, at first gave him considerable trouble. The action is as follows:

> Iolanta (soprano), the blind daughter of a fifteenth-century king of Provence, is picking fruit in her garden. She has never been allowed to know she is different from other people, and no stranger is allowed, on pain of death, to approach her. Her friends, Brigitte (soprano) and Laura (mezzo-soprano) and her maids, help her to find the fruit; her old nurse, Martha (contralto), holds the basket. Iolanta is tired and sad, and after trying to divert her with music and flowers her companions sing her to sleep and carry her into the castle. Horn calls are

heard. Martha's husband, the gate-keeper Bertrand (baritone), opens
the gates to Almerik, the King's armour-bearer (tenor), who announces
the arrival of King René (bass) with the Moorish doctor Ebn-Hakia
(bass) who is to attempt to restore Iolanta's sight. After looking at her,
Ebn-Hakia says a cure is possible but on one condition : Iolanta must
know she is is blind and *will* to see. The King refuses this condition.
Exeunt both.

Enter Robert, Duke of Burgundy (baritone), with Count Vaudemont
(tenor). Robert has been betrothed to Iolanta from childhood, but has
never seen her, is (like everyone else outside the castle) ignorant of her
blindness, and, being in love with another woman, is now making his
way to King René's court unwillingly and in the hope that René will
release him from his pledge. He and Vaudemont have come upon
Iolanta's hiding-place quite by accident. The two young men see the
still sleeping Iolanta, and Vaudemont is completely enchanted by her;
the Duke thinks they have wandered into a sorcerer's domain and
tries, in vain, to drag his friend away. Their voices awaken Iolanta.
Robert rushes off to fetch their followers and rescue Vaudemont from
the enchantment. Vaudemont soon discovers from his conversation
with Iolanta that she is blind, and inadvertently reveals the fact to her
too. Enter the King, Ebn-Hakia, and the rest; the King is overwhelmed
by the apparent misfortune of the revelation, but Ebn-Hakia points out
that his condition is now fulfilled. Yet Iolanta does not really long for
sight, for she does not know what sight means. To give her a motive
the King says that Vaudemont must die for disregarding the notice
forbidding entrance to the castle-grounds—unless Iolanta's sight is
restored. She says she will bear anything to save this young man with
whose voice she has fallen in love. She is led away by Ebn-Hakia and
the woman. The King tells Vaudemont that the threat was only a
device to work on Iolanta.

The Duke returns with his followers. General explanation : that
Robert does not love Iolanta but that Vaudemont does. Bertrand runs
in to announce that the treatment is completed. Ebn-Hakia leads in
Iolanta blindfold and removes the cloth from her eyes. She sees.
General rejoicing.

One wonders what attracted Tchaïkovsky to this subject, even
temporarily; perhaps the psychological point that the heroine's
physical abnormality can be removed only when she recognises it
and wills its removal strongly enough. But it is hardly surprising
that he felt considerable distaste for it and that his already quoted
confession to Fedotov that ' medieval dukes and knights and ladies
captivate my imagination but not my *heart* ' was written only a
month or two after he had finished scoring *Iolanta*. As in so many
earlier cases, he began with a crucial scene: in this case, the one
between Iolanta and Vaudemont. ' You've done this scene splen-
didly,' he wrote to Modest, ' and the music might have been very

beautiful, but I feel I haven't succeeded particularly well. I keep falling into self-repetition, so that a good deal in this scene is like *The Sorceress.*' In the same letter he complains that, after this ' light ' duet, there is ' too little music and nothing but explanation of the action.' A fortnight later (August 7/19, 1891) he reports that he is pleased with the Brigitte-Laura flower song and the lullaby. The whole work was completed in full score by mid-December.

Like *The Queen of Spades, Iolanta* reveals here and there affinities with *Nutcracker* on the one hand and the Sixth Symphony on the other. The dark colouring of the short orchestral introduction, which seems intended to suggest Iolanta's blindness and her sense of something lacking, is a weak anticipation—also mostly in B minor—of the Cimmerian darkness in which the last symphony opens. A great many passages in the opera belong to the harmonic world of the symphony, a world of increased harmonic tension. And when Vaudemont tells Iolanta ' Your wish is law to me ' and when later she uses the same words to him, each sings the words to bars 3–4 of Ex. 106c. But the relationship to *Nutcracker* is still closer. One notices it in the pseudo-orientalism, otherwise so rare in Tchaïkovsky, of Ebn-Hakia's ' Two worlds : fleshly and spiritual,' in Robert's ' Who can compare with my Mathilde? ' which might have come straight from the Confituremburg), in the charming orchestration of Iolanta's first conversation with Vaudemont (particularly when he empties the beaker of wine), and above all perhaps at the end when Ebn-Hakia takes the kerchief from Iolanta's eyes and a sweet but undistinguished tune first insinuates itself in the orchestra as she asks ' Where am I? ', is later sung by her as she sinks to her knees in grateful prayer (Ex. 108), and is used to clinch the final ' Hosannas ' as the curtain falls. But one feels that Ex. 108, if pretty and quite in place in a fairy ballet, is rather inadequate as the expression of the feelings of a lady who has just been almost miraculously given her sight. So with other passages. The women's flower song and the lullaby will pass muster, but the melody to which Vaudemont sings of light as ' the wondrous prime creation, first gift to the world by its Creator ' is less pretty and even more inadequate than Ex. 108. Yet this, too, is used again considerably in the last scene. That is the criticism one must level against the music of *Iolanta* as a whole : it is often pretty but dramatically inadequate and rather characterless. Not that the score is entirely lacking in unmistakably Tchaïkovskian melodies. Nothing could be more typical than the cantabile melody (Ex. 109) that accompanies the knights' discovery of the sleeping Iolanta, or the pretty canon on an oramented version of it a few pages later. (Here and elsewhere in *Iolanta*, as on some of the most impassioned pages of *The Queen of Spades*, the musical centre of gravity lies in the orchestra, while the voice part is merely declamatory; by the end of his life Tchaïkovsky was quite at home with the procedure which fourteen years earlier had scandalised him more than anything else in Wagner.) Naturally there is nothing Russian in the score— except the regal phrase heralding the reappearance of Robert with his armed followers, just as in *The Maid of Orleans* the King thanks his ' good people ' in decidedly Russian accents. But no one but Tchaïkovsky could have written, for instance, the passage where Vaudemont dries Iolanta's tears and that where she sings, a few pages later, ' Thou speak'st so sweetly! I have never known such happiness,' with its characteristic echoing of the voice by the orchestra. Both of these occur in the first scene to be composed, and one can only regret that, having written it, the composer's inspiration should have ebbed so completely. The ensemble following the discovery that Iolanta knows she is blind is an instance of that vulgarisation of his own melodic and harmonic idiom in which Tchaïkovsky sometimes forestalled the Arenskys and Rakhmaninovs who tried to imitate him.

In January 1891, a few months before Tchaïkovsky began the composition of *Iolanta*, Taneev had written to him: ' Apropos of opera in general. The question of how to write operas interests me in the highest degree and I've long wanted to exchange thoughts with you on this topic. Your views, so far as they are given concrete expression in your operas, do not completely satisfy me.' To this Tchaïkovsky replied with what in effect is a just summing-up of his aims as a stage-composer:

> The question how one should write operas I've always decided, do decide and shall decide extraordinarily simply. One should write them (just like everything else, for that matter) as God has put it in your soul to write them. I've always tried to express in music as truthfully and sincerely as possible what was in the text. Truth and sincerity aren't just the result of brain-work but the immediate product of inner feeling. So that the feeling should be warm and vital, I've always tried to choose subjects in which the characters are real living people, feeling as I do. That's why I find Wagnerian subjects, in which there's nothing human, intolerable; nor would I have chosen a subject like yours [Taneev's *Orestes*] with monstrous crimes, with the Eumenides and fates as actual characters. So, having chosen a subject and set about the composition

of an opera, I've given free rein to my feelings, neither resorting to Wagnerian methods nor striving to be original. In doing so I by no means prevented the spirit of the age from influencing me. I confess that if there'd been no Wagner I should have written differently; I admit there is even *Kuchkism*[1] in my operatic writings; probably also Italian music, which I passionately loved in childhood, and Glinka whom I adored in my youth, have strongly influenced me—to say nothing of Mozart. But I have never invoked either of these idols but allowed them to direct my musical inner being as they liked. It may be that as a result of this attitude there is no direct evidence in my operas that they belong to this school or that; it may be that one or another of these forces has predominated over the rest and I have fallen into imitations—but however that may be, it has all come about of its own accord, and if I am confident of anything it is that in my writings I have shown myself as God created me and as I have been formed by education, circumstances and the nature of the age and land in which I live and work. I have never been untrue to myself. But how I am—whether good or bad—let others judge.

[1] The spirit of the *Kuchka*, or ' handful,' of Balakirev's followers.

8

The Ballets

By

Edwin Evans

A HUNDRED YEARS AGO was a wonderful period for the ballet, but a singularly poor one for its music. One has only to recall Adolphe Adam's *Giselle*, a classic whose centenary was celebrated not long ago, and which still retains its place in the repertoire in spite of the banality of its music, which was characteristic of the age. So far as one may judge at this distance of time, the insipid quality of ballet-music was probably to be attributed to the tyranny of the *maître de ballet*, as ruthless a dictator as any modern film produced, who regarded the music as an accessory, unfortunately indispensable, but to be kept in its place. He was rarely himself musical, but disposed to resent anything that claimed a share in the attention to which his own work was entitled. He therefore preferred that the music should have just sufficient character to support the rhythms of his dancers, and no more. In this he had the support of a large section of the Press and the public. Otherwise it would be difficult to explain how some Parisian critics solemnly charged Delibes's delightful *Sylvia* with being too symphonic, and its composer with being a convert to the methods of Richard Wagner.

It was Delibes, a pupil of Adolphe Adam, who first raised the status of ballet music from the slough into which it had been allowed to fall. That he was permitted to do this in the face of the prevailing attitude seems to require some explanation. The opera house was then, as in many countries it still is, the traditional home of both opera and ballet, and I venture to suggest that, at a time when the quality of operatic performance was on the up-grade, and its music a topic of general discussion, the personnel of the ballet and their friends may have grown a little restive, not to say jealous, at hearing their own music dismissed as of no account. Be that as it may, Delibes eventually gained the day and the quality of ballet music soon came to be judged by his standard.

These preliminary remarks were necessary because Tchaïkovsky, a great admirer of Delibes, it will be remembered, has sometimes been said to have followed in his footsteps in further raising the status of ballet music. In his correspondence there is no mention of Delibes until the end of 1877, when he writes that he has heard the Vienna orchestra play the music of *Sylvia*, which he had previously known only in the piano arrangement. He hardly ever mentions *Coppélia*, the earlier ballet, and indeed remarks in a letter of January 1878 that he does not know it 'but will examine it at the first opportunity.' But whereas *Sylvia* was not produced until June 14, 1876, his own music for *The Swan Lake* was completed the previous March when he cannot have known the French work even in the unlikely event of its having been published immediately on production. The fact is that Tchaïkovsky had a strong intuitive inclination to music of a kind suited to the ballet, and when the opportunity presented itself to give free play to it, being the conscientious craftsman he was, the music had to be as good as was in his power to write. He needed no other prompting.

This intuitive inclination forms the theme of the interesting exchange of letters with Taneev, already quoted by Mr. Lockspeiser on page 20. This episode is in many ways illuminating. It shows how far removed Tchaïkovsky was from German pedantry, which dismisses as *Kitsch*, or mere ear-tickling, any music with a captivating tune. It implies that Tchaïkovsky regarded, as every musician should, the distinction between good and bad as cutting deeper than any antithesis of serious and light—or, to put it colloquially, ' classical ' and ' popular '—music. It explains how his ballet music came to be, not only among the best of its kind, but among the best he wrote. And finally it provides some justification for Massine's choreographic version of a Tchaïkovsky symphony, though not the Fourth but the Fifth, on which he based *Les Présages*.

Considering Tchaïkovsky's fame as one of the few great masters of ballet music, it is strange that he was not recognised as such until the last three years of his life. This was due to the ill-luck which beset his first venture in this field, *The Swan Lake*. It was in 1875, between Easter and the summer, that the Imperial Opera at Moscow commissioned this ballet for a sum of 800 rubles (then about £85), but owing to other work in hand he did not begin to compose it before August, when he completed two acts in a fortnight. He explained to Rimsky-Korsakov that he undertook this task partly because he needed the money, but also because he had long wished to ' try his hand ' at this kind of music. As already stated, the score was completed in March 1876, but for one reason or another production was delayed a whole year until February 20/March 4, 1877, when it was performed at the Bolshoy Theatre, Moscow, for the benefit of a dancer named Karparkova. It seems to have been more or less pitchforked on to the stage. The choreography was by a certain Julius Reisinger, of whom little else is known, the scenery and costumes were poor, and the orchestra was conducted by a semi-amateur named Ryabov, who confessed that never in his life had he seen so complicated a score. Several numbers—amounting, it is said, to a third of the whole—were omitted as not being sufficiently danceable (meaning, of course, that they were not of the banal type then favoured), and they were replaced with music from other ballets. Tchaïkovsky had not looked forward to this production with as much nervous excitement as he generally did to those of his operas; nor did he take its failure to heart, as he did not feel himself responsible for the shortcomings which had caused it—though eighteen months later, when expressing his admiration for Delibes, he declared *The Swan Lake* to be ' poor stuff ' compared with *Sylvia*. Not until after the composer's death was that unfortunate ballet rehabilitated, and then its success redeemed its first failure. As it cannot be said previously to have been heard in its entirety, its discussion will be deferred to the end of this chapter.

More than ten years elapsed before I. A. Vsevolozhsky, Director of the Imperial Theatres, at St. Petersburg, commissioned Tchaïkovsky, of whose works he was an enthusiastic admirer, to compose the music for a ballet of which he had himself prepared the scenario. It was based on the first of Charles Perrault's *Histoires ou Contes du Temps Passé*, the story beloved of children of all countries. *La Belle au Bois Dormant*, otherwise *The Sleeping Beauty*. He set to work with much enthusiasm, and the first four scenes were sketched by January 1889. It was completed and orchestrated during the following summer. His brother relates that he then found much pleasure in the company of a little girl of three, the child of Kondratiev's servant, Legoshin. He was fascinated by her prettiness and her charming ways, and would spend hours romping with her or listening to her chatter. Though this may not have influenced the work on which he was engaged, it probably helped to put him in the right mood by dispelling the despondency to which he was so much addicted. By all accounts he was immune from it during the composition of the ballet and for once he wrote to Nadezhda von Meck that he considered it one of his best works. It was completed in the autumn, and Ziloti's piano arrangement was published before the end of the year. The first performance took place at the Maryinsky Theatre, St. Petersburg, January 1/15, 1890, the choreography being by that master of the classic traditions, Marius Petipa.

Vsevolozhsky's scenario is remarkably faithful to its source. Even the number of the fairies invited to the Princess's christening is that indicated by Perrault, so that Petipa cannot be accused of ' showing-off' in introducing a masterly *pas de sept*. Originally consisting of a prologue and three acts the ballet as revived by Dyagilev in 1921 was presented in five scenes, the second act being divided into two.

The first scene is that of the christening, to which the wicked fairy Carabosse was not invited because nothing had been heard of her for more than fifty years and every one thought her dead. Far from it, she intrudes and utters the terrible curse. In the second scene the Princess Aurora, now sixteen, pricks her finger and falls asleep. The third begins as a hunting scene, but when the hunt has dispersed the Lilac-Fairy displays the Sleeping Princess in a vision to Prince Charming. The fourth is that of the awakening, and the fifth is taken up by the festivities connected with the wedding, which is attended by many notable personages from other familiar fairy-tales, such as Puss-in-Boots, Little Red Riding-Hood and Hop o' my Thumb. They serve to enhance the colour of the divertissement which so often formed the climax of a classical ballet.

The music, consisting of some thirty numbers, is undoubtedly Tchaïkovsky's masterpiece in this genre. Writing of it many years ago, before the improved status of ballet music had become general, Rosa Newmarch described it as ' though not deeper than the subject demands, melodious in the best sense of the word, fantastic, brightly coloured; while it never descends to the commonplace level of the ordinary ballet music.' The vindication contained in the last few words was necessary at a time when the only ballet music known to most of her readers was precisely of that ' ordinary ' kind. Happily those days are past. But there are still many who consider even a bad symphony better music than that of a ballet, which amounts to judging music by its pretensions instead of its quality. *The Sleeping Beauty* is good music considered from any angle. It has become familiar in our concert-halls by means of the usual Suite, which consists of the Introduction and Dance of the Lilac-Fairy; the Princess's Adagio; Puss-in-Boots; the panorama originally accompanying the change of scene during which the Prince is guided through the tangled forest to the castle (in the revival the entr'acte between Scenes

3 and 4); and the Valse from the beginning of Scene 2, in which the Princess is to prick her finger. It is unfortunate that the brevity of the many *variations* (in the choregraphic, not the musical sense), made them unsuitable for inclusion in a concert suite which they could have made scrappy, for most of them are deftly contrived and extraordinarily effective miniatures.

Some slight modifications were made in the revival which Dyagilev presented at the Alhambra Theatre, London, on November 2, 1921. Two numbers were omitted from the divertissement, their place being taken by others from *Nutcracker*, and two numbers omitted from the original production, and left unscored, were orchestrated by Stravinsky, who, on the eve of the production, wrote an ' open letter ' to Dyagilev in praise of Tchaïkovsky. It runs :

It gives me great happiness to know that you are producing that masterpiece, *The Sleeping Beauty* by our great and beloved Tchaïkovsky. It makes me doubly happy. In the first place it is a personal joy, for this work appears to me as the most authentic expression of that period of our Russian life which we call the ' Petersburg Period,' and which is stamped upon my memory with the morning vision of the Imperial sleighs of Alexander III, the giant Emperor and his giant coachman, and the immense joy that awaited me in the evening, the performance of *The Sleeping Beauty*. It is, further, a great satisfaction to me as a musician to see produced a work of so direct a character at a time when so many people who are neither simple, nor naïve, nor spontaneous, seek in their art simplicity, ' poverty ' and spontaneity. Tchaïkovsky in his very nature possessed these three gifts to the fullest extent. That is why he never feared to let himself go, whereas the prudes, whether *raffinés* or academic, were shocked by the frank speech, free from artifice, of his music.

Tchaïkovsky possessed the power of *melody*, centre of gravity in every symphony, opera or ballet composed by him. It is absolutely indifferent to me that the quality of his melody was sometimes unequal. The fact is that he was a creator of *melody*, which is an extremely rare and precious gift. Among us Glinka, too, possessed it; and not to the same degree, those others. And that is something which is not German. The Germans manufactured, and manufactured music with themes and leitmotives, which they substituted for melodies.

Tchaïkovsky's music, which does not appear specifically Russian to everybody, is often more profoundly Russian than music which has long since been awarded the facile label of Muscovite picturesqueness. This music is quite as Russian as Pushkin's verse or Glinka's song. Whilst not specially cultivating in his art the ' soul of the Russian peasant,' Tchaïkovsky drew unconsciously from the true, popular sources of our race.

And how characteristic were his predilections in the music of the past and of his own day! He worshipped Mozart, Couperin, Glinka, Bizet;

that leaves no doubt of the quality of his taste. How strange it is! Every time that a Russian musician has come under the influence of this Latin-Slav culture, and seen clearly the frontier between the Austrian-Catholic Mozart turned towards Beaumarchais, and the German-Protestant Beethoven turned towards Goethe, the result has been striking.

The convincing example of Tchaïkovsky's great creative power is, beyond all doubt, the ballet of *The Sleeping Beauty*. This cultured man, with his knowledge of folk-song and of old French music, had no need to engage in archælogical research in order to present the age of Louis XIV; he re-created the character of the period by his musical language, preferring involuntary but living anachronisms to conscious and laboured *pasticcio*; a virtue that appertains only to great creative minds. I have just read again the score of this ballet. I have instrumented some numbers of it which had remained unorchestrated and unperformed. I have spent some days of intense pleasure in finding therein again and again the same feeling of freshness, inventiveness, ingenuity and vigour. And I warmly desire that your audiences of all countries may feel this work as it is felt by me, a Russian musician.

Much to his own astonishment Stravinsky's perfectly natural, though perhaps over-emphasised gesture was greeted with surprise and even suspected of insincerity. It may be that this unwarranted charge prompted the tribute to Tchaïkovsky which took the form of his ballet, *Le Baiser de la Fée*. But next to Dyagilev himself the greatest enthusiast associated in this production was Leon Bakst, who, caught up in a fever of excitement, designed, in the incredibly short period of little over two months a special curtain, five elaborate scenes, and close upon three hundred costumes, which made this production, recorded in a handsome *édition de luxe*, a landmark in theatrical art. The ballet was thus presented in the most sumptuous manner and four great dancers—Trefilova, Sgorova, Lopokova and Spessiva (Spessivtseva)—took the principal part of the Princess Aurora in rotation. An interesting memory was recalled by the appearance, as the wicked fairy Carabosse, of Carlotta Brianza, who had created the rôle of the Princess Aurora thirty years before, in the original cast. Her husband, Enrico Cecchetti, was also in the original production, and to celebrate the fiftieth anniversary of his first appearance in a principal rôle, reappeared as the fairy Carabosse, for one night only, on January 5, 1922.

Having been warned that to an unsophisticated section of the English public the original title might suggest a Christmas pantomime, Dyagilev adopted that of *The Sleeping Princess* under which it had what, for another production, might be called a fairly long run; but which was not sufficient to recoup the lavish expenditure it had occasioned. There survived from it, under the title of *Aurora's Wedding*, a selection, mostly from the divertissement, but the greater part of Bakst's wonderful *mise en scène* had been allowed to perish and the costumes had to be eked out with some—including one worn by Nizhinsky—from the ballet of *Le Pavillon d'Armide*, dating from 1907. On February 2, 1939, however, the Sadler's Wells Ballet revived *The Sleeping Princess* in its entirety, perhaps the most ambitions of its feats of production. Although the fairy godmothers were reduced to six, as many as the width of the stage would allow to perform together, there was no serious flaw in its authenticity. But for the war it would doubtless have remained in the repertoire.

Once the remarkable quality of *The Sleeping Beauty* was recognised it was inevitable that Tchaïkovsky would soon be approached for another ballet. Again the subject was not of his own choosing but this time it did not prove to his liking, and he did not set to work with much alacrity. It was a version by Dumas, under the title of *Casse-Noisette*, of a story by E. T. A. Hoffmann, *The Nutcracker and the King of the Mice*. It was commissioned early in 1891, and the first act was sketched before the composer's departure for America, the rest in the summer, soon after his return; but another journey delayed the orchestration, and the score was not completed until March 1892. In another fit of depression the composer had confided to Vladimir Davidov, his nephew, that it was 'infinitely worse' than its predecessors. But when the Imperial Musical Society gave in the same month a preliminary performance of the concert suite from it, no fewer than five of its numbers had to be repeated in response to the applause. Much the same thing happened four years later when Henry Wood conducted the first performance in England at a Promenade Concert on October 17, 1896, and thereby inaugurated its immense popularity in this country. It must, however, be admitted that the suite comprises the best of the music.

The ballet is in two acts and three scenes:

President Silberhaus and his wife are giving a Christmas party for their children and those of their friends. The guests arrive, the candles are lighted and the children come in to receive their presents. But Councillor Drosselmeyer brings his in person. They are four mechanical dolls, Harlequin and Columbine, a Soldier and a Vivandière. To Clara, the daughter of the house, he gives in addition an old-fashioned

German nutcracker in the shape of a man who breaks the nuts in his capacious jaws. This pleases Clara more than all her other presents, but her brother Franz and the other boys snatch it away from her and break it. Clara bursts into tears, caresses the poor Nutcracker and fusses over it as an invalid. When the party is over and she has gone to bed she cannot sleep for thinking of her patient, so she creeps downstairs again. At midnight the room is invaded by mice, but all the toys come to life, and a battle royal is engaged which reaches its climax in a duel between the King of the Mice and the Nutcracker. At the moment when the King seems likely to be victorious Clara intervenes with a well-aimed slipper and the mice are defeated. The Nutcracker, whose life Clara has saved, now changes into a handsome Prince, who invites her to come with him to Confituremburg in the Kingdom of Sweets. They fly over the wintry forest, and to Clara all the snowflakes are living beings dancing round her. Arrived in the Kingdom of Sweets, where the Sugar-Plum Fairy is Queen, they are entertained with a divertissement in which Spanish, Arab and Chinese dancers represent respectively chocolate, coffee and tea, and there are other delectable dances, culminating in the well-known *Flower Valse*.

In the prominence given to eatables the theme might almost be said to anticipate Richard Strauss's *Schlagobers*. So far as I am aware the only composer attracted to the story was Karl Reinecke, who based on it a set of piano duets, *Nussknacker und Mausekönig*, Op. 46. It was obviously less calculated to appeal to Tchaïkovsky than the romantic fairy-tales which inspired his two major ballets. Nor can he have much relished submitting to Petipa's stringent instructions of which Modest Tchaïkovsky gives this specimen in his biography of his brother:

No. 1. Musique douce. 64 mesures.
No. 2. L'arbre s'éclaire. Musique pétillante de 8 m.
No. 3. L'entrée des enfants. Musique bruyante et joyeuse de 24 m.
No. 4. Le moment d'étonnement et d'admiration. Un *tremolo* de quelques mesures.
No. 5. Marche de 64 mesures.
No. 6. Entrée des Incroyables. 16 m. rococo (tempo menuet).
No. 7. Galop.
No. 8. L'entrée de Drosselmeyer. Musique un peu effrayante et en même temps comique. Un mouvement large de 16 à 24 m.
La musique change un peu de caractère, 24 m. Elle devient moins triste, plus claire et enfin passe à la gaîté.
Musique assez grave de 8 m. et temps d'arrêt.
La reprise des mêmes 8 m. et aussi temps d'arrêt.
4 mesures avec des accords d'étonnement.
No. 9. 8 m. d'un temps de mazourka. 8 autres m. de mazourka. Encore 16 m. de mazourka.
No. 10. Une valse piquée, saccadée et bien rhythmée 48 m. etc.

Petipa had been much less exacting over the composition of *The Sleeping Beauty*. As it happened, however, he was not to complete the choreography of *Nutcracker*. Soon after ·he had begun it he was taken ill, and he entrusted the rest to Lev Ivanov, who was afterwards to collaborate with him in the definitive version of *The Swan Lake*. The ballet was sumptuously staged and performed for the first time under Drigo on December 17, 1892, but despite the prestige now enjoyed by the composer of *The Sleeping Beauty* and the approval expressed by the Tsar at the dress rehearsal it had at first little success. The audience did not take kindly to the German story, so different from the type to which it was accustomed, nor did it welcome the appearance of children in ballet on such a scale. Moreover, Antoinetta Dell'Era, the Sugar-Plum Fairy, was a brilliant prima ballerina but with small claims to personal charm or beauty. Modest Tchaïkovsky ungallantly describes her as downright ugly. At the second performance she was replaced by A. F. Nikitina, one of Ivanov's pupils. It was really the music that saved *Nutcracker* and laid the foundation of its subsequent popularity. As already stated, the best of it is contained in the well-known concert suite. This comprises the Miniature Overture (a delicate piece without 'cellos or basses); the March which accompanies the arrival of the guests; the Dance of the Sugar-Plum Fairy, which is the best solo in the ballet; four numbers from the divertissement: Trepak, Coffee and Tea (represented by Arab and Chinese Dances) and the *Dance of the Mirlitons* (a home-made instrument familiar to French children); and the *Flower Valse*, which follows the divertissement. There are other numbers which may have gone under consideration, such as for instance the *Valse of the Snowflakes*, but there could not be room for two valses in the same suite, and the *Valse of the Flowers* was the right choice. For concert performance the suite leaves little to be regretted. An integral revival of the ballet was staged at Sadler's Wells Theatre on January 30, 1934.

The success of *The Sleeping Beauty* had the consequence of stimulating Vsevolozhsky's interest in the fate of *The Swan Lake*, and he obtained from the composer a promise to revise the score. But the last year of Tchaïkovsky's life was much occupied and he was unable to fulfil his promise before his death in October 1893. Thereupon Petipa requested the score, with anything that might exist of the revision, to be sent to him at St. Petersburg. He soon convinced himself of the importance of the work, and drafted a plan for its revival, which he submitted to Vsevolozhsky. It reinstated the cuts made at Moscow seventeen years before, and merely involved a certain reshuffling of the order in which the numbers were placed. Eventually, however, some additional numbers became necessary, and for these recourse was had to Tchaïkovsky's last set of piano pieces, Op. 72. Those incorporated were No. 12, *L'Espiègle*,[1] No. 11, *Valse Bluette* and No. 15, *Un poco di Chopin* (mazurka). I have no record of the orchestrator, but have always understood that it was Drigo, the conductor.

The Imperial Theatres were anxious to give a special memorial performance, and for this the second act was promptly got ready and presented at the Maryinsky Theatre on February 29, 1894. Nearly a year was to elapse before the first integral performance of this definitive version, which was given at the Maryinsky on January 27, 1895, for the benefit of Pierina Legnani. The style of the choreography and the individual dances were sketched by Petipa, who being much occupied at the time with another ballet, *Le Réveil de Flore*, entrusted L. I. Ivanov with the task of carrying out his general indications.

The story is woven round two girls, Odette and Odile, who resemble each other so closely that one can be mistaken for the other. Originally their rôles were entrusted to two dancers, but as there is only one brief moment when both are seen simultaneously it has long been customary for one prima ballerina to perform both parts, differentiating them by characterisation, facial expression and general style. The ballet is in four acts :

Act I. Prince Siegfried is celebrating his coming of age when his mother enters with her retinue and insists that he must choose a bride from the guests at a ball to be held the following day. Suddenly a flight of swans darkens the sky and the Prince suggests that he and his friends should end the festivity with a hunting-party.

Act II. The banks of the lake, on which the swans are for a moment seen swimming past, with their Queen at their head. The Prince's friends are eager for the chase, but he begs them to leave him, and while he is alone the Swan Queen appears to him in human form as Odette. She tells him that she and her friends are in the power of an evil magician, Von Rothbart, who has transformed them into swans. Only for a short time during the night are they allowed to resume human shape. The spell can be broken only by a lover who has never pledged his faith to another woman.

---

[1] One of the rare cases where one is justified in using a French instead of an English translation of a Russian title. There is no good English equivalent of ' Rezvushka.'—ED.

The Prince, with whom it is a case of love at first sight, proposes to kill the magician, who is to be seen in the form of an owl, but Odette tells him that Rothbart will not die until a lover kills himself for her sake. Meanwhile the hunting-party has returned and the rest of the act is taken up with dances until the swans return to their lake.

Act III. A ballroom, in which possible brides are paraded before the Prince without arousing his interest. Rothbart has a daughter, Odile, whom by his magic he disguises to appear Odette's double, and he brings her to the ball, where, despite the pleading of the Swan Queen from the window, the Prince is deceived into plighting his troth. Odile and her father then vanish and, realising that he has been tricked, the Prince hastens forth in search of Odette.

Act IV. The swans wait the return of their Queen, who tells them that the spell can nevermore be broken because of the Prince's innocent infidelity. Suddenly he appears and implores her pardon. This she grants but, as the magician reminds him, he is now pledged to Odile. Odette embraces him for the last time and throws herself into the lake. In despair the Prince follows her, thereby causing the magician's death and breaking his spell. The lake vanishes and the lovers are united.

Though less consistently rich than the music of *The Sleeping Beauty* that of *Swan Lake* contains many examples of Tchaïkovsky's melodic fecundity. One that haunts the memory is the oboe solo associated with Odette and her swans. It appears at the end of the first act, at the beginning and end of the second, and accompanies such glimpses as one has of Odette in the third. Her adagio in the second act is, as Mr. Abraham has related in the previous chapter, based on the love-duet in the last act of *Undine*. This forms the central movement of the concert suite, which comprises the opening scene of the second act, with the oboe solo mentioned above; the *Dance of the Cygnets* which, both choreographically and musically, is one of the ballet's most popular hits; the aforesaid adagio—or to be pedantically correct, andante non troppo; the Hungarian Dance, or Czardas, from the third act; and the Valse.

Performances of the ballet as a whole are comparatively rare, though it was revived by the Sadler's Wells Ballet on November 20, 1934, and again, in a brilliant new stage-setting by Leslie Hurry, on September 7, 1943, at the New Theatre. Otherwise what has most usually been presented is the second act, which, with some trifling modifications at the beginning and end, is really complete in itself. Under the Dyagilev régime for a time the third act was added for the sake of its divertissement and rounded off with a fragment of the fourth. That divertissement was the occasion on which Pierina

Legnani first displayed her thirty-two *fouettés*. The feat was then an unprecedented *tour de force*, but like many others—and not only in the art of the dance—it soon passed into the normal equipment of any highly accomplished artist. To-day many young dancers have performed it, among whom one may recall Baranova as the Top in Bizet's *Jeux d'Infants*.

The frequent abridgement of *Swan Lake* is better justified on the choreographic than on the musical side. Though the first act contains much that one would not care to lose, it is really little more than a prologue, with a disproportionate amount of miming and some rather naïve comedy for which the composer cannot be held responsible; and the fourth act is too much like the second to be acquitted of a certain redundancy, despite its dramatic *raison d'être*. Those who preferred to present the shorter version were not vandals, but actuated by sound theatrical motives. Nevertheless it gives much pleasure periodically to renew acquaintance with this ballet in its complete form. The Sadler's Wells Ballet has rendered signal service in including in its repertoire all three of Tchaïkovsky's ballets, as only thus can we realise his stature as the greatest master of ballet music in the classical traditions. The nearest approach to him is another Russian, Glazunov, also with three ballets : *Raymonda* (1898), *Ruses d'Amour* (1900), and *The Seasons* (1900)—the latter best known by the *Autumn Bacchanale* with which Pavlova startled London in 1910, the year before Dyagilev brought his Ballet to London. Arensky's *Une Nuit d'Egypte* (1908) was so unequal in quality that when Dyagilev took it over the year after its production, under the title of *Cleopatra*, he made extensive cuts and substituted music by other composers, making, as he was wont to say in later years, the only musical ' salad ' of which he had ever been guilty. Cherepnin's *Le Pavillon d'Armide* (1907), which he also took over at the same time, may be said to mark the end of that phase of ballet music, for although Stravinsky's *The Fire-Bird* (1910) is still formally in the tradition, in content it represents the dawn of modern ballet music, and was followed almost immediately by its first masterpiece, *Petrushka*.

English musicians who have Russian friends are sometimes surprised to find that to these the Tchaïkovsky of the theatre is more important than the composer of symphonies. That is partly because his operas and more particularly his ballets, with their rich flow of sumptuous sound, have the power to evoke a spectacular period in Russia's social history, which his concert works have not. But still more is it the expression of the Russian musical outlook, which has little in common with the æsthetics of German music, and much with that of the French, as is shown by Tchaïkovsky's own predilections. In their conception musical form is shapeliness rather than constructive elaboration, and they could if they chose quote in support the meaning of the Latin adjective *formosus*. It is the plastic and sensuous quality in Tchaïkovsky's music that appeals to them, as it does in that of Glinka, another great melodist, whom western critics seldom rank as high as their Russian confrères. The English musical world was so long exclusively swayed by Teutonic ideas that until comparatively recent times it accepted these as final and beyond challenge. Even now there are some who cling to those views and regard as heretics those who admit the possibility of there being other conceptions of the art of music. But much of the best music of non-German countries such as France and Russia testifies to another, more liberal creed. So let us frankly admire and enjoy the splendid shapeliness of Tchaïkovsky's ballet music and not judge it by standards which do not apply.

9

The Songs

By

A. Alshvang

(Translated by I. Freiman)

TCHAÏKÓVSKY'S CONTEMPORARIES not infrequently blamed him for his free treatment of the texts of his songs. Thus, the initial lines of Lermontov's poem ' The Love of the Corpse ' are presented by the composer, in his Op. 38, No. 5, as follows :

> Let me be covered by the cold earth. Oh friend,
> always, everywhere, my soul is with you, my soul
> always, everywhere, is with you. . . . [1]

Nekrassov's verses in the song ' Forgive,' Op. 60, No. 8, are changed by the threefold repetition of the words : ' Bless, and do not forget, do not forget, do not forget ' . . .

César Cui ridiculed what he considered to be the poor quality of the musical declamation in ' Not a word, O my friend,' Op. 6, No. 2, where the words ' not a sigh ' sound like ' not a si-i-i-gh.' The frequent repetition of separate words, and sometimes of whole sentences, was, in the opinion of the critics, evidence of carelessness and of the composer's adherence to antiquated traditions. Findeisen termed such carelessness ' inexcusable '—particularly after the achievements of Dargomïzhsky, who had created perfect examples of precise musical declamation true to the poetic subject-matter.

The fullest and most detailed of such critical remarks are Cui's in his book *The Russian Song* (1895) :

> His [Tchaïkovsky's] talent does not possess the flexibility required for real vocal music. . . . He did not acknowledge the equal rights of poetry and music. He regarded the text with despotic presumption. . . . Having chosen texts with no artistic value, Tchaïkovsky treated them without ceremony. . . . In the music, the punctuation is very badly observed . . . Tchaïkovsky could not be concise or laconic; he did not know how to write briefly. . . . Not particular in the choice of musical ideas, he nevertheless let go of them with difficulty and developed them

[1] The last six words are not in Lermontov's original.

197

in every possible way. But more often than not, this development consists of repetition and variation, effected with the skilful craft of the
experienced technician.

Tchaïkovsky exhaustively refuted all Cui's charges:

> Our musical critics, often losing sight of the fact that the essential in
> vocal music is truthful reproduction of emotion and state of mind, look
> primarily for defective accentuations and for all kinds of small
> declamatory oversights in general. They collect them maliciously and
> reproach the composer with an assiduousness worthy of a better cause.
> In this Cui has especially distinguished himself and he has gone on
> doing so on every occasion up to now. . . . Absolute accuracy of musical
> declamation is a negative quality, and its importance should not be
> exaggerated. What does the repetition of words, even of whole sen-
> tences, matter? There are cases where such repetitions are completely
> natural and in harmony with reality. Under the influence of strong
> emotion a person repeats one and the same exclamation and sentence
> very often. I do not find anything out of accordance with the truth
> when an old, dull-witted governess [in *The Queen of Spades*] repeats
> at every appropriate opportunity during her admonition her eternal
> ' refrain ' about decency. But even if that never happened in real life,
> I should feel no embarrassment in impudently turning my back on
> ' real ' truth in favour of ' artistic ' truth. The two are completely
> different. . . . For people to confuse them when contrasting speech and
> song is simply dishonest.

Tchaïkovsky also declared that he by no means proposed to submit
to the despotic demands of naturalism (the ' theories of realism,'
as he sometimes called the demands of naturalistic aesthetics). These
words of Tchaïkovsky's are true of all forms of vocal music; he
did not regard so-called ' accurate declamation ' as the key to the
attainment of artistic truth. Not that all the accusations of inexact
declamation are unfounded. Tchaïkovsky repeatedly laid himself
open to such attacks from Cui and others. But how petty is their
carping in comparison with the fullness of content, the incomparable
poetry, of Tchaïkovsky's songs! In the overwhelming majority of
cases he is exonerated for verbal repetition by the musical intention.

What some of his contemporaries did not notice in Tchaïkovsky's
songs—they perceived nothing but the subjective content—has now
become comprehensible to every attentive listener. Tchaïkovsky's
romantic songs are little poems of the kind that go deeper than
merely personal states of mind. These deeply truthful pages are
permeated by a philosophy of life. His songs are comprehensible
to everyone; they go ' from the heart to the heart.' Artistic simplicity, artlessness of musical language, perfection of form, variety

and originality of melody, richness of accompaniment: all these qualities are combined in Tchaïkovsky's musical style. Songs occupy an important place in his work. The fresh stream of song flows in an uninterrupted current, sparkling between the massive symphonies. Song also nourishes other genres of Tchaïkovsky's music; a great number of his operatic arias and cantilenas are closely related to his songs. And in his symphonic works, too, song is a fertilising element.

The songs are strikingly varied and embrace the most different genres : pure lyric and stark drama; solemn hymns and short songs of everyday life; folk tunes and valses. One need only recall the dramatic ' Corals,' Op. 28, No. 2, the exultant colouring of ' Does the day reign,' Op. 47, No. 6, and, finally, the solemn grandeur of the hymn of John of Damascus, 'I bless you, forests,' Op. 47, No. 5, and compare these vocal poems with lyrical miniatures of the type of ' Mid the din of the ball,' Op. 38, No. 3, in order to grasp the wide range of Tchaïkovsky's songs.

The composer draws his musical material in handfuls from the surrounding milieu. Now he takes an Italian street song (' Pimpinella,' Op. 38, No. 6), now the intonations of Russian and Ukrainian peasant *protyazhnïya* ('long-drawn' songs), now the elements of the so-called gypsy song (' Frenzied Nights '), Op. 60, No. 6.

But through all these borrowed and adopted genres runs the personal theme of the composer. It is customary to consider that this ' personal theme ' is the idea of ' fate ' weighing over man, the fear of death. Many of the composer's important works certainly contain figures of a tragic nature and give cause for such an interpretation of his works (themes of ' destiny ' in the Fourth, Fifth and Sixth symphonies, in *Manfred*, *Francesca*, in the operas *Oprichnik*, *Queen of Spades*, in some of the songs, etc.). Usually these are short, easily-memorised motives, and they are used invariably in definite, ' fateful ' situations. However there is no mystic content in these ' themes of fate.' Tchaïkovsky's tragic characters always adopt a positive attitude towards life, and this characteristic of his music is fully evident in his songs.

The composer's ' personal theme ' is displayed in the songs not so much in the actual idea of ' fate ' as in the unveiling of the inner life of a man obstinately fighting for personal happiness. The figure of such a man permeates Tchaïkovsky's lyrics, with their incomparable tranquillity and their sudden storms of a soul passionately longing for active life and insatiably thirsting for happiness.

All these shades of personal emotion are expressed in numerous songs. His creations stand before us in all their beauty and truth, free from the drawing-room affectations and cheap melodrama that some singers have infused into them.

The cycle of Tchaïkovsky's published songs opens with a group of six (Op. 6), composed at twenty-nine. Goethe's beautiful words, ' Nur wer die Sehnsucht kennt ',[1] inspired Tchaïkovsky in the Russian translation by Mey. This song makes its impression by the quiet, severe outline of its expressive melody and by its magnificent climax : ' . . . how I suffer.' The words ' My bosom burns,' which follow this outburst of passionate feeling, are pronounced very softly, and so by contrast reveal their deep emotion.

Heine's ' Warum sind denn die Rosen so blass,' expresses the sadness of love, born of great suffering. Tchaïkovsky's setting of Mey's translation, however, convinces one that the poet's ' cosmic pessimism ' was born exclusively of love's sadness. At the words, ' Why, oh tell me quickly, having abandoned me, did you forget me ? ' the composer produces an emotional explosion which leaves not the slightest doubt of the true content of Heine's poem. The melody now reproduces timid sighs, now reaches terrific strength.

The song ' Not a word, O my friend,' with words by Pleshcheev, is also full of youthful lyricism. Enchanted with the text, Tchaïkovsky here created an intimate elegy : a prototype of many of his popular songs, piano and other pieces (including the *Chanson Triste*, Op. 40, No. 2, and the Canzonetta from the Violin Concerto). A philosophical idea lies at the basis of A. K. Tolstoy's poem, ' Tears trembled in your jealous glance.' Unlike the other songs in Op. 6, it is dedicated, not to a personal emotion, but to the idea of the brotherhood of man. The slow declamation, tense development and brilliant climax are borrowed here from the operatic aria.

The six songs of Op. 16 (1872) are real masterpieces of the young Tchaïkovsky. It is sufficient to name such beautiful works as the ' Cradle Song ' and the ' New Greek Song,' with words by Maykov, and ' Have Patience ' to a text by Grekov. The wide fame of the ' Cradle Song ' is due to the perfection of the music in its organic unity with the text. The figures of the elements—the wind and the waves of the sea—taken from folk-lore, the slow, sad melody expressing the calm after the day's vexations, the light, slowly moving accompaniment—all this makes an irresistible effect.

[1] Beethoven wrote four different settings of this poem.

Grekov's 'Wait' was inspired by Shakespeare, partly by the night scene from *Romeo and Juliet*, partly by the moonlight scene in *The Merchant of Venice*. Tchaïkovsky's song, with its introductory recitative (up to the words ' But shall we see such a night again?'), the continuous rocking of the middle part (' Look, how the floor of heaven is thick inlaid with patines of bright gold . . .') and its philosophical summing-up—is full of charm. Particularly beautiful is the middle part of the song, where the summer-night reveals the limitless world of nature to the two lovers. The melody is saturated with a sense of peace; the ' sighs ' in the accompaniment are related to the horn-motive of the overture-fantasia *Romeo and Juliet*.

The ' New Greek Song ' introduces the sombre medieval ' Dies Irae '; in Berlioz and Liszt it expresses sombre, fantastic visions and the kingdom of death. Tchaïkovsky puts it in the mouth of the singer : ' In dark Hell beneath the earth the sinful shadows are languishing.'

' Gypsy ' themes occur especially often in Tchaïkovsky's songs of the '80s. In his earlier works the slightly melodramatic songs, ' Why did I dream of you?' and ' He loved me so much,' Op. 28, Nos. 3 and 4, are distinguished by this gypsy colouring. Almost at the same time the composer wrote ' The Fearful Minute,' Op. 28, No. 6, to his own words. Here melodrama reaches its height. ' Either you will pierce my heart with a knife or you will open paradise for me '—these words are sufficient evidence of the gypsy character of the whole text. In writing songs of this type, Tchaïkovsky simply paid tribute to his time.

During the same period the composer wrote some most valuable songs based on themes from the life of the people, such as the dramatic ballad, ' Corals ' (text by Syrokomla, trans. Mey), and ' Evening ' (Shevchenko, trans. Mey).

' The Corals ' (Op. 28, No. 2, 1875) is a ballad with a tragic subject. A girl asks her betrothed to bring her a string of corals from the war. The lad returns to his village with the string of corals and learns of his bride's death. The gripping dramatic content of the ballad, the variety of the pictures (the episode of the battle, the funeral ceremony, the scene at the girl's grave), the harmony of the form, the unity of the theme, the national colour of the basic melody—make it a real classic.

Among the songs of popular life should be noted the beautiful song—a plaint of a peasant girl : ' If I'd only known, if I'd only known,' Op. 47, No. 1 (words by A. K. Tolstoy). This song is dramatic in a high degree: it produces an enormous effect by preserving the monotonous manner of folk lamentation. To the setting of Schevchenko's, 'Wasn't I a little blade of grass in the field?' Op. 47, No. 7, Tchaïkovsky gave the character of a folk *protyazhnaya*, with a typical postlude. Both these songs date from 1881.

Tchaïkovsky listens eagerly to the voices of the people. In Italy he notes down the songs of a little street-singer and out of this material he creates his famous 'Pimpinella' (1878), for which the Russian text was written by himself. He shows great interest in the folk-poet Surikov (author of the translation of the above-mentioned Shevchenko poem, 'Wasn't I a little blade of grass in the field?')[1] He writes to Nadezhda von Meck: 'Is a Moscow poet, Surikov, who died this spring from tuberculosis, known to you? He was a self-educated poet; his real job was sitting in a miserable ironmonger's shop selling nails and horseshoes. There he remained till the end of his life, a shop-assistant, but he has real talent and his plays are permeated by genuine feeling.'

'Nightingale,' with words by Pushkin ('Nightingale, my nightingale, little bird of the forest,' Op. 60, No. 4, 1884), is evidence that even in the last period of his work, the composer clung to figures from folk-lore; as regards purity of the style 'The Nightingale' is perhaps his best song of the folk-type.

Watching year by year the changes in Tchaïkovsky's output, we observe a notable extension of his themes and an enrichment by new genres. At the same time the figures of poetic love and of vivid grief, in which the early songs of Tchaïkovsky are rich, are not absent from his later ones. An invariable sense of moderation, beauty of musical form, simplicity and laconicism, mark all his songs. The further he went, the quieter became the character of the emotion. Even despair finds a balanced, artistic expression. At the same time, the poetic forms are saturated more and more with philosophic thought. One of the most perfect songs of this genre, 'Mid the din of the ball,' with words by A. K. Tolstoy (1878), is an example of an almost salon type of song that is nevertheless philosophical in its real meaning. This hidden meaning lies in the artist's tragic loneliness; he feels this particularly acutely at the moment when true beauty' touches him with its wing and then disappears, leaving an ineffaceable mark on his soul. The content of

[1] Shevchenko wrote in Ukrainian.—ED.

this short song does not fit into the conventional formula of the amorous subject. The strange woman who suddenly flashes before the artist's eye embodies a poetic dream—which vanishes like Euphorion, the son of Faust and Helen.

The sweet recollection of youthful love provides the content of some of the mature Tchaïkovsky's songs. In Op. 38 (1878), there is a charming song ' It was in the early spring,' with words by A. K. Tolstoy. The text of the song is an echo of the poetry of the young Heine; the music is reminiscent of the most poetic episodes of Schumann's love songs. The bravura in ' Don Juan's Serenade ' is distinguished by great brilliance and ' theatricalness '; it is almost an operatic aria; the genre is superbly caught. One is forced involuntarily into a comparison of the ' Serenade ' with the well-known air of Robert in the opera *Iolanta*, written fourteen years afterwards. Both pieces are compellingly successful and brilliant; both are related in character, in spite of the difference in the texts.

Of outstanding interest is Tchaïkovsky's great vocal poem, ' I bless you, forests ' (Op. 47, No. 4). The words of the song are borrowed from A. K. Tolstoy's poem *John of Damascus*. Escaping from the magnificent palace of Damascus, John renders solemn homage to nature. He calls upon humanity to fraternise and love and unify itself with nature. The hymn resounds majestically, powerfully, inspiringly. In the same Op. 47 we find another brilliant composition, the song, ' Does the day reign,' with words by Apukhtin. After the delicate watercolours of the early songs, this hymn of triumphant love sparkles with liberated passion, as if its melody had absorbed the animating warmth and light of the sun. It flies and bounds in the air like a bird intoxicated by gleaming space.

' On the golden cornfields ' is filled with profound psychological content. A. K. Tolstoy's text expresses the weariness of separation; Tchaïkovsky's music evokes the distant ringing of bells amid the twilit fields; the quiet evening colouring contrasts with the drama of the sad exclamation : ' My soul is full through separation from you. . . .'

New features characterise also the late songs of the gypsy type. The famous ' Song of a Gypsy,' Op. 60, No. 7, to words by Polonsky (1886), is unusually concentrated; its basic motive is an echo of Carmen, of her ' fate ' theme. The same gravity of content distinguishes ' Frenzied Nights,' Op. 60, No. 6, to words by Apukhtin. The bitter dregs from days spent uselessly, from drunkenness, from suppressed passion, from longing for happiness but disbelief in it —this is the circle of emotion which generated the atmosphere of this song, weighed down by oppressive images. ' The mild stars shone for us,' with words by Polonsky, and especially the last cycle of songs (Op. 73 : 1893), all to words by D. M. Rathaus (' We sat with you,' ' Night,' ' In this moonlight,' ' The sun has set,' ' 'Mid sombre days,' ' Again as before, alone ')—are full of intimate lyricism, psychologically true, human, full of ardent love of life.

The composer, not infrequently agitated by weariness and oppressed by suffering, never sank into sombre abysses of despair in his creative work. He constantly strove toward an optimistic acceptance of life. For his music is born of a living acceptance of reality, of a passionate desire for the highest and of belief in this highest.

It remains to analyse in detail some of the masterpieces among Tchaïkovsky's songs, beginning with Op. 6, No. 1 (1869), based on a poem by A. K. Tolstoy :

> Do not believe, my friend, do not believe, when in a fit of grief
> I say that I no longer love you.
> Do not believe, in the hour of the ebb-tide, do not believe in the
>   treachery of the sea.
> It will return full of love to the land.
>
> I am already longing for you, full of the old passion.
> I shall give up my freedom to you again.
> And already the waves are rolling back with a roar
> From afar to the beloved shores.
>
> Do not believe, my friend, do not believe,
> Do not believe, my friend, do not believe, when in a fit[1] of grief
> I say that I no longer love you.
> Do not believe, in the hour of the ebb-tide, do not believe in the
>   treachery of the sea.
> It will return full of love to the land.

Tchaïkovsky liked Alexey Tolstoy's poetry and frequently turned to his texts; he was apparently attracted by the philosophy which inspires Tolstoy's best poems. One's general impression of this particular song is of the wholeness, the organic nature of the music, of perfection of form, fine elegiac quality and graceful sadness. Analysis confirms this immediate impression and reveals the expres-

---

[1] Tchaïkovsky introduced a small alteration into the text, evidently aiming at greater euphony : ' In a fit,' instead of ' in an abundance of grief.'

sive means which produced this result. Thus the musical unity is conditioned by a key plan akin to sonata form : I. exposition : C sharp minor—E major; II. development : A minor—C sharp minor—F sharp minor—B minor—D sharp minor—G sharp minor; III. reprise : C sharp minor.[1] The elaboration of the accompaniment is due to the variety of chords available in the minor mode, some of them quite remote. Free use is made of alterations and of functional chords founded on the chromatically moving bass. So, for example, the beginning of the voice part is accompanied by chords in C sharp minor on the bass : C sharp, B, A sharp, A, G sharp, F sharp, E, E, E sharp, F sharp, etc.; in the development, the harmonies four times form compact chromatic sequences on the bass : A, A sharp, B, B sharp, C sharp, etc.

This complexity of minor harmony produces an effect of elaboration. But the vocal melody is distinguished by *great simplicity*, and is easy to sing and to memorise. It never goes beyond the limits of the seven notes of the natural minor scale, while the accompaniment from beginning to end is characterised by continual chromatic alterations and other extensions of the natural scale. This contrast between simple vocal melody and complicated accompaniment, with its wide interpretation of the scale and its technical layout, which frequently has an independent, expressive significance, is characteristic of Tchaïkovsky. In the second part of the development section (' and already the waves are rolling back with a roar from afar to the beloved shores '), the semiquaver arpeggio passages are characteristic; in all the other episodes the movement is only in quavers; obviously this different lay-out was dictated by the image of the sea's full tide. Consider too the special characteristics of the vocal melody. The very first four bars reveal its rich content (Ex. 110). The tender first motive perfectly sets the elegiac tone of the music. Such ' looping ' intonations on small intervals (in this case, the minor third : E—C sharp) are among Tchaïkovsky's most expressive motives. Generally speaking, the composer achieved amazing expression by means of motives within the narrow limits of the minor and major thirds, fourths and fifths.

The second motive, with its thrice-repeated G sharp, its leap of a fourth higher and final ' sigh ' (B—A), corresponds to many of the ' themes of inevitability ' so typical of Tchaïkovsky. Here the ' inexorable force of necessity ' is modified by the whole surround-

---

[1] The composer repeated, without alteration, the first quatrain at the end; however, he did not transform the song into a *da capo* aria. Hence the reproach of word-repetition is avoided.

ing: the warm emotion of the first motive, followed by the 'sigh' and, finally, the movement of the accompaniment. However, this 'motive of necessity' preserves its significance throughout the song; it is imitated by the accompaniment marcato; the vocal part of the whole development section is built on its pattern (the repeated note and the upward leap of an octave). The 'sigh' motive acquires a particularly expressive significance in the last four bars of the piano postlude, where it runs parallel in two parts (C sharp—B sharp and A—G sharp). The first motive, with its passionate elegiac quality, dominates the exposition, the reprise, and also the introduction and interlude.[1]

The strained, restless melody with its 'sighs,' its uneasy impulses and theme of 'inevitability' hardly agrees with the completely 'happy' content of Alexey Tolstoy's poem. The composer saturates the music with a substantially different, sad and 'suffering' expression. For Tchaïkovsky, Tolstoy's text was only a pretext for unveiling an incomparably more complicated and sensitive soul-state. We may define the song as *an elegy of love*, a genre overburdened by Tchaïkovsky with an excess of painful emotion, despite the sincerity and complete absence of rhetoric and pretentious pathos.

'To forget so soon' (words by Apukhtin—no opus-number, 1870), possesses outstanding features and was the first example of a new type. Not everything in this song is perfect; only later did Tchaïkovsky succeed in raising the dramatic truth expressed here to the limits of the highest art. But that does not impair the significance of the first impulse towards the creation of a new psychological type of song.

> To forget so soon, my God
> All the happiness of life!
> All our meetings, talks, to forget so soon, to forget so soon!
>
> To forget the emotion of the first days,
> The hour of meeting in the shadow of the branches! the silent
>   speech of the eyes,
> To forget so soon, to forget so soon, so soon.
>
> To forget how the full moon looked upon us through the window.
> How the blind gently swayed . . .
> To forget so soon, to forget so soon, so soon.

[1] I say nothing of the other vocal intonations which do not undergo any development or change—and sometimes are very feeble: for example, the strange progression in thirds at the words ' It will come back towards the land again.'

To forget the love, to forget the dreams,
To forget those vows, do you remember, do you remember, do
  you remember?
In the sad time of the night, in the sad time of the night.
To forget so soon, so soon, my God!

'To forget so soon' successively reveals three different psychological states. The first and third parts are closely connected by community of thematic material. But the second part also organically follows from the first and flows into the third quite naturally.

The content of the music is immeasurably richer than the text. The tonal design is as follows: I. F major; II. D flat major; III. F minor. In the first part there are deviations in the direction of D flat (bars 16 *et seq.*). The second part, which corresponds to the slow movement of a cyclic work, is free from such deviations. It is entirely in D flat major, with the exception of the stringendo passage leading into the third part. The last part, with its 'suffocating' rhythm in the piano accompaniment, and its long piano postlude, consists of two sections very different in character—the vocal and the purely instrumental. This allegro, full of passion and sombre excitement, is a vocal episode unprecedented in force and impetuosity. Short as it is, it is unusually intensive in key development. The harmony changes at almost every half-bar. The recapitulatory passage begins at bar 12 and the tonal development becomes less intensive; the harmonies change only with each whole bar. The tonal plan of this section is: F minor—A flat major—C minor—F minor. The second, purely piano section, in contrast, is not marked by any changes of key: it is in F minor, with sequences on the basic motive.[1]

Thematically, the principal part is played by the initial motive of 'inevitability' (Ex. 111), which is frequently repeated later. This thematic kernel appears fully in the first and third parts, in the major and minor respectively. The complete contrast of the second part is produced by, among other things, the absence of this motive; indeed the second part represents a moment of oblivion when the reminder of heavy loss is no longer heard. The melody becomes fluid and smooth, and even the words 'To forget so soon,' which are

[1] The very first bars contain the notes of the harmonic minor, which with the deviations into D flat show the free treatment of the major scale. In the second part, D flat major too is coloured by the harmonic minor, which occurs also in the voice (bars 15–16). Finally, the third part, the most complicated in its first (vocal) section, is in bold harmonic effects, with chromatic alterations and 'ellipses' which widen the frames of the minor. This variety of tonal language entirely disappears in the last section, where the minor key prevails.

sung piano-pianissimo, are pronounced automatically, as though in sweet oblivion.

The rough pencil sketch of the song, found in the first volume of sketches for the opera *Voevoda*,[1] is instructive.

The first and second parts of this sketch agree in fundamentals with the final version. (The accompaniment is by no means completely written out, nor is the voice sometimes; and the introductory piano bars are wanting, as is usually the case in the composer's song-sketches.) But the third part is written down in such a way that it reveals Tchaïkovsky's creative purpose. The ' suffocating ' rhythm appears immediately : the first three bars are an exact replica of the corresponding place in the piano-accompaniment with its restless pattern. The following three bars—crossed out—point to an attempt to continue on the same lines, but one sees at once that these crossed-out bars lack the intense harmonic development which constitutes the chief charm of the sombrely excited music of the third part. The following bars, after the crossed-out ones, give the same picture of a rather ' sticky ' harmonic background in F minor (two bars), with a vocal solo corresponding to the last exclamation, ' To forget so soon,' immediately before the piano postlude. This variant is pale and colourless in comparison with the bold design of the final version. Evidently the composer was not satisfied with the harmonic structure of the bars crossed out. The desired intensity, the broad development of the third part, did not come at once. But the climax in the vocal solo appears with full clarity, and the composer hastens to write it down in rough outline, leaving the composition of most of the preceding lines ' for afterwards.' On the other hand, the piano postlude is written down fully and exactly; it coincides, down to the smallest details, with the final version.

From these few observations an important deduction can be made. The general form of the accompaniment-movement in the third part was found at once. The routine continuation of this movement, in a minor key, evidently did not agree with Tchaïkovsky's intention. Owing to the brevity of the remaining text, broad development of the third part presented a difficulty. But it was necessary to write down the climax immediately because it represented the corner-stone of the whole structure. Indeed the place for the climax had been found already; hence the piano postlude

[1] The sketch, kept in the archives of the Tchaïkovsky Museum, was written down by the composer considerably later, apparently, than the sketches for *The Voevoda*. This is evident, incidentally, from the fact that the sketch appears on a few blank pages dividing the sketches for the First and Second Acts.

emerged easily, freely and naturally. Now the problem was clear : it was necessary to discover as far as possible a broader harmonic development in the third part preceding the climax. The composer undertook this directly after the conclusion of the last bars of the postlude. The sketch shows a detailed working-out of the accompaniment and vocal part directly after the three strokes marking off the end of the postlude; and these bars written in at the end of the sketch represent a direct continuation of the first three bars of the third part (before the crossed-out passage). It is true there is still no voice part, though it appears in the last bars of the sketch; but it is evident that this is a direct continuation, which essentially agrees with the final version. Unfortunately it breaks off at the fourteenth bar, and we do not know how Tchaïkovsky arrived at the extremely expressive final version of the climax itself (bars 15—23).

The composer evidently could not satisfy himself even with so skilful a solution of the problem of enlarging the form : the first section of the third part (including the climax) is still too short, and the slow postlude which emphasises the ' inevitability ' theme and also the fundamental minor tonality, can only partly compensate for this considerable defect. In its final version, the composer made a ritenuto (bars 8 *et seq.*), enlarged—by comparison with the original sketch—the climactic solo (six bars instead of four), and, finally, introduced in the third bar of the postlude the last words of the voice part (' My God ') so as to extend it.

But, with all this, the form as a whole is uneven. And the element of disappointment and desperation comes out all the more. In the first part, the fundamental idea of disappointment and suffering emerges movingly and simply; it is full of perplexity; the soul cannot comprehend its hurt. Then comes the recollection of the happiness experienced : the moonlit night, the swaying of the blind—two or three strokes of the pen which portray the intimacy of completely reciprocal love. The lips are still whispering words of resentment, but the imagination is drawing pictures full of undisturbed happiness. This is expressed in the beautiful nocturne-like music of the second part, with its crystallised charm of remembrance.[1] Then suddenly comes a restlessly gloomy, passionately disquieted state of mind. Pain burns unexpectedly. A poignant cry is uttered, a remembrance of vows ' in the dark night.' The voice of passion overwhelms all other voices; only the heavy blows

[1] The whole passage is based on a pedal D flat and contains neither modulations nor extensions of the major key.

of ebbing passion, the sad repetition of the same tiresome motive, drown this cry.

The rhythmic patterns of the song are interesting : instead of squareness we get a constant alteration of two-bar and three-bar patterns. For example, the very first vocal phrase falls into two groups ('To forget you so soon, my God'—three bars; 'All the happiness of life'—two bars). This structure is the basis of the entire first part. In the second part, after two three-bar patterns, four-bar and two-bar groups appear. The same alternations characterise the first (vocal) section of the third part.

This song was not understood at first. For his friends and admirers, Tchaïkovsky was apparently only a lyrical composer, an exponent of tasteful elegiac art. The tragic dissatisfaction of the artist and his tireless struggle for happiness remained beyond the comprehension of many of his contemporaries during his whole creative life.[1]

The structure of this type of song originates in the classical aria. The first part corresponds to the dramatic recitative, the second part to the slow, lyrical episode, full of deep feeling, and the third part to the final allegro. But this does not explain the essentially new content of the song : its thematic unity, its tonal design, the very character of the expressed passion, and so on. All these character istics go beyond the limits of the classical aria : this is the birth of a new type of song. It is essentially a dramatic monologue, cyclic in form, short in duration, deeply psychological in content. The furthest development of this genre is seen in the song, 'If I'd only known' (1880), with its monothematism, contrasted development, cyclic form and fine psychological characteristics.

The dramatised ballad, 'In dark Hell' ('New Greek Song,' words by Maykov, Op. 16, No. 6, written in 1872) is one of the most important of Tchaïkovsky's earlier works. Its dark colouring, its vividness and its theme, forcibly recall Liszt's sonata, *Après une lecture de Dante* (1837) on the one hand, and Tchaïkovsky's own *Francesca* on the other.

> In dark Hell beneath the earth, the sinful shadows are languishing,
> The maidens are lamenting, the women are crying, and all are sad
>   and all are grieving
> That the news does not reach the infernal boundaries.

---

[1] Cui chose this song as a target for attacks on the continual repetition of the same words, especially the last words, 'My God': ' " My God " is just what the listener desperately repeats after Tchaïkovsky.' The critic forgot that these incriminating words occur in the first line of Apukhtin's poem. Their repetition at the end of a highly dramatic musical interpretation is fully justified.

The women are crying and lamenting : is there a blue sky?
Is there a wide world? Are there God's churches in the world?
And golden ikons? And, as before, behind the looms,
Are the young maidens weaving? Are the young maidens weaving?
In deep dark Hell beneath the earth the sinful shadows are
    languishing,
The maidens are lamenting, the women are crying, and all are sad
    and all are grieving!

The 'New Greek Song' is written on the variation principle,
the theme being the thirteenth-century 'Dies irae' which by the
clarity of its melody, its brevity and sombre strength, has attracted
the attention of so many romantic musicians. In the 'New Greek
Song,' Tchaïkovsky has given an entirely original musical embodi-
ment to the poetic myth of infernal torment, on this same melodic
basis. He was influenced by Liszt. But, as so often happened with
Tchaïkovsky, the obvious influence of the musical language of
other composers has by no means robbed his work of originality.

The variations follow each other in uninterrupted succession in
the same metre and tempo. The individual variations are outstanding in metro-rhythmical, melodic and harmonic inventiveness.
The voice does not always take the predominant melodic part; it
appears mostly as a counter-melody in a way that occurs extremely
seldom in Tchaïkovsky's vocal works. The course of the 'endless
melody,' passing frequently from voice to accompaniment in an
unbroken chain of melodic variations, is original in the highest
degree. The metrical displacements, throwing the original down-
beats of the melody on weak parts of the bar, are characteristic. The
variations gradually grow away from the theme so far that only its
most general forms of movement remain, and only the end,
balancing the beginning, brings back the theme exactly. Thematic
unity is carried through so carefully, that even the melodic semiquaver figuration in the accompaniment is built on the 'Dies
irae' motive (cf. Ex. 112).

No less interesting is the harmonic structure of the song. By
using different aspects of the minor key—natural, harmonic, full,
by recourse to simple modulations and enlargements of function
(for example, double dominants), by introducing new colours in the
scale by chromatic alteration, Tchaïkovsky achieves a striking range
of harmony fully justified by the inner content of the text. The
introduction presents the theme of the sombre sequence in the
simplest, natural minor harmony, with a predominance of plagal
inflections. The minor dominant, the diminished triad on the

second degree of the scale, the flattened leading note, all combine to give the ancient melody a hard, virile character. The next four bars transfer the melody to the voice, while alterations, the sharpened leading-note and the double dominant appear in the accompaniment. But these novelties appear only in the second part of the four-bar period and are quite unobtrusive : the music retains the character of severity. The continuation is bolder at the words, ' The maidens lament, the women are crying and are sad and grieving,' the theme plays the part only of a cantus firmus. Against its background (scarcely audible), the piano develops a complicated, harmonic design over a chromatically-descending bass. The whole conception has, as its basis, a variant of the famous Protestant *Choral* ' Weinen, Klagen ' used by Bach and revived by Liszt. On the foundation of this continuous movement of descending semitones, the composer builds ingenious chords, whose sequence takes us definitely beyond the limits of major and minor. The harmonic sequence repeats the same augmented and diminished triads, alternating with six-four chords.

Thus the variant of the Protestant *Choral*, telling of the tears and grief of mankind, supplements the harsh old Catholic sequence. Tchaïkovsky usually softens his numerous ' themes of fate' by introducing the factor of ' human suffering.' The same occurs here : a prayer for mercy immediately follows the inflexible *Choral* with its reminder of the Last Judgment. The three-part variation, ' Weinen, Klagen,' resembles Liszt's variations on the same theme.

Thus in the very first eight-bar period after the voice enters, the central idea of the song is revealed; sombre, oppressive forces and a prayer for mercy. It is interesting to note that the ' Weinen, Klagen ' episode corresponds with the sense of the words : both dealing with the tears of oppressed souls. The complicated thematic fabric of the accompaniment, ' Dies irae ' in combination with ' Weinen, Klagen,' and the complicated harmonic sequence— all this, in a strictly three-part structure—did not hamper Tchaïkovsky in the design of his voice part : the intonations express the whole weight of grief of the unhappy lost souls. This four-part episode (three parts on the piano and the singer's part), represents an ideal, almost Mozartean perfection of part-writing and shows Tchaïkovsky's superb technical mastery.

The episode ends with a cadence in G flat major, the G flat triad replacing the relative minor, E flat minor, which is apparent in the next two chords (dominant and tonic in E flat minor). Thus the episode just considered leads away from the solid tonic section of the song (E flat minor, first twelve bars). The second episode is an eight-bar period; harmonically it consists of a modulation to the minor dominant, i.e. to B flat minor; the 'Dies irae' theme appears now in the accompaniment, now in the voice, undergoing substantial changes and preserving only the first four notes, which serve merely as a starting-point for the further free development of the theme. The new key is strengthened by the scale-movement of the highest and lowest parts of the accompaniment in contrary motion. This method of 'strengthening' tonality was, as is well known, worked out by Schumann, whose influence on Tchaïkovsky is beyond doubt although it still awaits proper study by musicologists.

The greatest interest is presented by the third section, with its metro-rhythmic displacement of the 'Dies irae' theme; with accompaniment figuration illustrating the words 'and, as before, behind the looms are young maidens weaving'; with a gradual 'deformation' of the theme; and with chromatic contrary motion of the outside parts (left-hand of the accompaniment) making it impossible to define whether the mode is major or minor. This repeated harmonic progression is borrowed from Liszt (see his *Mephisto-Valse*, bars 165–172). The fact that these progressions are obvious extensions of the scale does not give us the right to conclude that the whole episode represents a complete scheme of extended tonality. It is doubtful if such a formal key principle was at any time thought of by Tchaïkovsky. It is safer to suppose that he saw in such unusual constructions only empirical 'harmonic progressions' which could be concluded with a cadence of the traditional type. But the tendency to these unusual forms of harmonic thinking in this episode is indisputable. Compare also the final episode of the third section (Ex. 112). The typical slowing down in Ex. 112, through sestolets, groups of four, triplets and groups of two, effects the transition back to the initial episode : the 'Dies irae.' The music being reduced to a single line in Ex. 112, the previous harmonic colouring by diminished chords fades out and the ornamental figure, moving within a very narrow range, melts naturally into the E flat minor of the last section.

The fourth section does not introduce any new element, but completes the symmetry and brings the listener back to the original image of harsh judgment. A painful impression is left only by the noisy piano postlude with its sombre bravura. In other respects the 'New Greek Song' is an example of perfect art—from its

213

thematic unity and its broad treatment of the subject to its mass of detail. The musical content, as almost always with Tchaïkovsky, goes beyond the poetic text. But the words are expressed and supplemented by music so superb that even Cui, with all his ill-will towards Tchaïkovsky, was obliged to recognise the ' Song ' as a flawless work of art.

' Reconciliation,' with words by N. Shcherbina, Op. 25, No. 1 (1875), is of great interest both in type and in form—which introduces a new principle of unification of parts. Shcherbina's text is full of melancholy and is dictated by a feeling of desperation, of profound disillusionment, acknowledgment of weariness, and longing for rest and oblivion :

> Oh fall asleep, deeply my heart !
> Do not awake the past.
> Do not call back what is far away.
> Do not love what you loved before.
> Let not your sleep and peace
> Be troubled by hope and false dreams.
> For you, the past is irrevocable.
> There is no hope in the future.
> You did not know peace in happiness;
> Calm yourself, then, on your bed of suffering.
> And try not to remember in the winter
> That you plucked roses in the spring !
> Oh fall asleep, my heart, deeply !
> Do not awake the past.
> Do not call back what is far away.
> Do not love what you loved before.
> Let not your sleep and peace
> Be troubled by hope and false dreams !
> And try not to remember in the winter
> That you plucked roses in the spring !

This kind of lyrical poetry is the basis of many songs of everyday life in the second half of the nineteenth century, songs with sentimental melodies, with the simplest cadence-formulas, and with a dash of emotional unrestraint (which was emphasised by the customary manner of performance).

' Reconciliation ' is the earliest example of the gypsy genre in Tchaïkovsky's work. The range of the voice part, covering almost two octaves, from the low A to G in alt (sung forte) with its big jumps; the simplest harmonic accompaniment, almost banal in its guitar-like turns and cadences; the introduction and postlude consisting of a continual repetition of the same motive and the same plagal cadence: all these features are characteristic of the gypsy songs, so different from the reserve and economy of Tchaïkovsky's other songs.

Tchaïkovsky's mastery of harmonic resource allows him to hide the many banal touches by complicated alterations, by evenly descending basses, and by modulations. The varied rhythm of the vocal part and the skilful sequences help to give distinction; the bare couplet structure of the ordinary gypsy songs is replaced by one more strongly welded; above all, ' Reconciliation ' is distinguished from the popular gypsy folk songs by its organic unity of form : the recapitulation sums up the metres of the first and second sections.

The source from which Tchaïkovsky drew—the ordinary gypsy songs—is obvious. Take the opening phrase of the voice part, ' O fall deeply asleep, my heart! ' (Ex. 113). One of the distinguishing characteristics of that phrase is that the A remains unresolved over the firm harmonic basis (subdominant, dominant, tonic); this, with the wide range of the melody (the major sevenths : B flat—A), gives the whole phrase a melodramatic colouring very typical of the gypsy genre.

Before leaving Tchaïkovsky's earlier songs for those of his maturity, I should like to mention one of his few essays in the folk-song genre : ' As they kept on saying, " Fool!" ' (words by Mey, Op. 25, No. 6, 1875) :

> As they kept on saying, ' Fool! Keep away from ·the Tsar's
>   tavern.'[1]
> So they say : ' Drink water and not wine.
> Go and bow to the little river, learn from the quick one.'
> I shall go to the river, I shall speak to it.
> " They tell me you are clever : I shall bow very low to you.
> Teach me how to behave so as not to shame people by my
>   drunkenness.
> Not to shame people by my drunkenness.
> How to drown in you, my river, my anguish which is like a serpent.
> If you will teach me that, then I will say : ' Long life to you, river !
> You have enticed the fool away from the Tsar's tavern !'

The word *romans*[2] certainly does not apply to this composition with its clearly expressed naturalism. Scenes from the everyday life of the people do not occupy an important place in Tchaïkovsky's work as a whole, but there are some fine examples in *Vakula the*

---

[1] i.e. the *vodka* shop.
[2] The common Russian—or rather adopted French—word for the *Lied* or art-song.—ED.

Smith, written at the same period as this song. The song itself is an extremely good one, its sad irony cloaked with humour but emphasised by the tragic element in the music. Tchaïkovsky has left no other song like it, though he touched the same field to some extent in some of his children's songs and in a few projects which never materialised (sketches for settings of Pushkin's 'Vurdalak' and 'The Amazing Case' by an unknown poet).

The music corresponds most nearly to the dance-songs of the peasants. 'Only the Russian dancing songs have rhythms with square-cut and regularly-stressed bars,' wrote Tchaïkovsky to Leo Tolstoy (December 24th, 1876). But not only the regular stresses show the dance character of the tune: the accompaniment is, for the most part, a typical strummed folk-dance accompaniment: stamping lower parts on the string beats, with treble chords on the weak ones. This background throws the mournful content of the song into high relief. The use of a particular type of music—folk dance, *protyazhnaya*, march, or even operatic bravura—to express subject-matter foreign to the type is a most effective artistic device. Striking examples of it will be found in Mussorgsky's *Songs and Dances of Death*, where types of music associated with human *life*—a cradle song, a folk-dance, a march—become expressions of the idea of *death*.

The melodic outline of Tchaïkovsky's song is distinctly akin to folk-song. The typical intonations of peasant song had already been studied by Sokalsky (whose book, *Russian Folk Song*, was in Tchaïkovsky's library), and in recent times Kastalsky has clearly defined the melodic peculiarities of Great Russian songs. And the characteristic melodic cadences and scale-structures of the peasant tunes are presented by Tchaïkovsky in their original forms. Thus the last phrase of the song ('from the Tsar's tavern') (Ex. 114) is a genuine bit of folkish 'natural' minor, typical in its downward leap to the tonic (E flat, D, C, G). The whole melodic line of the song is full of such patterns. In one passage, 'Teach me how to behave so as not to shame people by my drunkenness,' Tchaïkovsky uses the change from 4/4 to 3/2, often found in Slavonic folk-songs, though keeping the basic movement in crotchets. Although this is borrowed from folk-lore, it is done here to compress the rhythm, giving peculiar expressiveness to the declamation. Despite this intention, which goes beyond the limits of folk-melody, it is carried out through the adaptation of a true folk-method and does not disturb the stylistic unity of the song. The allegation that Tchaïkovsky took no interest in peasant song, but reproduced the characteristics only of the popular songs of the cities, rests on no sound foundation.

We have now examined in detail five songs by the young Tchaïkovsky, all published between 1869 and 1875, and our analysis has shown some of the typical methods of his realistic art. In these early songs he had already covered a large range of musical types. In his mature period he developed his earlier discoveries and mastered new types of song. Let us turn now to the analysis of some individual, outstanding songs composed by Tchaïkovsky during the fifteen-year period, 1878–1893. But first let us stop to consider a work written in 1875. This is ' The Corals,' with words translated by Mey from the Polish of Syrokomla (Op. 28, No. 2).

As I went with the Cossacks,
Hanna said:
' By my tears I succeeded in moving
God to help you:
You will return from the first battle,
Cheerful and in good health.
Bring, then, to me for my prayers
A string of corals.'
God gave us a chieftain.
Immediately we smashed soundly
The whole of the Khan's army,
Captured the town,
Burst open the strong gates.
A feast, a feast, for the Cossacks!
I have only one worry—
The string of corals!

Suddenly, they were flashed before my eyes,
Apparently, apparently, the All-Highest helped,
And the corals were suddenly plunged into the hollow of my hand,
Like a blood-red, large cherry.

I pressed the prey tightly,
And took to my heels:
I rushed straight to Hanna across the steppe
With the string of corals.
I didn't stop to seek a ford, a dam or a bridge. . .

The bells are ringing in our parish;
The people are thronging out of the cemetery,
And the whole mass of people are shouting to me
With a hundred voices:
' Hanna is there—but she doesn't need
The string of corals!'

217

My heart contracts, sinks,
In my broken breast.
And, weeping, I fall from my horse,
Before the ikon.
Silently, I beg for mercy,
And hang on the frame of the ikon . . .
The string of corals!

The author of the text, the well-known Polish poet-democrat, Syrokomla (the pseudonym of L. Kondratowicz), won a wide reputation by folk poems depicting the wretched life of the Polish peasant. 'The Corals' is a simple narrative of a girl's death; there is nothing specifically folk-like in it; but the very tone of the narration, the tragic simplicity with which the story is told, the way of life that underlies these few words, the very choice of words and expressions—all this speaks of peasant grief. The happiness of the young peasant is mercilessly shattered, and the modest gift so eagerly awaited by the girl becomes an expression of her unhappy fate. Tchaïkovsky perceived the folk basis of Syrokomla's poem. His music is deep and persuasive, distinguished by rare vigour and roundness of imagery. The composer has revealed everything that remained unexpressed in the words : the foreboding of the tragic end is felt at the very beginning of the song.

'Corals' goes beyond the limits of the *romans*. The complexity of the theme, the narration of different events following one upon the other, the alternation of subjective experiences with pictures drawn from life—all this justifies one in calling it a *folk-ballad*. The musical themes are fundamentally national. Thus the short melody (Ex. 115), which is the thematic basis of the whole, is marked by patterns typical of the peasant songs of the Slavonic peoples. From this moving melody, which in different forms passes from the melancholy to the active and dramatic, the composer has evolved a magnificent folk-song-like narrative. Artistically it stands on the same level as Tchaïkovsky's best symphonic and operatic compositions.

The first section (the first strophe of the text) is devoted to Hanna turning to her betrothed as he departs for the war. She will pray for him; he will return safely and bring her a string of corals. The melody quoted as Ex. 115 constitutes a sort of leitmotive for Hanna; it underlies the whole of her simple words. A funereal tolling accompanies them, predicting her fate in an almost requiem-like episode. The gloom is deepened by the monotonous change of harmony—subdominant/tonic on a tonic pedal in F sharp minor.

Is not this the prototype of the finale of the Sixth Symphony? The music does not in the least correspond with the cheerful sense of Hanna's words; the contrast is complete. The tragic character of the music is a premonition of the girl's fate, a shadow cast by coming events—such as we often find in Tchaïkovsky. The listener *expects* something evil. Hanna's final words, ' a string of corals,' on the last notes of her theme, hang ominously in the air; the motive is taken up by the accompaniment and dies away in the deep bass. And so this mournful moderato reaches its conclusion. Hanna's motive appears later as a refrain, repeated at the end of each episode.

The second section, allegro con spirito, gives a picture of the battle. The 2/4 march time,[1] the march-like figures in the accompaniment (two semiquavers—crotchet), the martial words, the aggressive musical theme (Ex. 116): all these features make the music of the second section almost illustrative. Yet over the whole animated melodic design lies a tragic shadow : the sharply marked march figures (bars 13–14 and 16–17 from the beginning of the second section)[2] are echoed in a transition passage in the first movement of the Sixth Symphony, composed eighteen years after ' The Corals.' The same gloomy colouring marks the analogous figures of the brass (trumpet, trombone, tuba), at a moment of extreme ' pressure,' of maximum intensity (un poco animato, pages 10–11 of the Eulenburg miniature score). A sense of ominous challenge characterises this symphonic wave, suddenly boiling up with its threatening intonations and cutting through the complicated polyphony. The battle picture in ' The Corals' is on an incomparably smaller scale, of course—not only in length, but harmonically, tonally and rhythmically. Nevertheless one recognises the intonations of ominous anxiety common to the two very different works. Immediately after the battle scene, the refrain in F sharp minor reappears—Hanna's theme. Typical is the slower movement of the melody, interrupted by the piano accompaniment, now prompting, now imitating, the voice part (meno mosso. Tempo 1). This recollection of the promised gift is a stimulus to further action.

The third part (allegro non tanto), is a development section. Its accompaniment is built on an almost continuous pedal E, with a typical ' disquieting ' texture (alternation of lower and higher voices

---

[1] The second section is the only one where triple time is replaced by duple.

[2] Constituting a minor variant of the similar patterns in the second and fifth bars of the same section.

in quavers). The keys change (B minor, C sharp minor, D major); the motives of the voice part are closely linked by sequences. The growing tension is expressed by stretto-like compression of the rhythm. These melodic variations result from the fusion of a variant of the intonations of the second section (a sort of continuation of the battle picture), with the metrical figures (minim-crotchet) typical of the first section. The hero has got possession of the string of corals; that is the culmination of his military adventures. The third section, like the second, depicts the outside world, far from the village and from Hanna. It is a world full of anxiety, activity, movement; where one must watch and fight and hunt for what one wants. And only the thought of the corals—a sort of refrain at the back of the hero's mind—is connected with Hanna. Thus the melody of the third section knits intimate lyricism with images of the outside world.

The fourth section allegro con fuoco, constitutes the climax of the drama. The piano accompaniment drops its usual modest function, becoming almost symphonic in its tension, its rich imitative polyphony, its syncopated basses moving downward, its powerful climaxes. This is the tragic finale, predicted by the funereal moderato : the hero rushes back to his native village and is met by Hanna's funeral. In its highest register the voice gives the shouts of the crowd : ' Hanna is there but she doesn't need the corals!' Hanna's theme dies away in the piano part.

As regards key-system, there is a characteristic duality : the beginning of the fourth section presents a balance between D major and its relative B minor, which is also maintained later on, in spite of slight deviations (F sharp minor). Only at the very climax is the basic key (F sharp minor), as a sort of resultant of all the previous keys, clearly defined : the triads of D major, B minor, C sharp minor, take their place in the ' natural ' F sharp minor. This suppression of the fundamental key, with its appearance only at the end as a resultant of various related keys, is a beautiful means of attaining formal unity.

The dramatic concentration is admirable; in thirty seconds the composer paints a picture of people and hero, expresses a feeling of despair, and depicts the central incident of the drama. The picture is rounded off in the piano part with its mournful postlude. Tchaïkovsky contrived this compactness of form by masterful interweaving of motives, by his striking key-scheme, and, finally, by the exceptionally powerful climax on the high F sharp and A in the voice part, accompanied by his favourite subdominant-tonic cadence with a typical alteration : the 6/5 chord on the fourth degree of the scale, with the sixth sharpened.

In the following andante a new repetition of Hanna's theme attains the significance of an independant episode (up to the words, ' and weeping, I fell from my horse before the ikon '). Her theme is heard over a pedal F sharp; but this time its last figure (bar 2 of Ex. 115) unfolds in two sequences. There is a modulation to the subdominant, B minor; the whole development is achieved by plagal patterns and by the upward movement of all the parts, except the pedal in the bass. In the second part of the andante the mournful vocal intonations are not strikingly significant; they merge into the general movement imperceptibly, just as the part of Isolde in the last scene of *Tristan* is almost engulfed in the symphonic web. This expressive ritornello leads directly to the epilogue (poco più mosso), where the music exactly corresponds with the ' agitated ' texture of the third section : the same pedal point, the same ' imploring ' figure in the tenor. The key is A major, with a dominant pedal E; only in the second half of the epilogue does it reach the basic F sharp minor[1] The last phrases of the voice part are interrupted by pauses; there is an especially long pause before the last phrase, ' the string of corals '—three whole bars, all on the same unfolding motive of bar 2 of Ex. 115. The motive is imitated by the piano; in the last two bars the imitation is inexact (D—D—C sharp—A—F sharp); its pace is retarded and it passes into the deep bass, suggesting distance and disappearance.

The significance of the motives worked out through the whole song should be noted. Thus the ' unfolding ' melody, several times referred to, appears in the voice part only with the words, ' the string of corals.' Besides this leitmotive we also find the well-known ' theme of fate ' (or ' inevitability '). It appears in the vocal part of the fourth section in its classical form : C sharp—C sharp—C sharp/E—C sharp, F sharp—F sharp—F sharp/A and even in the form consecrated by Beethoven : B—B—B—G. The almost complete absence of Tchaïkovsky's usual ' sigh ' intonation is in accordance with the stern simplicity of the music. As regards key-scheme, the whole ballad is solidly constructed; the modulations are controlled by the demands of formal unity : first section, F sharp minor;

[1] The pedal E is combined throughout with an F sharp : evidence of the bi-tonal character of the epilogue, a balancing between A major and F sharp minor. The latter gets the upper hand only at the very end.

refrain, F sharp minor; second section, D major—B minor; refrain, F sharp minor; third section, B minor—C sharp minor—D major; fourth section, D major—B minor; refrain, F sharp minor; fifth section, E major—F sharp minor; refrain, F sharp minor. The richness of the tonal language is shown by the abundance of 'balancing.' tonics and its unity by the refrains, all based on the same motive and all in the same key. In the sections where subjective experiences predominate, plagal progressions are heard almost exclusively (first section, all the refrains). Where the outside world is illustrated, authentic progressions, dominant-tonic, predominate (second, third, fourth sections).

The rhythmic structure of 'The Corals' is peculiar; it is by no means square-cut but flexibly follows the intonations of the spoken word. Two of the most important refrains stand out, not only by tempo, key and thematic content. In distinction from the other sections the refrains are constructed in three-bar patterns: in the first case—two three-bars; in the second—three three-bars. The pauses, the broadening of the metre, the tight drawing together of the motives—all show the narrative character of even the piano part.

Thanks to the artistic quality of the ballad as a whole, the unequal value of some of its melodic elements passes almost unnoticed. Besides the fine themes of Hanna and the battle scene, appear paler, more mediocre elements. But the unity, the impetus, the wholeness of the content, the harmony of the thought expressed —by a variety of means—entirely justify Tchaïkovsky's frequent use of themes and melodies of unequal value. As a dramatic ballad 'Corals' has no precise prototype in Tchaïkovsky's work. True, the 'New Greek Song' is also a sort of ballad, but its variation-design and consequent lack of thematic contrast, distinguishes it from the many-sided, and in subject realistic, 'Corals.' The exceptional terseness of the music in conjunction with the complicated musico-psychological and pictorial content, makes 'The Corals' unique in the heritage of Russian song.

The soprano song, 'If I'd only known,' Op. 47, No. 1 (1881), a setting of words by A. K. Tolstoy, is an example of a type of folk-lamentation used by Tchaïkovsky in earlier songs. But the theme of the song and the approach are entirely original:

> If I'd only known, if I'd only known
> I wouldn't have looked out of the window
> At the bold lad,
> As he went down our street,

Putting his hat on sideways,
As he threw his spirited, light bay,
Sound-legged, long-maned, .
Horse on its haunches opposite the window!
If I'd only known, if I'd only known,
I wouldn't have dressed myself up for him,
I wouldn't have twisted my long plait
With a red ribbon with a golden border,
I wouldn't have risen before daybreak,
I wouldn't have hurried along the fields,
I wouldn't have wet my feet in the dew,
I wouldn't have looked at the cross-roads,
To see if he would pass along this road or not,
Holding a many-coloured hawk in his hand.
If I'd only known, if I'd only known!
If I'd only known, if I'd only known!
I wouldn't have sat in the late evening
Depressed, on the bench near the well,
Waiting and anticipating
Whether he'd come or not, my enchanting one,
Whether he'd come or not, my enchanting one.
Ah, ah! whether he'd come, my enchanting one,
To water his horse in the cold water!
If I'd only known, if I'd only known!
If I'd only known, if I'd only known, ah!

The chief weakness of the song lies in the long introduction (15 bars, allegro moderato), which is repeated at the end as a postlude. Although the music of the introduction contains important thematic elements, it does not correspond in the least with the subject of the song. The sonority of the upper register of the piano suggests little bells or a musical-box, but nothing with any immediate relation to the text. Yet this episode, however inappropriate, was conceived by Tchaikovsky as an indispensable element of the song, as we see from his first pencil sketch in the margin of the volume of A. K. Tolstoy's poems (Ex. 117).[1] The splendid expressive monologue coming after this immediately destroys the 'toylike' impression created by the introduction. It is vigorous and human and full of significance in every part. It is constructed symmetrically: first moderato, then molto più mosso, vivace, and finally, after a stormy interlude, moderato as at the beginning. It is based on the principle of motive-development.

The whole of the first part is built on free, rising sequences of the same three-bar motive. The motive itself (Ex. 118) shows some

[1] The definitive version is in half note-values and the semiquaver pattern is modified. The missing key-signature is three flats.—ED.

relation with Russian folk-lamentations. Beginning with the third three-bar period, a chain of sequences gradually rises to the upper register of the voice, with a gradual dynamic increase. The main charm of these rising lamentations lies in their alternation with the laconic chord-groups in the piano accompaniment—on one sustained note (mainly G). The monotonous construction gives the whole slow sequence a character of passionate concentration on one thought, on one bitter recollection; the increasing range—together with the sustained note—suggests almost an obsession, which reaches its maximum development in the middle part : poco più mosso, vivace. This agitated, strenuous music shows a close thematic affinity with the preceding part. But the separate, 'amputated' motives of the previous designs are now expressed vehemently, almost feverishly, with strained breath, in a new and more broken-up rhythmic design; all of which justifies us in speaking of complete motive-transformation. In tempo, time-signature (3/8), and lay-out of the piano accompaniment, in its whole character of extreme emotion, a sort of nakedness of feeling—this music is akin to the third part of 'To forget so soon.' But how the composer had developed in ten years! In the earlier song the sense is weakened by its final section.

In 'If I'd only known,' on the contrary, there is a sound, psychologically justified development : after twelve excited, short and continuously mounting phrases in the same somewhat 'gypsy-like' rhythm[1] (on two pedal-points), comes a meno mosso on high notes, *ff,* which by its emphasis introduces an element of despair ('I wouldn't have wet my feet in the dew'); then, without interruption, comes a vivace bringing the expression of this feeling of despair to its logical conclusion. (The phrase-construction, 4+4+2+5, gives a sort of summing-up of the previous short patterns). The emotional wave—the impetuous rise, the climax, the cry of pain—is kept in due proportion, is expressed *protractedly* and constitutes an organic, musical form. The transition to the reprise is effected with the same psychological precision : the unspent energy of despair is finally discharged in an instrumental recitative typical of Tchaïkovsky (Ex. 119). Its beginning repeats the running string-figure which accompanies Tatyana's appearance in the third scene, and Onegin's in the final scene, of *Eugene Onegin.* Its end anticipates the gloomy phrase of the violas in the introduction of the Sixth Symphony. There are three motives in this recitative which together express the

[1] The same rhythm as in the popular 'Black Eyes,' well known at that time.

idea of fate: the motive of 'suddenness' (bars 1–2), the motive of poignant suffering (bars 3–7), and the motive of stern implacability (bars 8–13), hardening into an evil, interrogative intonation.

The reprise differs from the first part in key plan: the harsh succession of C minor and its minor dominant (C minor—G minor —C minor) is now softened; the modulations do not go beyond the flattened supertonic. The reprise is skilfully extended: after an extended melodic recitative, there appears a phrase ('Whether he'd come, my enchanting one, to water his horse in the cold water!') quoted as Ex. 120. The mood of loving expectancy and hope is emphasised by the slower tempo, the more compact motive-structure, the more passionate expression. But, after the fermata, the moderato reappears and the momentary burst of passion of the preceding phrase sinks into hopeless dejection: 'If I'd only known, if I'd only known . . .'

'If I'd only known' is a remarkable synthesis of the folk-lamentation with the intonations of the passionate *romans*, a synthesis which reflects the corresponding one in A. K. Tolstoy's poem. On the basis of this synthesis, Tchaïkovsky has painted a picture of a Russian peasant girl's sufferings, a theme elaborated by many Russian composers—from Dargomïzhsky to Rimsky-Korsakov—but which was given the widest possible development by Tchaïkovsky.

New tendencies appear in the splendid cycle of six songs, to words by D. Rathaus (Op. 73), written in the year of the composer's death, 1893. They are lyrical 'mood-songs.' 'Night,' No. 2, is an impressionistic miniature. It confirms how sensitive Tchaïkovsky was, to the end of his days, to new artistic methods, how sharply he reacted in particular to the new tendencies of French artistic thought —transforming it, however, into something deeply individual, not so much rejecting as extending his favourite themes and modes of expression.

It is not possible within the scope of this essay to prove that the six songs of Op. 73 constitute a true cycle. But even the examination of a single song from this cycle will show the essential newness of the genre discovered by Tchaïkovsky at the end of his life.

> The feeble light of the candle is vanishing . . .
> Gloomy darkness descends . . .
> And anguish possesses my breast with inconceivable force.
> Sleep quietly descends upon my sad eyes . . .
> And at this moment my soul begins to converse with the past.
> It languishes with deep sorrow . . .
> Appear then, oh my distant friend, if only in a dream . . .

The unrelieved predominance of sub-dominant harmonies stamps this unique song with deep melancholy. The dominant occurs only as an accessory function of the subdominant key of B flat minor. All the other progressions, without exception, are expressed by the formula : subdominant/tonic. The harmonic background rests entirely on one note (a continuous pedal F, in regular bell-strokes sounded on every third beat in the deep bass and resolved, as a rule, on to the tonic on the second beat of the next bar). The piano part is ' completely immobile, even when the oppressive, monotonous chords are shot through with melancholy interjections or with imitations of the vocal melody.

The intonations of the voice are remarkable above all for the matching of the poetic words : the same phrase-construction, the same rise and fall. The perfect declamation in this song easily refutes the criticisms aimed at Tchaïkovsky for his ' neglect of the text.'

The very first strophe shows absolute perfection of vocal enuncia- tion ('The feeble light of the candle is vanishing. Gloomy dark ness descends and anguish possesses my breast with inconceivable force ') (Ex. 121).

We have already noted Tchaïkovsky's typical synthesis of recitative ' speech ' with genuinely melodic phrase structure. Here is one of the best examples of this mood. The unusual intonation, on a diminished triad (C—E flat—G flat), is completed by an equally unusual chromatic progression (G flat—F—E—E flat—D flat). The second motive presents a complete contrast to this; it is an impersonal, typically melodic rounding-off on the tonic with a suspension and is almost exactly repeated to the words, ' with inconceivable force '; it lacks any individual feature. The third motive (' and anguish possesses my breast ') is very expressive; it is a purely melodic design, one of those passionate outbursts so typical of Tchaïkovsky. It is elementary : the notes of the minor triad and the tetrachord C— D flat—E.flat—F exhale gloomy power. The octave drop and the cadence remind one of the end of the voice part of the song, ' On the golden cornfields.'

In this strophe may be observed a characteristic trait of Tchaï- kovsky's melody : a succession of varied motive-intonations, often quite different in nature and artistic quality. Nevertheless this vocal melody is distinguished by its unity. And this results not only from the monolithic accompaniment, the harmonic background, but much more from the actual succession of the intonations, their rise and fall and their rhythm,[1] which in turn is rooted in the content of the words and in the mood of the music evoked by them. Thus the various intonations—refined and banal, passionately intense and coolly impersonal—are inextricably entwined and form a true melodic whole.

The melody of the other two strophes contains few new motive-intonations. Even the climax with its passionate prayer ('Appear, then, if only in a dream . . .') consists of the first motive of the voice part, with its striking, impassioned progression and its chromaticism transferred an octave higher.

Of the new motives, the initial one of the second and third verses (Ex. 122) impresses one by its tenderness; it is full of spiritual pain, of deepest melancholy. The composer achieves this by blending the simplest elements : a drooping line, predominantly diatonic but with chromaticism creeping in, and a final sigh—a suspension—and all this within the narrow limits of a fourth. The remaining motive-intonations are in themselves of little importance; but they serve to maintain and strengthen the fundamental melancholy:

The rough draft of 'Night'[2] is interesting primarily for the metrical variations of the ostinato F in the deep bass, on the third beat of each bar. At first Tchaïkovsky wrote it in minims, but later changed the minim to a crotchet and a crotchet-rest; then he tried a quaver until he hit on the final solution : a crotchet tied to a quaver, with a quaver-rest. Such is the precision for which all great artists strive.

Among Tchaïkovsky's vocal works, the sixteen *Songs for Children* (Op. 54, 1883) occupy a special place. This collection shows the tender humour, the peculiar warmth that inspired Tchaïkovsky's work wherever he touched the theme of childhood. He saw childhood as a happy, golden age; in his memories he involuntarily idealised everything connected with his mother whom he adored and with the house at Votkinsk. Such is the personal colouring of these charming little songs. 'The Cuckoo' Op. 54, No. 8 (text by A. Pleshcheev) is perhaps the most popular of all Tchaïkovsky's songs for children. The reason lies in the interest of the story, the ingenuity of the choice of means of musical expression, the skilful control of the dialogue and the delightful sound-imitations. One recognises the unusually ingenious musical characterisation at the

[1] It may be noted that the metre of the whole strophe and of the remaining strophes, equals $1 + 1 + 2$, which in turn contributes to the impression of unity.

[2] In S. I. Taneev's archives in the Tchaïkovsky Museum at Klin.

very first hearing. The starling's words are very spiteful; they begin each time with the same intonation, a drop of a minor seventh, that Tchaïkovsky generally uses to express either deep and powerful feeling ('Nur wer die Sehnsucht kennt') or caricatured zeal (Larina in the first act of *Eugene Onegin*). Here the intonation expresses mockery of the cuckoo's conceit. Very witty is the 'speech' of the enraged cuckoo, when in impotent rage it repeats eighteen times without interruption, on the same notes, the same 'cuckoo'—with ever louder and more complicated accompaniment, until the piano postlude concludes this most original piece with its repeated 'mocking' seventh.

The 'Lullaby in a Storm' (Op. 54, No. 10, words by Pleshcheev) is a sad, penetrating melody, and despite its outward tranquillity full of concealed alarm; it would seem that behind its apparent simplicity is concealed a deeper and wider meaning than one expects to find in a lullaby.

Ah, be quiet, storm,
Do not make a noise, pines!
My little one is slumbering
Sweetly in his cradle.
Do not wake the child,
O thunderstorm of God.
Rush past, black clouds!
In future, perhaps, there will be
Still more storms,
And repeatedly anxiety
Will disturb his sleep.
Sleep quietly, my child . . .
See, there, the thunderstorm abates.
When you awake to-morrow
And open your little eyes,
You will meet the sun again,
And love, and caresses!

The middle section tells of the storms of life which the child must expect in the future. It is not a new idea : one comes across it in many cradle songs. Accordingly Tchaïkovsky introduces a variation of the chief melody in the same rhythm. The music of the first and third sections consists of repetitions of the same eight-bar phase. Such thematic unity is close to folk-song structure. The main eight-bar melody, twice repeated, recalls the build of the Ukrainian song, the *vesnyanka*: 'Come here, come here, Ivanka!' which served Tchaïkovsky as the basic melodic idea of the finale of the Piano Concerto in B flat minor. There the endlessly revolving movement is conditioned by the idea of the dance; here these repetitions express an idea—the image of human life. The lulling tune, with its two-fold refrain appearing in the introduction and postlude, is a presentiment of the future. The pleasant melancholy of the monotonous tune, the predominance of one minor key, the numerous sustained notes and certain individual motive-intonations, and the character of the accompaniment : all this expresses the sweet sadness of recollection. The ' Lullaby in a Storm ' is a little masterpiece, full of Tchaïkovsky's most intimate and purest lyricism.

Tchaïkovsky composed seven duets for various combinations. The last of them, sketched by the composer shortly before his death, the duet from *Romeo and Juliet*, was completed and scored by S. I. Taneev. The remaining six form Op. 46 (1881). Their character is extremely varied. Side by side with the fateful ' Scottish Ballad '[1] is the amusing duet, ' In ·the garden near the ford.' All six duets are essentially *Lieder* for two voices. The last of the six duets, ' Dawn ' (with words by Surikov), is a model of beautiful writing, the subject being a finely conceived picture of an early summer morning. Slow valse rhythm, rich in syncopations and sometimes even losing all connection with its dance model, is the constructive principle of the whole piece. The precision of the basic colouring —clear light, the deep peace of a full life, of a mature human soul, almost happiness—is not at all disturbed by the great emotional outburst and the rhythmic stretto on the words, ' Be quick, and let us set out . . .' On the contrary, the climax near the end serves as the second and not less important constructive principle of this fine piece of sound-architecture. Continuing the analogy with architecture, one recognises the originality of the phrases between the couplets, sung by both voices on the same note in octaves— arches leading to the return of motives previously heard.

The purely melodic material of the duet has no independent significance and should be considered only in relation to the harmony. The latter is extremely simple : the simplest functions of the major key predominate and the separate insignificant chromaticisms do not affect the general key-structure. But there is one feature which makes ' Dawn ' stand out from Tchaïkovsky's other works composed at the same period : the abundance of dominant chords and the extremely insignificant role of subdominant functions which— as is well known—are usually allowed the utmost predominance in Tchaïkovsky's music. Hence the greater mobility of the harmonic language and the absence of characteristic Tchaïkovskian stagnation.

[1] A setting of A. K. Tolstoy's translation of ' Edward.'—ED.

10

Religious and Other Choral Music

By

Gerald Abraham

TCHAÏKOVSKY'S CHORAL COMPOSITIONS fall into three main categories: (*a*) church music, (*b*) cantatas, with soloists and orchestral accompaniment, written for special occasions, (*c*) short *a cappella* or piano-accompanied choruses, again including·some *pièces d'occasion*. The two latter classes call for no more than passing mention. The only one of the big cantatas published so far is *Moscow*, written for the coronation of Alexander III, but it would be interesting to see the setting of parts of K. S. Aksakov's[1] translation of Schiller's *An die Freude*, which was Tchaïkovsky's 'leaving exercise' at the St. Petersburg Conservatoire in 1865. It is known to be in six movements :

I. Orchestral introduction (C minor).
II. Chorus : ' Freude, schöner Götterfunken ' (allegro non troppo, E major).
III. Solo Quartet : ' Deine Zauber binden wieder ' (adagio molto, G major).
IV. Soloists and chorus : ' Freude trinken alle Wesen ' (allegro, B flat major).
V. Bass solo and chorus : ' Festen Muth in schwerem Leiden ' (andante non troppo, F major).
VI. Soloists and chorus : ' Seid umschlungen, Millionen ' (allegro giusto, C major).

One would also like to see the 1872 Cantata for the opening of the Polytechnic Exhibition in Moscow, for according to Taneev[2] the introduction and finale are based almost entirely on the finale of the First Symphony. The orchestral introduction to the cantata consists of the folk-song andante lugubre of the symphonic movement, expanded to nearly twice its original length by exact or varied repetitions, plus the first twelve bars of the allegro moderato and fifty newly composed bars leading into the first tenor solo, ' As across the

---

[1] A son of the author of the famous Family Chronicle.
[2] Letter to M. I. Tchaïkovsky, March 26, 1901.

dark and cloudy vault of heaven.' The final chorus of the cantata, 'That our way may be straight,' is set to the same folk-song theme, at first sung unaccompanied; at bar 29 the strings enter, and then the full orchestra. According to Taneev, this tutti is simply the conclusion of the First Symphony (from letter M onward) with chorus parts added.

The best of Tchaïkovsky's short choruses is perhaps his *a cappella* arrangement (1889) of his well-known *Legend* ('The Christ-child had a garden'), Op. 54, No. 5, originally written for voice and piano. But his choral writing has no interest for its own sake. His setting of Lermontov's beautiful little lyric 'The golden cloud had slept' (1887), for instance, is in block chords throughout, like an English hymn-tune, though the irregular phrase-lengths, the feminine endings and the Æolian mode lend it a certain charm.

The religious music is more important, though here we approach a field—the liturgical music of the Russian Orthodox Church—so specialised that an English critic must tread warily indeed, so specialised that Tchaïkovsky himself is alleged, as we shall see, to have often tripped. Although all Tchaïkovsky's church music dates from the period 1878–85, it would be false to deduce that they sprang from any special religious crisis or tendency during this period. Tchaïkovsky's religious views underwent natural modifications in the course of his life, but his general attitude to Christianity—characteristic of a great many educated Russians of his day—may be summed up in three phrases: acceptance of Christian ethics, regretful rejection of the doctrines of the Orthodox Church, artistic (or sentimental) pleasure in the ritual of that Church. He had a great admiration for the Orthodox 'Liturgy of St. John Chrysostum,' holding it as literature to be 'one of the greatest works of art in existence,' but the earliest mention of his proposed setting of it that I can trace, in a letter from Florence, dated February 14/26, 1878, to the publisher Jurgenson, suggests neither religious fervour nor strong artistic excitement. Having explained that he would like a real rest after the Fourth Symphony and *Onegin* but is bored by complete idleness, he goes on:

> I'd like to try to write a series of easy pieces, *Kinderstücke*.[1] It would be pleasant for me, and for you even profitable, i.e., relatively. What do you think about this? Tell me in general what small-scale compositions you'd like to have. I'm strongly disposed just now to take on any small-scale work by way of relaxation. Only I abso-

[1] The *Children's Album*, Op. 39, was completed in May, like the *Liturgy*.

lutely refuse to take on translations. Wouldn't you find *religious* pieces useful? If so, tell me what texts. Would it pay you to bring out a whole liturgy composed by me? There is a job that would be particularly pleasant for me. Can you print religious music,[1] and can you hope to find a market for it? But I should very much like to occupy myself with it.

Only at the end of April, in a letter to Nadezhda von Meck, do we get a further glimpse of his motives:

> If I continue in the right frame of mind, I should like to try to do something for church music. In this direction lies an enormous and as yet hardly touched field of activity for a composer. I recognise some merit in Bortnyansky, Berezovsky and others, but how little their music harmonises with the Byzantine style of architecture and ikons, with the whole structure of the Orthodox service!

He entered upon the composition—or, rather, compilation—of his *Vesper Service*, based on old liturgical melodies, in a precisely parallel period of creative relaxation in May 1881. On the 7th/19th, he tells Jurgenson:

> I'm doing absolutely nothing. No desire to compose. Have I asked you to commission something? Really, don't you want anything? Have you no ideas in which I could collaborate?[2] If so, please write. Some such external jolt might set me going again.

Next day he writes to Madame von Meck, that ' in the religious mood in which he finds himself,' it would be a good thing to bury himself in Russian church music; he is studying old melodies and would like to try to harmonise them. And on the 9th/21st, Jurgenson heard:

> (1) I want to try to write a vesper service, and for this I need a full *text* of it; I'd like to know whether one can buy some such book as a *Short Exposition of the Liturgy for Laymen*, if there is one, please send it me. I've got a book with morning and evening services, but that isn't what I want; I need a *vesper* with all the *ekteniya* and everything that has to be sung. (2) I've begun to study the *obikhod* [ritual], but to understand it properly I need Razumovsky's book (*History of Church Music*), so I beg you to send me a copy.

Further letters to Madame von Meck, Modest and others reveal the difficulties Tchaïkovsky met with both in harmonising the modal

---

[1] The publication of religious music in Russia was at that time regarded as the monopoly of the Imperial Chapel and publication of Tchaïkovsky's *Liturgy* involved Jurgenson in a lawsuit, which, however, he won.

[2] Jurgenson's direct reply to this was to commission Tchaïkovsky to edit the complete church music of Bortnyansky and to suggest a set of songs for children: the genesis of Op. 54 two years later.

melodies and in discovering what was and was not allowed in the ritual and its musical treatment.

Tchaïkovsky's last crop of religious music—the three *Cherubic Hymns* (1884), the arrangement of the old Czech *Hymn to St. Cyril and St. Methodius* (1885) and the six *Church Songs* (1885)—was the direct consequence of a hint from the Tsar that he would like his favourite composer to write for the Church.

There is little in the substance of Tchaïkovsky's church music to blur this impression that the impulse to write it was as much external as internal, and Russian critics give whatever confirmation may be needed that the composer had 'crammed' his deeper knowledge of Russian church tradition and was far from being really saturated with it. Nevertheless his contribution is acknowledged to be of historical importance, coming as one of the heralds of an artistic revival in Russian church music, and one competent critic, N. Kompaneysky,[1] went so far as to declare that the third *Cherubic Hymn* is as important in Russian sacred music as *A Life for the Tsar* in Russian secular music : 'both freed Russian thought from slavish dependence on foreigners.' It was as remarkable for Tchaïkovsky to harmonise and seek to imitate the old monodic chants of the true Russian ecclesiastical tradition as it had been for Glinka, nearly half a century earlier, to harmonise and seek to imitate Russian folk-songs; the true tradition had been lost in the sentimental Italian-ism of the late eighteenth century, the less sentimental but still Italianate style of Bortnyansky and his school, and the harmonic Teutonism of Lvov and Bakhmetev. Neither Glinka nor Tchaï-kovsky was an absolute pioneer, but each was the first to achieve anything artistically worthwhile. But in Russian church music there were far more serious limitations to the artistically worthwhile than in Russian opera. The veto of the Orthodox Church on all forms of instrumental accompaniment was in general a *condition* rather than a limitation, of course, though to Tchaïkovsky personally it was a fettering condition; and one cannot help wondering what would have happened to both Catholic and Protestant church music after the great age of polyphony if the same condition had been imposed by the Churches of the West. The real limitation was the rigid tradition of subordination of music to text, of refusal to allow church music any independent beauty or significance. In the whole of his *Liturgy of St. Chrysostom* Tchaïkovsky allows himself only five brief deviations from block-harmony, ever so slightly orna-

[1] In an article in the *Russkaya Muzïkalnaya Gazeta*, October 31, 1904.

mented, with the melody in the treble : the four opening bars of the
' Kheruvimskaya ' and a few bars of its last section, two bars of
imitation in the ' Milost mira,' four bars of quasi--imitation between
treble and tenor near the end of the 'Dostoyno est,' and the
'alleluias' in the 'Khvalite.' Anything equivalent to the great
Catholic masses, to the German Protestant church cantata or even to
the Anglican anthem, except in its very simplest forms, was thus out
of the question in Russian church music.

The harmony of the *Liturgy* is also of the plainest, though
Tchaïkovsky does allow himself one or two chromatic incongruities,
and he has actually been criticised for changing the harmonies under
a treble monotone—though he seldom sins in this respect. But the
main criticisms of not unfriendly Russian purists are that he is care-
less or ignorant in his handling of verbal accent—the text, of
course, is Church Slavonic, not modern Russian—that he admits
faulty melodic progressions such as the tritone and leaps that are
foreign to the true church style, and that in harmonising old melodies
he betrays imperfect knowledge of modal harmony and frequently
changes the harmony on what are really only ornamental notes.[1]

He has stated his own point of view in the preface to his *Vesper
Service* (1882):

> The present work is an attempt at a four-part harmonisation of a
> number of unmodified, with a few modified, liturgical melodies. Some
> of these genuine church chants (borrowed from the musical publications
> of the Most Holy Synod) I have left untouched; in others I have
> allowed myself a few insignificant changes; in others, again, I have in
> places altogether abandoned the originals and followed my own musical
> feeling. In the harmonisation I have kept to the narrow limits of the
> so-called strict style, i.e., I have absolutely avoided chromaticism and
> only in an extremely limited number of cases allowed myself the use of
> dissonances.

That he was sensitive to accusations of ignoring verbal stress is
suggested by his footnote to the seventh number, where he explains
that an apparent lapse is the result of trying to bar a melody that
is naturally barless; in other numbers he wisely abandons bar-lines
altogether for long stretches.

On the whole, partly because of the beauty of the borrowed
melodies but also because of the finer workmanship, the *Vesper
Service* strikes the non-Orthodox critic as a much better work than
the *Liturgy*. But the three *Cherubic Hymns* and the six choruses

[1] M. Lisitsin gives numerous examples of all these faults in his essay on Tchaïkovsky
as a religious composer in the *Russkaya Muzïkalnaya Gazeta* for September 1897.

written in 1885 are the most approachable of all: freer in style and revealing something of a creative personality, though unspoiled by subjective emotion even in the opening of the ' Nïne silï nebesnïya ' (' Now the heavenly powers be with us ') which perhaps comes nearest to it (cf. Ex. 123). The first of the three settings of the ' Kheruvimskaya ' (Cherubim, mysterious forms, singing to the life-giving Trinity their thrice-holy song '), a simple one in F, is sometimes heard as an anthem in English churches. I quote the opening, after two preludial bars, of the third setting in C, the one to which Kompaneysky attached so much importance, as a fine example of Tchaïkovsky's treatment of an old melody, in this case a Kiev chant which also attracted Balakirev, Rimsky-Korsakov, Kastalsky and others (cf. Ex. 124). The division of parts and frequent use of submediant chords in both these examples are thoroughly characteristic.

CHRONOLOGY

1840. Born at Votkinsk (Vyatka Government), April 25/May 7.[1]

1845. First music lessons.

1850. At preparatory school in St. Petersburg.

1852. Enters School of Jurisprudence.

1854. Mother's death.

1859–63. Clerk in Ministry of Justice.

1861. First visit to the West; takes private lessons from Zaremba.

1862–65. Student at Petersburg Conservatoire.

1864. Overture to *The Storm*.

1865. Piano Sonata in C sharp minor.

1866–78. Professor of Harmony at Moscow Conservatoire.

1866. First Symphony.

1868. *Fate; The Voevoda* (opera); attracted by Desirée Artôt.

1869. *Romeo and Juliet* (first version).

1871. First String Quartet.

1871–76. Music critic of *Russky Vedomosti*.

1872. Second Symphony (original version); *The Oprichnik*.

1873. *The Tempest*; *Snow Maiden* music.

1874. Second String Quartet; *Vakula the Smith*.

1875. Third Symphony; B flat minor Piano Concerto.

1876. At Bayreuth; *Francesca da Rimini*; *Rococo Variations*; *Swan Lake*; Third String Quartet.

1877. Beginning of friendship with Nadezhda von Meck; marriage to Antonina Ivanovna Milyukova (July 6/18); attempted suicide; Fourth Symphony.

1878. *Eugene Onegin*; Piano Sonata in G; Violin Concerto.

1879. *The Maid of Orleans*.

1880. Second Piano Concerto; Italian Capriccio; *1812* Overture; Serenade for Strings.

1882. Piano Trio.

[1] The first date is the Russian one, ' old style '; the second the equivalent according to the Western calendar. Compositions are mentioned under the year of composition (or completion).

1883.   *Mazeppa.*

1884.   Third Orchestral Suite.

1885.   Takes a house of his own at Maidanovo; *Manfred* Symphony.

1887.   *The Sorceress; Mozartiana.*

1888.   First European tour as conductor; move to Frolovskoe; Fifth Symphony; *Hamlet* Overture.

1889.   *The Sleeping Beauty.*

1890.   *The Queen of Spades*; end of friendship with Mme. von Meck.

1891.   American tour; *Iolanta.*

1892.   Move to Klin; *Nutcracker*; String Sextet.

1893.   *Pathétique* Symphony; death at St. Petersburg (October 25/ November 6).

BIBLIOGRAPHY

The main sources for Tchaïkovsky bibliography are the list of works in the Klin Museum, published at the end of the volume *Proshloe Russkoy Muzïki*: *I.—P. I. Chaykovsky* (Petrograd, 1920) and the exhaustive catalogue of *Literatura o P. I. Chaykovskom za 17 let* (1917–34) compiled by N. Shemanin for the volume *Muzïkal'noe Nasledstvo* (Moscow, 1935). The bibliography given below is selective rather than exhaustive; it includes books and articles dealing with the music rather than with the man; the primary biographical sources, including important correspondence, are all given, but other purely biographical works are ignored. The preponderance of Russian works is inevitable; they are usually much more valuable than those in Western languages, and the increasing number of students of Russian leads one to hope that the listing of studies in Tchaïkovsky's own language is by no means as useless as it would have been a few years ago.—Ed.

ABRAHAM, GERALD: ' The programme of the *Pathétique* Symphony ' and ' *Eugene Onegin* and Tchaïkovsky's marriage ' (in the volume *On Russian Music*. William Reeves, 1939).
    ' Peter Ilyich Tchaïkovsky : Some Centennial Reflections ' (in *Music and Letters*, April 1940).
ALSHVANG, A.: *Tvorchestvo P. I. Chaykovskovo* (in preparation).
    ' Romansï Chaykovskovo '[1] (in *Sovetskaya Muzïka*, 1939, No. 9–10, and 1940, No. 1).
ASAFEV, B.: ' O Chaykovskom : k 40-letiyu so dnya smerti ' (in *Sovetskoe Iskusstvo*, 1933, No. 56).
    Article ' Chaykovsky ' in *Bolshaya Sovetskaya Entsiklopediya* (Moscow, 1934).
    (See also under ' Glebov, I ').
BALAKIREV, M. A.: *Perepiska M. A. Balakireva s P. I. Chaykovskim* (St. Petersburg, 1913).
BAZÏLEV, A.: ' Operï Chaykovskovo ' (in *Muzïkal'naya Nov'*, 1924, No. 9).
BLOM, ERIC: *Tchaïkovsky : Orchestral Works* (Oxford University Press, 1927).
    Chapter ' The Early Tchaïkovsky Symphonies ' in *Stepchildren of Music* (Foulis, n.d.).

---

[1] Translated in the present volume in a slightly abridged form.

BOGDANOV-BEREZOVSKY, I. : *Chto nado znat ob Opere ' Evgenny Onegin '* (Leningrad, 1933).
　Chto nado znat o Balete ' Spyashchaya Krasavitsa (Leningrad, 1933).
BRAUDO, E. : ' Muzikalnaya Chast *Pikovoy Damï*' (in *Sovremenny Teatr*', 1928, No. 2).
CARSE, ADAM : Chapter XIII of *The History of Orchestration* (Kegan Paul, 1925).
　First Symphonies : Studies in Orchestration. IV. Brahms–Tchaïkovsky (in *Musical Opinion*, September, 1920).
CHERNOV : *Simfonii Chaykovskavo, s tematicheskim ukazatelem* (St. Petersburg, 1904).
DANILEVICH, L. : ' O Simfonizme Chaykovskovo ' (in *Sovetskaya Muzika*, 1940, No. 1).
DVINSKY, M. : ' Opera, ne napisannaya Chaykovskim ' (in *Vechernaya Krasnaya Gazeta*, 1933, No. 122).
EVANS, EDWIN : *Tchaïkovsky* (Dent, 1906; revised edition, 1935).
FELBER, R. : ' Tchaïkovsky and Tolstoy ' (in *The Chesterian*, 1931, No. 91).
FINDEISEN, N. F. : *Kamernaya Muzika Chaykovskovo* (Moscow, 1930).
　Article ' Tchaïkovsky ' in Cobbet's *Cyclopædic Survey of Chamber Music* (Oxford University Press, 1930).
　Chapter XII, 'P. I. Chaykovsky,' of *Russkaya Khudozhestvennaya Pesnya* (St. Petersburg, 1905).
　' Zhenskie Tipi Operakh Chaykovskavo ' (in *Russkaya Muzikal'naya Gazeta*, 1903, p. 998).
　' Chaykovsky i Rimsky-Korsakov (Opït paralleli) ' (Supplement to *Niva*, January, 1910).
FISKE, ROGER : ' Tchaïkovsky's Later Piano Concertos (in *Musical Opinion*, October, November and December, 1938).
GENIK, R. : ' Fortepiannoe Tvorchestvo P. Chaykovskavo ' (series of articles in *Russkaya Muzikal'naya Gazeta*, 1908).
' GLEBOV, I.': *Instrumentalnoe Tvorchestvo Chaykovskovo* (Petrograd, 1922).
　P. I. Chaykovsky. Evo Zhizn i Tvorchestvo (Petrograd, 1922).
　' Pikovaya Dama ' and ' Operï Chaykovskovo ' (in the volume *Simfonicheskie Etyudi*, Petrograd, 1922).
　' Tridtsatletie *Shchelkunchika* ' (in *K Novïm Beregam*, 1923). No. 1.
　(*ed.*): *Chaykovsky. Vospominaniya i Pisma* (Leningrad, 1924).
———— and YAKOVLEV, V. (*ed.*): *Proshloe Russkoy Muziki—I. P. I. Chaykovsky* (Petrograd, 1920).
GROMAN-SOLOVTSOV, A. : ' Neskolko Mïsley o Chaykovskom ' (in *Sovetskaya Muzika*, 1934, No. 2).
JURGENSON, B. : *Catalogue Thématique des Oeuvres de P. Tschaikowsky* (Moscow, 1897).
KARATÏGIN, V. : ' Chaykovsky i Rakhmaninov ' (in *Zhizn Iskusstva*, 1923, Nos. 40 and 41).
KASHKIN, N. : *Vospominaniya o Chaykovskom* (Moscow, 1896).
KAYGORODOV, D. : *P. I. Chaykovsky i Priroda* (St. Petersburg, 1907).

KLEVEZAL', E. : ' Patologicheskie Chertï Tvorchestva Chaykovskovo ' (in *Uralsky Meditsinsky Zhurnal*, 1929, No. 5).

KLIMENKO, I. A. : *Moi Vospominaniya o P. I. Chaykovskom* (Ryazan, 1908).

KNORR, IWAN : *Peter Tschaïkowsky* (Berlin, 1900).

KOMPANEYSKY, N. : ' Kheruvimskaya Pesn No. 3 P. Chaykovskovo ' (in *Russkaya Muzikalnaya Gazeta*, 1904, No. 44).

KOPTYAEV, A. : *Istoriya Novoy Russkoy Muziki v Kharakteristikakh* : *Vip. I—P. Chaykovsky* (St. Petersburg, 1909).

LAROCHE, H. A. : *Sobranie Muzikalno–Kriticheskikh Statey*. Vol. II (in two parts) (Moscow, 1922 and 1924).

  ' Pamyati Chaykovskavo ' (in *Ezhegodnik Imper. Teatrov*, 1892–3; off-print, St. Petersburg, 1894).

  ' Chaykovsky, kak Dramatichesky Kompozitor ' (in *Ezhegodnik Imper. Teatrov*, 1893–4; off-print, St. Petersburg, 1895).

——— and KASHKIN, N. : *Na Pamyat o Chaykovskom* (Moscow, 1894).

LEE, E. MARKHAM : *Tchaïkovski* (John Lane, 1906).

  ' The Amateur's Repertoire (Tchaïkovsky's *Dumka*, Op. 59) ' (in *Musical Opinion*, November 1929).

LISITSIN, M. : ' P. I. Chaykovsky kak Dukhovny Kompozitor ' (in *Russkaya Muzikal'naya Gazeta*, 1897, No. 9).

LEVINSON : ' Chaykovsky v Balete ' (in *Zhizn Iskusstva*, 1918, No. 1).

LOGE : ' Chaykovsky i Narodnaya Pesnya ' (in *Zhizn Iskusstva*, 1921, No. 811).

MARTÏNOV, I. : ' Chaykovsky i Glinka ' (in *Sovetskaya Muzïka*, 1940, No.1).

NEWMAN, ERNEST : ' The Essential Tschaïkowsky ' (in *Contemporary Review*, June 1901).

NEWMARCH, ROSA : *Tchaïkovsky, his Life and Works : with extracts from his writings* (Grant Richards, 1900).

  Chapter XIII, ' Tchaïkovsky,' in *The Russian Opera* (Herbert Jenkins, 1914).

  ' Tchaïkovsky's Early Lyrical Operas ' (in *Zeitschrift der int. Musikgesellschaft*, 1905).

NIKOLSKAYA, G. : Chaykovsky v Muzikalnoy Literature Revolyutsionnïkh Let (in *Muzika i Revolyutsiya*, 1928, No. 11).

OSTRETSOV, A. : *P. I. Chaykovsky (Sotsiologicheskaya i Muzikalnaya Kharakteristika)* (Moscow, 1929).

POPOV, S. M. : ' Perepiska P. I. Chaykovskovo s M.M. Ippolitovïm-Ivanovïm i evo Zhenoy (1885–93) ' (in *Iskusstvo*, 1927, IV).

POPOV, S. S. : ' Novoe o zabïtïk muzikalnïkh proizvedeniyakh P. I. Chaykovskovo ' (in *Sovetskaya Muzïka*, 1933, No. 6).

P——V, S. : ' Pervaya Opera Chaykovskovo ' (in *Kultura Teatra*, 1921, No. 5).

PSHIBÏSHEVSKY, B. : ' O Chaykovskom. Kompozitor i Epokha ' (in *Sovetskoe Iskusstvo*, 1933, No. 42).

RUKAVISHNIKOV, N. : ' Pushkin v Biblioteke P. Chaykovskovo ' (in *Sovetskaya Muzïka*, 1937, No. 1).

SHAVERDYAN, A. I. (*ed.*) : *Chaykovsky i Teatr* (Moscow, 1940).

SHEMANIN, N.: 'Literatura o P. I. Chaykovskom za 17 let (1917–34)' (in the volume *Muzikal'noe Nasledstvo*, Moscow, 1935).

STASSOV, V. V.: *Sobranie Sochineniy, Vol. III* (St. Petersburg, 1894).
'V. V. Stasov i P. I. Chaykovsky' (letters) (off-print from *Russk. Misl'*, St. Petersburg, 1909).

STEIN, R.: *Tschaïkowskij* (Berlin and Leipzig, 1927).

STEINITZER, M.: *Tschaïkowsky* (Leipzig, 1925).

SUBERT: *Moje Izpoménky* (Prague, 1902).

TANEEV, S. I.: 'Neopublikovannoe Pismo' (on Tchaïkovsky's Trio) (in *Sovetskaya Muzika*, 1936, No. 6).

TCHAÏKOVSKAYA, ANTONINA: 'Vospominaniya Vdovi P. I. Chaykovskavo' (in *Russkaya Muzikal'naya Gazeta*, 1913, No. 42).

TCHAÏKOVSKY, M. I.: *Zhizn P. I. Chaykovskavo* (3 vols.) (Moscow, 1900–02); slightly abridged German version by Paul Juon, *Das Leben P. I. Tschaïkowskys* (2 vols.) (Moscow and Leipzig, 1900–02); drastically abridged English version by Rosa Newmarch, *The Life and Letters of Peter Ilich Tchaïkovsky* (1 vol.) (John Lane, 1905).
Pisma P. I. Chaykovskavo i S. I. Taneeva (Moscow, 1916).

TCHAÏKOVSKY, P. I.: *Dnevniki P. I. Chaykovskovo*: 1873–91 (Moscow, 1923).
Muzikaln'nie Feletoni i Zametki (Moscow, 1898); German version, *Musikalische Erinnerungen und Feuilletons* (trans. by Stümcke) (Berlin, 1899); selection published as *Erinnerungen eines Musikers* (Leipzig, 1922).
"Perepiska Chaykovskovo s Besselem' (in *K Novim Beregam*, 1923, No. 1 and 2).
'Pisma P. I. Chaykovskovo k Besselyu' (in *Muzikal'naya Nov'* 1923, Nos. 1 and 3).
'Neizdannie Pisma P. I. Chaykovskovo k V. V. Besselyu' (in *Sovetskaya Muzika*, 1938, No. 6).
Perepiska s N. F. von Meck (3 vols.) (Moscow, 1934–36).
'Pisma P. I. Chaykovskovo k I. V. Shpazhinskomu' (in *Kul'tura i Teatr*, 1921, No. 6).
Perepiska s P. I. Jurgensonom (Vol. I. 1877–83) (Moscow, 1938).
Pisma k Rodnim, Vol. I (Moscow, 1940).
'Perepiska P. I. Chaykovskovo s V. V. Stasovim' (in *Russkaya Misl'*, 1908).

TIDEBÖHL, ELLEN VON: *Mazeppa* (in *Monthly Musical Record*, August, 1918).

TOLSTOY S.: 'Lev Tolstoy i Chaykovsky' (in the volume *Istoriya Russkoy Muziki*, edited by K. A. Kuznetsov, Moscow, 1924).

VLIET, W. VAN DER, and THEAKSTON, J.: *Tschaïkowsky* (Copenhagen, 1929).

VOLÏNSKY, A.: 'Spyashchaya Krasavitsa' (in *Zhizn Iskusstva*, 1923, No. 48).

WALTER, VIKTOR: 'Kamernaya Muzika P. I. Chaykovskavo' (in *Russkaya Muzikalnaya Gazeta*, 1913, No. 42).

WESTRUP, J. A.: 'Tchaikovsky and the Symphony' (in *Musical Times*, June, 1940).

YAKOVLEV, V. : ' P. I. Chaykovsky i N. G. Rubinstein (1866–81) ' (in the volume *Istoriya Russkoy Muziki*, edited by K. A. Kuznetsov, Moscow, 1924).

'Chaykovsky v Poiskakh Opernovo Libretto' (in the volume *Muzïkal'noe Nasledstvo*, Moscow, 1935).

Chaykovsky na Moskovskoy Stsene (Moscow, 1940).

(*ed.*): *Dni i Godï P. I. Chaykovskovo*: *Letopis Zhizni i Tvorchestva* (Moscow, 1940).

———— and BELYAEV, V. : *Evgeny Onegin* (Moscow, 1924).

YARUSTOVSKY, B. : 'O Rabote Chaykovskovo nad Opernïm Libretto' (in *Sovetskaya Muzïka*, 1940, No. 1).

ZHEGIN, N. : 'P. I. Chaykovsky i E. K. Pavlovskaya' (in *Sovetskaya Muzïka*, 1934, No. 8).

ZHITOMIRSKY, D. : ' O Simfonisme Chaykovskovo ' (in *Sovetskaya Muzïka*, 1933, No. 6).

Chapter XXI, ' P. I. Chaykovsky ' (in Vol. II of the *Istoriya Russkoy Muzïki*, edited by M. S. Pekelis, Moscow, 1940).

LIST OF COMPOSITIONS
(with page-references)

Opus No.   ORCHESTRAL WORKS

None. Andante ma non troppo in A, for small orchestra (1863–64).

None. Agitato in E minor, for small orchestra (1863–64).

None. Allegro vivo in C minor (1863–64).

76. Overture to Ostrovsky's *Storm* (1864): 76–8, 80, 123, 129.

None. *The Romans in the Coliseum* (1864 ?).

None. *Characteristic Dances* (afterwards revised and used in opera *The Voevoda*) (1865)[1]: 130–1.

None. Overture in F for small orchestra (1865). (Re-scored for large orchestra in 1866): 94.

None. Concert Overture in C minor (1866): 78, 123, 130.

13. Symphony No. 1 in G minor (1866; revised 1874): 13, 30, 32–6, 40, 44, 59, 75, 87, 230–1.

15. Festival Overture on the Danish Hymn (1866)[1]: 94–5.

77. Symphonic Poem, *Fate* (1868): 76–9, 83, 138.

None. Overture *Romeo and Juliet* (1869) (completely revised—new introduction, largely new development section, new close, and much re-scoring—in 1870; cut, further revised and re-styled ' overture-fantasia ' in 1880): 14, 54, 76, 78–84, 86–7, 93, 137, 201.

17. Symphony No. 2 in C minor (1872) (first movement entirely re-written, scherzo radically altered and finale cut, 1879)[1]: 30–3, 36–7, 39, 66–7, 84, 87, 106, 123, 132.

None. Serenade for small orchestra (for Nicholas Rubinstein's name-day) (1872).

18. Fantasia, *The Tempest* (1873): 76, 81–3, 93.

29. Symphony No. 3 in D (1875): 30, 33–4, 36, 43–4, 83, 178.

31. Slavonic March (1876)[2]: 95–7.

32. Fantasia, *Francesca da Rimini* (1876): 76, 83–7, 89, 92, 96, 124, 147, 199, 210.

36. Symphony No. 4 in F minor (1877): 12, 14, 17, 19–21, 25–8, 31–5, 39–40, 42–4, 72, 75, 84, 97, 177, 185, 199, 231.

43. Suite No. 1 in D minor (1879)[1]: 99–100.

45. *Italian Capriccio* (1880)[1]: 96–7.

None. Musical Picture, *Montenegrin Villagers receiving news of Russia's declaration of war on Turkey* (1880).

49. Festival Overture, *The Year 1812* (1880): 86, 94–7, 123.

None. Coronation March (1883)[2]: 96.

[1] Arranged for piano duet by the composer.
[2] Arranged for piano solo by the composer.

Opus No.

53. Suite No. 2 in C (1883)[1] : 99, 101.
55. Suite No. 3 in G (1884)[1] : 62, 71, 99, 101–2.
58. Symphony, *Manfred* (1885)[1] : 76, 89–94, 96, 99, 102, 124, 126, 199.
None. *Jurists' March* (1885) : 96.
64. Symphony No. 5 in E minor (1888): 31, 33–4, 39–40, 43–4, 63, 102, 118, 176, 185, 199.
67a. Overture-fantasia, *Hamlet* (1888): 76, 79–82, 87, 92, 178–9.
78. Symphonic Ballad, *The Voevoda* (1891): 76, 81, 87–9, 94.
71a. Suite, *Nutcracker* (1892)[2] : 190, 192.
74. Symphony No. 6 in B minor (*Pathétique*) (1893)[2] : 23, 31, 33–4, 37, 39–41, 43–4, 63, 67, 72, 75, 97, .176, 181, 199, 219, 224.

WORKS FOR SOLO INSTRUMENT WITH ORCHESTRA[3]

23. Concerto No. 1, in B flat minor, for piano and orchestra (1875): 47–58, 60, 65, 69, 83, 107, 115, 228.
26. *Sérénade mélancolique*, for violin and orchestra (1875): 70–1.
33. Variations on a Rococo Theme, for 'cello and orchestra (1876): 71–2.
34. Valse-Scherzo, for violin and orchestra (1877): 70–1.
35. Concerto in D, for violin and orchestra (1878): 58, 68–70, 104, 200.
44. Concerto No. 2, in G, for piano and orchestra (1880; revised and cut by Ziloti with the composer's agreement, 1893): 58–60, 65.
56. Concert-Fantasia for piano and orchestra (1884): 60–3.
62. *Pezzo capriccioso*, for 'cello and orchestra (1887): 72–3.
75. Concerto No. 3 in E flat (in one movement) for piano and orchestra (1893): 63–6.
79. Andante and Finale, for piano and orchestra (1893), orchestrated by Taneev. (Op. 75 and Op. 79 originated as movements of a symphony in E flat): 63–4, 66–7.

WORKS FOR STRING ORCHESTRA

48. Serenade in C (1880) (arranged for piano duet by the composer): 97–8, 106, 123.
None. Elegy (for the jubilee of the actor I. V. Samarin) (1884) (afterwards included in the incidental music to *Hamlet*): 99, 178.

CHAMBER MUSIC

None. Adagio in F, for wind octet (1863–64).
None. Introduction and allegro in A, for two flutes, string quartet and double-bass (1863–64).
None. Allegro in C minor, for string quartet, double-bass and piano (1863–64).

---

[1] Arranged for piano duet by the composer.
[2] Arranged for piano solo by the composer.
[3] The composer made piano arrangements of the orchestral parts of all the works in this category

Opus No.

None. Adagio molto in E flat, for string quartet and harp (1863–64).

None. Allegro ma non tanto in G, for string quartet and double-bass (1863–64).

None. Prelude in E minor, for string quartet and double-bass (1863–64).

None. Fragment of andante molto in G, for string quartet (1863–64).

None. Allegro vivace in B flat, for string quartet (1863–64).

None. Allegretto in E, for string quartet (1863–64).

None. Adagio in C, for four horns (1863–64).

None. Allegretto in D, for violin, viola and 'cello (1863–64).[1]

None. String Quartet in B flat (only the first allegro survives) (1865): 115.

11. String Quartet No. 1 in D (1871)[2]: 104–8, 110, 113, 123.

22. String Quartet No. 2 in F (1874): 106–8.

30. String Quartet No. 3 in E flat minor (1876)[3]: 108–10.

42. *Souvenir d'un lieu cher* (Meditation, Scherzo and Melody for violin and piano) (1878): 68, 104.

50. Trio for piano, voilin and 'cello (1882): 104, 110–1, 117.

70. String Sextet (*Souvenir de Florence*) (1887–90; revised 1892): 104, 111–3.

Piano Music

None. Valse (1854).

None. Piece (on the theme ' By the River, by the Bridge ') (1862).

None. Fragment of an allegro in C minor (1863–64).

None. Theme and Variations in A minor (1863–64): 117.

80. Sonata in C sharp minor (1865): 40, 115, 120.

1. Scherzo à la Russe and Impromptu in E flat minor (1867): 115.

2. *Souvenir de Hapsal* (Nos. 1 and 3, 1867; No. 2, 1865): 115–6.

None. Potpourri on Motives from P. Tchaïkovsky's opera *Voevoda* (published pseudonymously as the work of ' H. Cramer ') (1868): 130.

4. Valse-Caprice in D (1868).

5. Romance in F minor (1868): 100, 116.

7. Valse-Scherzo in A (1870): 116.

8. Capriccio in G flat (1870): 116.

9. Rêverie, Salon Polka and Salon Mazurka (1870): 116.

10. Nocturne and Humoresque[4] (1871): 63, 116.

19. Six Pieces (1873)[5]: 116–7.

21. Six Pieces on a Single Theme (1873): 116–7.

37b *The Seasons* (twelve pieces) (1876): 118.

40. Twelve Pieces (of moderate difficulty) (1876–78): 118, 200.

---

[1] Although these student exercises have all been classed as chamber music, some of them are probably orchestral sketches; the Allegro ma non tanto even has a passage for four 'cellos divisi.

[2] Slow movement (andante cantabile) scored for 'cello and orchestra about 1888.

[3] Slow movement (andante funebre) later arranged for violin and piano.

[4] The Humoresque was arranged for violin and piano about 1877.

[5] Op. 19, No. 4 (Nocturne), scored for 'cello and orchestra about 1888.

Opus No.

None. Funeral March for piano duèt (on motives from *The Oprichnik*)
(1877): 15.
37. Sonata in G (1878): 115, 121–2.
None. March, *The Russian Volunteer Fleet* (published pseudonymously
as the work of ' P. I. Sinopov ') (1878): 96.
39. Children's Album (twenty-four easy pieces) (1878): 118–9, 123, 231.
51. Six Pieces (1882): 119.
None. Impromptu-Capriccio (1885).
59. Dumka (1886): 119.
None. Valse-Scherzo, No. 2 (1889).
None. Impromptu in A flat (1889).
None. Military March (for the 98th Yurevsky Infantry Regiment) (1893):
96.
72. Eighteen Pieces (1893): 119–20, 193.
None. *Momento lirico,* completed by Taneev.

OPERAS[1]

3. *The Voevoda* (1868): 123, 126, 129–32, 135–7, 154, 208.
None. *Undine* (1869): 33, 39, 126, 131–4, 139, 154, 194.
None. *The Oprichnik* (1872): 10, 15, 77, 123, 130–1, 133–8, 144–6, 154,
159, 165, 199.
14. *Vakula the Smith* (1874) (drastically revised as *Cherevichki* = *The
Slippers*) (1885) (no opus number): 141–7, 153–4, 159–60, 166,
168, 177, 215.
24. *Eugene Onegin* (1878) (Ecossaise for sixth scene added in 1885): 12,
14, 17, 19–21, 71, 138, 146–54, 158, 161, 163, 166, 171, 175–7, 224,
228, 231.
None. *The Maid of Orleans* (1879) (various alterations made in 1882):
154–60, 163, 165, 182.
None. *Mazeppa* (1883): 160–6, 168.
None. *The Sorceress* (1887): 128–9, 154, 166–71, 175, 181.
68. *The Queen of Spades* (1890): 71, 145, 152, 154, 172–8, 181–2, 198–9.
69. *Iolanta* (1891): 178–82, 203.

BALLETS

20. *Swan Lake* (1876): 83, 131–2, 137, 185–6, 192–5.
66. *The Sleeping Beauty* (1889): 186–90, 192, 194.
71. *Nutcracker* (1892) (arranged for piano solo by the composer): 72,
88, 115, 177, 179, 181, 188, 190–2.

INCIDENTAL MUSIC

None. To Ostrovsky's *Dmitry the Pretender* (Introduction to Act 1 and
mazurka only) (before 1870).
12. To Ostrovsky's *Snow Maiden* (1873) (vocal score arranged by
composer): 123–4, 133, 137–42, 154, 178.

[1] The vocal scores of all the operas, except *Iolanta*, were made by the composer.

OPUS No.

None. Cradle Song for Octave Feuillet's play *La Fée* (1879).

None. Melodrama for small orchestra, for the *domovoy* scene in Ostrovsky's *Voevoda* (1886): 131.

67b. To *Hamlet* (1891): 99, 124, 178–9.

OTHER STAGE MUSIC (FRAGMENTS OF OPERAS, ETC.).

None. Fountain Scene from Pushkin's *Boris Godunov* (1863–65?): 129.

None. Couplets for P. S. Fedorov's vaudeville *The Tangle* (1867).

None. Recitatives and Choruses for Auber's *Domino Noir* (1868).

None. Chorus of Flowers and Insects for projected opera *Mandragora* (1870) (vocal score arranged by composer).

None. Couplets 'Vous l'ordonnez' from Beaumarchais' *Le Barbier de Séville* (1872): 153.

None. Recitatives for Mozart's *Marriage of Figaro* (1876).

None. Duet from *Romeo and Juliet* (Shakespeare, translated Sokolovsky) (possibly a sketch for an opera on the subject and partly based on the overture-fantasia; completed by Taneev) (1881?): 160, 229.

CANTATAS, CHURCH AND CHORAL MUSIC, ETC.

None. An unnamed oratorio (1863–64).

None. Chorus *a cappella*, *To Sleep* (Ogarev) (1863–64).

None. Another version of the same, slightly altered and with orchestral accompaniment (1863–64).

None. *An die Freude*, Cantata for four soloists, chorus and orchestra (Schiller, trs. K. S. Aksakov) (1865): 230.

None. *Nature and Love* (composer) for two sopranos, contralto, chorus and piano (1870).

None. Cantata for tenor solo, chorus and orchestra, for the Opening of the Polytechnic Exhibition in Moscow (Polonsky) (1872) (vocal score arranged by composer): 230–1.

None. Cantata (hymn) for tenor solo, chorus and orchestra, for the jubilee of the singer O. A. Petrov (Nekrasov) (1875).

41. Liturgy of St. John Chrysostom (four-part mixed chorus) (1878)[1]: 231–4.

52. Vesper Service (harmonisation of 17 liturgical songs for mixed chorus) (1882)[1]: 232, 234.

None. *Evening* (composer?), three-part male chorus *a cappella* (1881).

None. Cantata (four-part women's chorus *a cappella*) for the pupils of the Patriotic Institute) (1881).

None. *Moscow*, Coronation cantata for mezzo-soprano and baritone soli, chorus and orchestra (Maykov) (1883) (vocal score arranged by composer): 230.

None. Three Cherubic Hymns (in F, D and C) (1884)[1]: 233–5.

None. Hymn to St. Cyril and St. Methodius for *a cappella* chorus (based on an old Czech melody) (Russian words by the composer) (1885)[1]: 233.

[1] Arranged for piano solo by the composer.

OPUS NO.

None. Six Church Songs, for four-part chorus (1885) *Tebe poem, Dostoyno est, Otche nash, Blazheni yazhe izbral, Da ispravitsya* (trio with chorus), and *Nine sili nebesnïya*)³ : 233–5.

None. *The Pure Bright Flame of Truth*, chorus, *a cappella* for the Fiftieth Anniversary of the Imperial School of Jurisprudence (composer) (1885).

None. *The Golden Cloud had Slept* (Lermontov) for mixed voices, *a cappella* (1887): 231.

None. *Blessed is he who Smiles*, male chorus, *a cappella* (dedicated to the students of Moscow University) (Grand Duke Constantine) (1887).

None. *The Nightingale* (composer) (*a cappella* chorus) (1889).

None. *Greeting to A. G. Rubinstein* (*a cappella* chorus) (Polonsky) (1889).

None. *'Tis not the Cuckoo in the Damp Pinewood* (*a cappella* chorus) N. G. Tsïganov) (1891).

None. *The Merry Voice Grew Silent* (male chorus *a cappella*) (Pushkin) (1891).

None. *Without Time or Season* (women's chorus *a cappella*) (N. G. Tsïganov) (1891).

None. *An Angel Crying* (*a cappella* chorus) (date unknown).

None. *Spring* (women's chorus *a cappella*) (date unknown).

SONGS

None. *My Genius, My Angel, My Friend* (Fet) (1857–58?).

None. *Zemfira's Song* (Pushkin) (1857–60).

None. *Who Goes* (Apukhtin) (1857–60).

None. *Mezza Notte* (Italian words; author unknown) (1860?).

6. Six Songs (1869): 1, *Do Not Believe, My Friend* (A. K. Tolstoy); 2, *Not a Word, O My Friend* (Pleshcheev, from the German of M. Hartmann); 3, *Painfully and Sweetly* (E. P. Rostopchina); 4, *A Tear Trembles* (A. K. Tolstoy); 5, *Why?* (Heine's *Warum sind dann die Rosen so blass?* translated Mey); 6, *No, Only He Who's Known* (Goethe's *Nur wer die Sehnsucht kennt*, translated Mey)¹ : 197, 200, 204–6, 228.

None. *To Forget So Soon* (Apukhtin) (1870): 206–10.

16. Six Songs (1872): 1, *Cradle Song* (Maykov); 2, *Wait* (Grekov); 3, *Accept Just Once* (Fet); 4, *O Sing That Song* (Pleshcheev, after Mrs. Hemans);² 5, *Thy Radiant Image* (composer); 6, *New Greek Song* (Maykov) (Nos. 1, 4 and 5 were arranged for piano solo by the composer; No. 4 was also arranged by him for violin and piano): 200–1, 210–4, 222.

None. *Take My Heart Away* (Fet) (1873).

None. *Blue Eyes of Spring* (Mikhaylov, after Heine) (1873).

¹ Also known in this country as *None but the Weary* (or: *Lonely*) *Heart* and *E'n Though My Heart Should Break*; the translations given in this list are the closest possible equivalents of the Russian originals.

² Perhaps her ' Mother ! Oh, Sing Me to Rest '; but if so, Pleshcheev's version is not so much free as licentious.

³ Arranged for piano solo by the composer.

OPUS No.

25. Six Songs (1874): 1, *Reconciliation* (N. F. Shcherbina); 2, *As O'er the Burning Ashes* (Tyutchev); 3, *Mignon's Song* (Goethe's *Kennst du das Land?* translated Tyutchev); 4, *The Canary* (Mey); 5, *I Never Spoke to Her* (Mey); 6, *As They Kept on Saying, 'Fool'* (Mey): 214–6.

None. *I Should Like In a Single Word* (Mey, after Heine) (1875).

None. *We Have Not Far to Walk* (Grekov) (1875).

27. Six Songs (1875): 1, *To Sleep* (Ogarev); 2, *Look, Yonder Cloud* (Grekov); 3, *Do Not Leave Me* (Fet); 4, *Evening* (Mey, from the Ukrainian of Shevchenko); 5, *Was it the Mother Who Bore Me* (Mey, from the Polish of Mickiewicz); 6, *My Spoiled Darling* (Mey, from the Polish of Mickiewicz): 201.

28. Six Songs (1875): 1, *No, I Shall Never Tell* (de Musset's 'Chanson de Fortunio,' translated Grekov); 2, *The Corals* (Mey, from the Polish of Syrokomla); 3, *Why Did I Dream of You?* (Mey); 4, *He Loved Me So Much* (anon.); 5, *No Response or Word of Greeting* (Apukhtin); 6, *The Fearful Minute* (composer): 199, 201, 217–22.

None. *The Underdog* (musical joke) (composer) (1876).

38. Six Songs (1878): 1, *Don Juan's Serenade* (A. K. Tolstoy); 2, *It Was in the Early Spring* (A. K. Tolstoy); 3, *Mid the Din of the Ball* (A. K. Tolstoy); 4, *O, If Thou Couldst For One Moment* (A. K. Tolstoy); 5, *Love of a Corpse* (Lermontov); 6, *Pimpinella* composer, from an Italian popular song): 43, 118, 197, 199, 202–3.

47. Seven Songs (1880): 1, *If I'd Only Known* (A. K. Tolstoy); 2, *Softly the Spirit Flew Up to Heaven* (A. K. Tolstoy); 3, *Dusk Fell on the Earth* (N. V. Berg, from the Polish of Mickiewicz); 4, *Sleep, My Poor Friend* (A. K. Tolstoy); 5, *I Bless You, Forests* (A. K. Tolstoy); 6, *Does the Day Reign* (Apukhtin);[1] 7, *Was I Not a Little Blade of Grass in the Field* (Surikov, from the Ukrainian of Shevchenko)[2]: 199, 202–3, 210, 222–5.

54. Sixteen Songs for Children (No. 16, 1881; Nos. 1–15, 1883): 1, *Granny and Grandson* (Pleshcheev); 2, *Little Bird* (Pleshcheev, from the Polish); 3, *Spring* ('The Grass Grows Green') (Pleshcheev, from the Polish); 4, *My Little Garden* (Pleshcheev); 5, *A Legend* (Pleshcheev, from the English);[3] 6, *On the Bank* (Pleshcheev); 7, *Winter Evening* (Pleshcheev); 8, The Cuckoo (Pleshcheev, from the German of Christian Gellert); 9, *Spring* ('The Snow's Already Melting') (Pleshcheev); 10, *Lullaby in a Storm* (Pleshcheev); 11, *The Flower* (Pleshcheev, after L. Ratisbon); 12, *Winter* (Pleshcheev); 13, *Spring Song* (Pleshcheev); 14, *Autumn* (Pleshcheev); 15, *The Swallow* (Surikov,

---

[1] Accompaniment orchestrated by the composer in 1888.

[2] Accompaniment orchestrated by the composer in 1884.

[3] I have failed to trace the English original of this well-known *Legend* ('The Christchild had a garden'); Tchaïkovsky orchestrated the accompaniment in 1884 and rearranged the piece for mixed chorus, *a cappella*, in 1889.

Opus No.

from the Polish of Teofil Lenartowicz); 16, *Child's Song* (K. S. Aksakov) : 227–9, 231–2.

57. Six Songs (1884) : 1, *Tell Me, What in the Shade of the Branches* (Sollogub); 2, *On the Golden Cornfields* (A. K. Tolstoy); 3, *Do Not As*k (Goethe's *Heiss mich nicht reden*, translated Strugovshchikov); 4, *Sleep !* (Merezhkovsky); 5, *Death* (Merezhkovsky); 6, *Only Thou* (Pleshcheev, after A. Kristen) : 203.

60. Twelve Songs (1886) : 1, *Last Night* (Khomyakov); 2, *I'll Tell Thee Nothing* (Fet); 3, *O, If You Knew* (Pleshcheev); 4, *The Nightingale* (Pushkin, after the Serbian of Stefanovic); 5, *Simple Words* (composer); 6, *Frenzied Nights* (Apukhtin); 7, *Gypsy's Song* (Polonsky); 8, *Forgive !* (Nekrasov); 9, *Night* (Polonsky); 10, *Behind the Window, in the Shadow* (Polonsky); 11, *Exploit* (Khomyakov); 12, *The Mild Stars Shone for Us* (Polonsky) : 197, 199, 202–3.

63. Six Songs (Grand Duke Constantine) (1887) : 1, *I Did Not Love Thee at First;* 2, *I Opened the Window;* 3, *I Do Not Please You;* 4, *The First Tryst;* 5, *The Fires in the Rooms Were Already Extinguished;* 6, *Serenade* (' O Child, Beneath Thy Window ').

65. Six French Songs (1888) : 1, *Aurore* (E. Turquety); 2, *Déception* (Paul Collin); 3, *Sérénade* (Paul Collin); 4, *Poème d'octobre* (Paul Collin); 5, *Les Larmes* (A. M. Blanchccotte); 6, *Rondel* (Paul Collin)

None. Musical Jest (plea to the composer's nephew, V. L. Davïdov) (composer) (1892).

73. Six Songs (D. M. Rathaus) (1893) : 1, *We Sat Together*; 2, *Night*; 3, *In This Moonlight*; 4, *The Sun Has Set*; 5, *Mid Sombre Days*; 6, *Again, As Before, Alone* : 204, 225–7.

Vocal Duets

46. Six Duets (1880) : 1, *Evening* (Surikov); 2, *Scottish Ballad* (' Edward,' translated A. K. Tolstoy); 3, *Tears* (Tyutchev); 4, *In the Garden Near the Ford* (Surikov, after the Ukrainian of Shevchenko); 5, *Passion Spent* (A. K. Tolstoy); 6, *Dawn* (Surikov)[1] : 229.

Arrangements of Works by Other Composers

None. First movement of Beethoven's Piano Sonata, Op. 31, No. 2, orchestrated (1863).

None. Scherzo from Weber's Piano Sonata in A flat, Op. 39, orchestrated (1863–64).

None. First movement of Beethoven's *Kreutzer* Sonata, orchestrated (1863–64).

None. *Adagio* and *Allegro brillante* from Schumann's *Etudes Symphoniques*, orchestrated (1863–64).

[1] Afterwards orchestrated by the composer.

Opus No.

None. A valse by Gung'l, orchestrated (1863–64).

None. K. I. Kral's *Triumphal March,* orchestrated (1867).

None. Dargomïzhsky's *Kazachok,* arranged for piano solo (1868).

None. Dubuque's *Romance de Tarnowsky,* arranged for piano duet (1868).

None. Dubuque's polka, *Mariya-Dagmar,* orchestrated (1869).

None. Potpourri on Meyerbeer's *Pardon de Ploërmel* for piano duet, by 'H. Cramer' (1868?).

None. Fifty Russian Folk-songs, arranged for piano duet (1868–69): 122–3, 131, 137, 140–1.

None. Rubinstein's 'musical picture' *Ivan the Terrible,* arranged for piano duet (1869).

None. Rubinstein's 'musical picture,' *Don Quixote,* arranged for piano duet (1870).

None. Stradella's aria, *O del mio dolce,* orchestrated (1870).

None. Trio from Cimarosa's *Il matrimonio segreto,* orchestrated (1870?).

None. Dargomïzhsky's trio, *The Golden Cloud Had Slept,* orchestrated (1870?).

None. Piano accompaniments for M. Mamontova's collection of *Children's Songs,* on Russian and Ukrainian melodies (1872 and 1877).

None. *Perpetuum mobile,* from Weber's Piano Sonata in C, Op. 24, arranged for left hand with fresh right-hand part (1874).

None. *Gott erhalte Franz den Kaiser,* orchestrated (1874).

None. Liszt's *König von Thule,* orchestrated (1874).

None. *Gaudeamus igitur,* arranged for male chorus and piano (1874).

None. *Slavsya* from Glinka's *Life for the Tsar,* simplified and linked with the former Russian national anthem (chorus and orchestra) (1883).

61. Suite No. 4, *Mozartiana* (Mozart's Gigue (K.574), Minuet (K.355), Liszt's transcription of the *Ave Verum Corpus* (K.618), and Mozart's *Variations on a Theme by Gluck* (K.455), slightly altered and orchestrated) (1887): 99, 102–3.

None. Overture Fantasia by H. A. Laroche, orchestrated (1888).

None. *Night* (composer). Vocal quartet (S.A.T.B.) based on the *andantino* of Mozart's Fantasia in C minor, K.475 (1893).

None. Sophie Menter's *Ungarische Zigeunerweisen,* orchestrated (1893).

None. A ballad by Schumann, orchestrated (date unknown).

LITERARY WORKS

Translation of Gevaert's *Traité d'Instrumentation* (1865).

Translation of the text of the Page's cavatina from *Les Huguenots* (1868).

Translation of Schumann's *Musikalische Haus-und Lebensregeln* (1868).

Translation of J. C. Lobe's *Musical Catechism* (1869).

Translation of texts of Anton Rubinstein's *Twelve Persian Songs,* Op. 34 (1869) and nineteen other songs by Rubinstein (1870–71).

Guide to the Practical Study of Harmony (1871).

Short Manual of Harmony, adapted to the study of religious music in Russia (1874).

OPUS No.

Translation of libretto of *The Marriage of Figaro* (1875).
Translation of Italian texts of five songs by Glinka (1877).
Text for a vocal quartet by Glinka (1877).
Autobiographical Description of a Journey Abroad in 1888.
Musical criticisms (collected as *Musical Feuilletons and Notes*),[1] parts of
the libretti of his own *Voevoda, Oprichnik, Eugene Onegin,
Maid of Orleans, Mazeppa* and *Queen of Spades*, verses for
occasional cantatas, for some of his own songs, etc.[2]

·[1] See Bibliography, p. 241.   [2] See under compositions.

Musical Examples

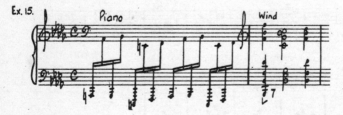

Ex. 16.

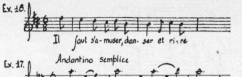

Il faut s'a-muser, dan-ser et ri-re

Ex. 17. **Andantino semplice**

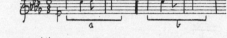

a   b

Ex. 18. **Allegro**

Ex. 19. **Prestissimo**

Ex. 20. **Allegro (poco meno mosso)**

Ex. 21. **Allegro**

Ex. 22.

Piano

Orch

Orch

etc. (Pf. arpeggi)

257

Ex.23. Molto vivace

Ex.24 Poco meno

twice

Ex.25

twice

Ex.26 Allegro brillante

Ex.27. Un poco ritenuto
Horns

Ex.28

pf

Str

Ex. 29. Allegro maestoso

Ex. 30. Andante

Ex. 31. Allegro vivacissimo

Ex. 32.

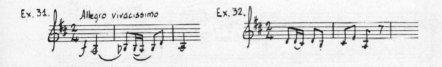

Ex. 33. Moderato assai

Ex. 34. Con molto espress.

Ex. 35. Moderato semplice

Ex. 36.

Ex. 37. (Moderato assai)   rit.   più mosso, largamente

Ex. 38. (Molto Allegro)

Wind

(Percussion omitted.

Strings

Ex. 39. (Molto·Allegro)

Wind

Strings

Ex. 40. (♩=88)

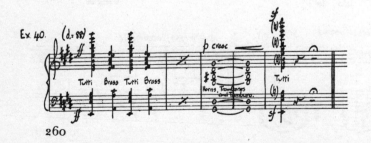

Tutti Brass Tutti Brass

Horns, Trombones
and Tambura.

Tutti

260

Ex. 41.

Ex. 42.

Ex. 43.

Ex. 44.

Ex. 45.

262

Ex. 50 (Allegro vivo)

Ex. 51. (Andante cantabile non troppo)

Ex 53. (Allegro vivo)

etc

Ex. 54. (Andante cantabile non troppo)

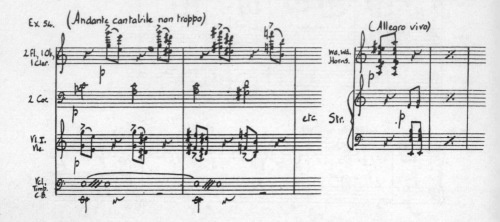

Ex. 55 Allegro vivacissimo (♩.♩ = 208)

Ex. 56. (Allegro vivacissimo)

264

Ex. 57. (Allegro vivacissimo)

265

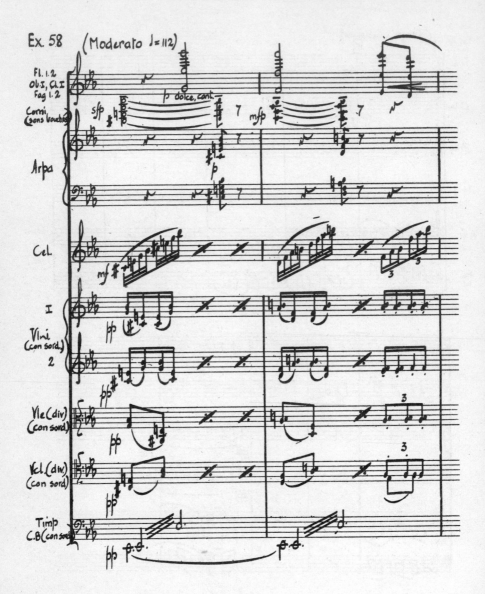

266

Ex. 59 — Allegro moderato

Ex. 60 — Lento lugubre

Ex. 61. — Moderato con moto (♩=100)

Ex. 62. — Andante

Ex. 63   Andante con duolo (♩= 69)

Ex. 64   L'istesso tempo

Ex. 65.   Andante con moto (♩ = 144)

Ex. 66.   (Andante)

268

Ex. 67.

Ex. 68.

Ex. 69.

Vivacissimo (♩=168)

Ex. 70.

Ex. 71.

Ex. 72.

Allegro giusto

mf

Ex. 73.

mf largamente

etc.

Ex. 74.

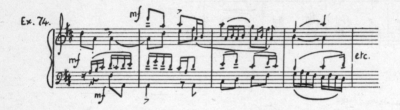

mf

mf

mf

etc.

Ex. 75.

Allegro moderato

p dolcissimo

Ex. 76.

p piangendo e molto espr.

Ex. 77.

THEME
Andante con moto

Tempo di mazurka

p cantabile

etc.

f con brio

etc.

270

Ex. 78.

Ex. 79.

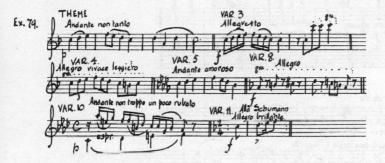

Ex. 80.

Ex. 81.

Ex. 82.

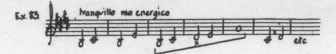

Ex. 83. **Tranquillo ma energico**

Ex. 84. **Moderato e risoluto**

Ex. 85. **Allegro vivace** con espress.

Ex. 86.
(a) **Andante** espress. etc.
(b) **Allegro non troppo e tranquillo** p grazioso etc.

Ex. 87. **Andante non troppo**

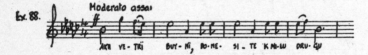

So - lo - vush - ko v bu - bra - vush - ke Gro - mko — svi — schet Gro - mko svi — sachet

Ex. 88. **Moderato assai**

Akh ve - trï buy - ni, po - ne - si - te k na - w dru - gu

Ex. 89. **Allegro giusto**

Ex. 90. **Allegro moderato**

Mi - ly sin ti me - nya o - di - no - ku - yu v Gor - koy do - le mo - ey ne po - ki - day

Ex. 98.

Ex. 99.

Ex. 100.

Ex. 101

Ex. 102
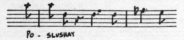

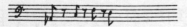

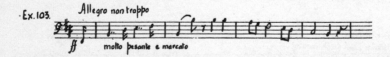

Ex. 103.

Ex. 104.

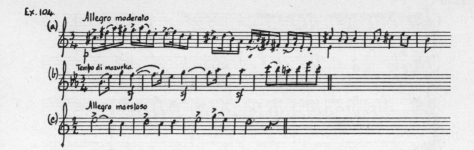

(a) Allegro moderato

(b) Tempo di mazurka.

(c) Allegro maestoso

Ex. 105.

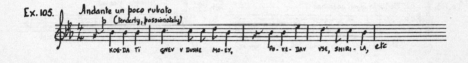

Andante un poco rubato
p (tenderly, passionately)

KOG-DA TI GNEV V DUSHE MO-EY,   PO-KE-DAV VSE, SHIRI-LA, etc

Ex. 106. Queen of Spades

(a) Allegro

of three cards, ... of three cards, of three cards!

Onegin
(b) Andante, quasi adagio
a piena voce

What has the coming day in store!

6th Symphony.
(c) Adagio

f   mf=p   f   mf

Ex. 107. Andante mosso

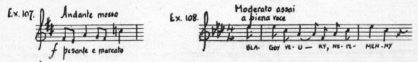

f pesante e marcato

Ex. 108.

Moderato assai
a piena voce

BLA- GOY VE- U — KY, NE-IZ- MEN-NY

Ex. 109.

f cantabile

Ex. 110.

NE   VER, MOY DRUG, NE   VER. KOGDA V PO- RIVE GO- RYA

Ex. III.

275

Ex. 112.

Ex. 113.

Moderato quasi andantino

_ O ZAS- NI, MO-E SERD. TSE, GLU- BO- KO!

Ex. 114.

Allegro giocoso

OT TSH-RE-VA KA-BA-KA!

Ex. 115.

Moderato assai

p

Ex. 116.

Allegro con spirito

f

Ex. 117.

Ex. 118.

Allegro moderato

KA- Bï ZNALA YA, KA Bï VIDELA

Ex. 119.   Vivace

Ex. 120.   Meno mosso

NE PRI—DET LI ON, NE NA—GRYADNY MOY NA-PO——IT KO-NYA STUDE—NOY VO BOY!——

Ex. 121.   Adagio

MERKHET SLA-BY SVET SVE-CHI, BRODT MRAK U-NILY I TO-SKA SZHI-NA-ET GRUD C NE-PO—NYAT-NOY SI-LOY

Ex. 122.   mf

TS—TO MI-LA-SYA O-NA—

Ex. 123.   Slow   poco cresc.   mp

Trebles
Altos

MI—NE SI-LI-NE-BE   SHI-YA, S NA-MI   etc

Tenors
(Basses
tacet)

Ex. 124.   Slow

Trebles
Altos

I——ZHE KHE-RU——VI——   Mi, KHE——RU-VI—

cresc.

I-ZHE KHE-RU-VI, Mi,

Tenors
Basses

I-ZHE KHE-RU-VI, Mi, I ZHE KHE——RU-VI

Mi

dim

MI